THE DIGITAL TRANSFORMATION OF THE EUROPEAN BORDER REGIME

The Powers and Perils of Imagining Future Borders

Paul Trauttmansdorff

BRISTOL
UNIVERSITY
PRESS

First published in Great Britain in 2024 by

Bristol University Press
University of Bristol
1-9 Old Park Hill
Bristol
BS2 8BB
UK
t: +44 (0)117 374 6645
e: bup-info@bristol.ac.uk

Details of international sales and distribution partners are available at bristoluniversitypress.co.uk

© Bristol University Press 2024

British Library Cataloguing in Publication Data
A catalogue record for this book is available from the British Library

ISBN 978-1-5292-3520-3 hardcover
ISBN 978-1-5292-3521-0 ePub
ISBN 978-1-5292-3522-7 ePdf

The right of Paul Trauttmansdorff to be identified as author of this work has been asserted
by him in accordance with the Copyright, Designs and Patents Act 1988.

Cover design: Liam Roberts Design
Front cover image: iStock/koto_feja
Bristol University Press uses environmentally responsible print partners.
Printed and bound in Great Britain by CPI Group (UK) Ltd, Croydon, CR0 4YY

FSC
www.fsc.org
MIX
Paper | Supporting
responsible forestry
FSC® C013604

Contents

List of Figures iv

List of Abbreviations v

About the Author vii

Acknowledgements viii

1 Introduction 1

 First Interlude: Doing Research From Within the 21
 Border Regime

2 The Imaginary of Digital Transformation 26

 Second Interlude: Three Empirical Vignettes 44

3 Assembling a Fractional Europe 51

 Third Interlude: Another Vignette—The Golden Age? 68

4 Crafting the Epistemology of Smart Borders 71

5 Interoperability: Making a New Policy Fiction 96

6 Justification, Techno-Determinism, and Sanitized 113
 Realities: The Perils of Imagining Future Borders

7 Coda 127

Appendix A: Overview of Existing and Future Large-Scale IT 131
Systems Under eu-LISA's Management

Appendix B: List of Conducted Interviews and Sites of Participant 138
Observation

Notes 140

References 150

Index 177

List of Figures

2.1	"Transformation", a slide presented at the ID@Borders conference (April 2019) by eu–LISA	34
2.2	Indicative timeline for the establishment of smart borders	40
2.3	eu–LISA's HQ in Tallinn, Estonia	44
2.4	eu–LISA's HQ and the old Seaplane Harbour (in the back left)	45
2.5	Rue de Schengen in Strasbourg, the street behind eu–LISA data centre	48
2.6	eu–LISA data centre in Strasbourg	49
3.1	A livestreamed speech by eu–LISA's former Executive Director at the annual conference of eu–LISA (2019)	56
3.2	Screenshot of eu–LISA's announcement of its anniversary conference (October 2022) in Tallinn, Estonia	64
3.3	Conference setting at eu–LISA's annual conference (2019) at Tallinn, Estonia	69
4.1	"What's next?", a slide presented at the ID@Borders conference (April 2019) by eu–LISA	81
4.2	"Stay Open, Stay Secure", a slide presented at the ID@Borders conference (April 2019) by eu–LISA	87
4.3	A flyer for the eu–LISA industry roundtable in 2019	94

List of Abbreviations

Organizational entities

EC	European Commission
EDPS	European Data Protection Supervisor
EP	European Parliament
EU	European Union
EUAA	European Union Agency for Asylum, formerly European Asylum Support Office (formerly EASO, until 19 February 2022)
eu-LISA	European Union Agency for the Operational Management of Large-Scale IT Systems in the Area of Freedom, Security and Justice
EUROPOL	European Union Agency for Law Enforcement Cooperation
FRA	Fundamental Rights Agency
Frontex	European Border and Coast Guard Agency (frontières extérieures)
HLEG	High-Level Expert Group on Information Systems and Interoperability
INTERPOL	International Criminal Police Organization
LIBE	Committee of the European Parliament on Civil Liberties, Justice and Home Affairs
OSCE	Organization for Security and Co-operation in Europe

Information systems and technological components

CIR	Common Identity Repository (Interoperability component)
ECRIS-TCN	European Criminal Record Information System for Third-Country Nationals
EES	Entry/Exit System
ESP	European Search Portal (Interoperability component)

ETIAS	European Travel Information and Authorisation System
Eurodac	European Dactyloscopic Database
MID	Multiple Identity Detector (Interoperability component)
RTP	Registered Traveler Program
sBMS	shared Biometric Matching Service (Interoperability component)
SIS II	Schengen Information System—"second generation"
SIS	Schengen Information System
VIS	Visa Information System

About the Author

Paul Trauttmansdorff is a researcher in Science and Technology Studies whose work has explored controversies surrounding technological and infrastructural innovation, the evolution of large-scale IT systems, and the transformations in border and mobility regimes. His particular interest revolves around inquiries into the societal, political, and ethical repercussions of digital transformations, as well as the collective imaginaries that underpin them.

Paul Trauttmansdorff obtained his MSc degree in Political Sociology from the London School of Economics and Political Science and completed his PhD in Science and Technology Studies at the University of Vienna. He held a fellowship with the Austrian Academy of Sciences from 2018 to 2021 and was a recipient of the Marietta-Blau scholarship from Austria's Agency of Education and Internationalization. Between 2022 and 2023, he worked as a postdoctoral researcher at the Department of Philosophy and Communication Studies, University of Bologna, and as a fellow on the ERC Starting Grant Project "Processing Citizenship—Digital registration of migrants as co-production of citizens, territory and Europe". In October 2023, he joined the European New School of Digital Studies, European University Viadrina Frankfurt (Oder), as a research fellow. Paul Trauttmansdorff is the co-editor of *Technopolitics and the Making of Europe. Infrastructures of Security* (with Nina Klimburg-Witjes, Routledge).

Acknowledgements

I want to express my appreciation for the invaluable contributions, ideas, and input provided by colleagues and friends at various stages and in diverse locations and settings, as they have significantly shaped the content of this book. I extend my gratitude to everyone at the Department of Science and Technology Studies, University of Vienna, which has served as my intellectual home for my years as PhD student. I am particularly grateful to Ulrike Felt, who offered her continued support and guidance as my supervisor of my thesis. I am also indebted to the Department of Philosophy and Communication at the University of Bologna, where I had the privilege of collaborating with exceptional colleagues as part of the Processing Citizenship project led by Annalisa Pelizza.

During my research journey for this book, I have found inspiration from numerous researchers in the fields of Science & Technology Studies, Critical Migration Studies, as well as Critical Security and Border Studies. I am thankful for the ongoing exchange of ideas and the rich intellectual environment fostered by the STS-MIGTEC network, especially during the COVID-19 pandemic. Here and elsewhere, numerous outstanding colleagues have contributed to shaping the ideas and arguments for this book, offered generous feedback, or provided valuable comments.

I extend my gratitude to Paul Stevens from Bristol University Press for his generous support throughout the editing and publication process. Additionally, I would like to thank the reviewers, who provided insightful comments and feedback on both the book's proposal and the manuscript, which were instrumental in refining its content.

I offer my heartfelt thanks to all the counterparts and individuals who generously participated in interviews and conversations, shared their knowledge and experiences, and to those who kindly granted me access to crucial empirical sites, events, or materials.

Furthermore, I am thankful for the financial and institutional support I received from various funding bodies and academic departments over the years of writing, revising, or editing this book: the Austrian Academy of Sciences, Austria's Agency for Education and Internationalisation (OeAD), the Faculty of Social Sciences and the Vienna Doctoral School of Social

Sciences at the University of Vienna, and the European New School of Digital Studies at the European University Viadrina.

Parts of the Introduction of this book have been printed in *Tecnoscienza, Italian Journal for Science & Technology Studies*, available at http://www.tecno scienza.net/index.php/tsj/article/view/531. This is available open access under Creative Commons Attribution 4.0 International License (https://doi.org/10.6092/issn.2038-3460/17584).

Chapter 2 is a modified version of an article written and published together with Ulrike Felt, in *Science, Technology, and Human Values*, 17 November 2021, available online: https://journals.sagepub.com/doi/full/10.1177/01622439211057523.

Chapter 5 is derived from an article in *Critical Policy Studies*, Taylor & Francis, 15 November 2022, available online: https://www.tandfonline.com/doi/full/10.1080/19460171.2022.2147851.

1

Introduction

Any traveler who enters or transits through Europe today will encounter multiple sociotechnical infrastructures that regulate their mobility. Infrastructures prevent, facilitate, or arrest movement; they shape its form, direction, and speed. They formalize and sometimes create some of the most commonly used terms to describe mobile people and categories of belonging—citizens, third-country nationals, immigrants, refugees, tourists, or bona fide travelers. As hybrid networks of people, technologies, regulations, and standards, infrastructures determine what kinds of mobility are considered legitimate or illegitimate, regular or irregular, legal or illegal. Infrastructures are often said to operate in the invisible background (Star and Ruhleder 1996), but they also perform collective visions, values, social life, and order. Their design and construction display governmental powers, such as the capacity for grand planning, organizing public space, or safeguarding security. Infrastructures have therefore been ascribed a constitutive role in the formation of states and European communities—in whichever ways the term "Europe" signifies the different legal, political, or sociocultural compositions on the continent (Easterling 2014; Klimburg-Witjes and Trauttmansdorff 2023; Opitz and Tellmann 2015a; Schipper and Schot 2011).

In the European Union (EU), Schengen member states and Schengen associated countries have constructed digital infrastructures to collaborate with each other on the governance of mobility. One of the most salient ways this is pursued is through the build-up and maintenance of large-scale transnational databases. EU member states' national authorities not only share and process data and information with each other; they also agreed to establish a joint institution for administering and developing these information systems—the eu-LISA Agency.

eu-LISA is the curious official acronym of the European Union Agency for the Operational Management of **L**arge-Scale **IT** **S**ystems in the **A**rea of Freedom, Security and Justice, which began its activities on 1 December 2012.[1] Since then, the Agency has been undergoing remarkable development, consistently growing and expanding its scope and power. This book will provide insights into the inner-workings of an actor who has played a key role in developing collective visions of border security while managing the necessary digital infrastructures that must bring these visions into being. The book thereby draws on four years of research that, at its core, consisted of extensive document analysis, interviews, and ethnographic observations to explore the Agency's main sites, projects, and practices in the management of large-scale databases in the Schengen Area. My overall intention is to analyze forms of sociotechnical imagination that undergird some of the most fundamental technological developments in the European border regime.[2]

In a "Foreword" of one of its early official brochures, the Agency describes the broader context of its mission in the following manner:

> The internal security of countries is changing enormously. Guaranteeing their security and that of their people can no longer just be done through physical resources on the ground. The "virtual world" of IT is now part of the equation, as authorities are increasingly reliant on data and information. In today's complex and globalised world, a single state cannot look after its security alone. Hence the importance of sophisticated, flexible and integrated IT systems and solutions – designed to enable law enforcement cooperation and integrated border management at EU-Level. (eu-LISA 2014, 1)[3]

Let us depart from questioning three powerful and interrelated assumptions in this statement. The first assumption holds that we live in an evermore "complex and globalised world" that produces transnational threats and insecurities that single nation-states cannot cope with on their own. The very concept of the "internal security of countries" has changed and it must no longer be safeguarded solely within the traditional boundaries of the state.

The second implicit assumption concerns the heterogeneous and dispersed character of borders themselves. The recognition of our complex, globalized world—as well as its patterns of global mobility—undermines not only the traditional imagination of the modern sovereign state, which is in control of its territory and population within well-defined geographical boundaries. Contemporary state borders can no longer be safeguarded by so-called "physical resources on the ground". States have been forced to rethink borders and security—internally, externally, nationally, and intergovernmentally. It brings to mind what Mezzadra and Neilson (2013) have once accurately described as the proliferation of borders in our globalized world.

The third assumption relates to a solution and is crystallized in the notion of a "virtual world" in which law enforcement and border management are empowered to mobilize "data and information" and rely on "sophisticated, flexible and integrated IT systems and solutions". The virtual world must then restore today's seemingly fragile constitution of state security. Data and information become "part of the equation"—a phrase that articulates the ideal of an equilibrium, imagined and instituted once adequate responses to the complex threats and challenges of our world are applied. The Agency's statement wonders how borders can be operated, mobility governed, and security safeguarded in the future if not through this world of the virtual, the world of data.

In this statement, the futures promised by digital technologies are inseparable from the orders and disorders imagined in the present. As will become increasingly explicit in this book, the assumptions made here are more than ever integral parts of the powerful collective sociotechnical imaginations that undergird the contemporary transformations of the European border regime. They direct us to investigate digitization as an arena of emerging (border) politics, "a space in which old orders may be shaken up and changed, sometimes in subtle and sometimes in dramatic ways" (Hilgartner, Miller, and Hagendijk 2015, 5). This arena is one that encompasses networks of humans and nonhuman elements, visions of future borders, hopes and promises for technology, multiple interacting institutional actors, material artefacts and large-scale infrastructures. They have become part of a transformation that ties the complex processes of bordering inevitably to data and information systems.

The border multiple, then and today

To begin understanding this transformation, let us first rewind to the early 1990s, a time when author and management theorist Kenichi Ohmae (1990) wrote an influential book that captured the zeitgeist of that era, proclaiming the arrival of a "Borderless World". In this entrepreneurial diagnosis, he pondered the widespread optimism and expectation of a flourishing and liberated global economy after the fall of the Berlin Wall and the end of the Cold War—characterized by the victory of liberalism over communism, the globalization of customer demands, and the restructuring of nation-state interests beyond national boundaries. Ohmae's book perfectly epitomized what Boltanski and Chiapello (2018 [1999]) would later call the "New Spirit of Capitalism" that promoted information technologies as core drivers in the networked world of global flows. Today, his book's far-fetched diagnosis is often used as a counterpoint to the observation that "borders are back" (Mau 2021, 11): after the global spread of the COVID-19 pandemic that led to radically restricted forms of mobility, the worldwide construction of new border walls and fences, states of emergency along militarized border zones, and the continuing securitization of mobility.

It is important to note, however, that Ohmae's theory was never consistent with the reality and development of borders (see Mezzadra and Neilson 2013; Paasi 2018). Border security has never solely concerned the ability to control a geographical line along a state's national territory—as if drawn on a map and physically secured on the ground. Instead, borders have diffused into heterogeneous practices, techniques, biopolitical strategies, and technologies of inclusion and exclusion. In critical border studies, it has therefore become a common denominator to perceive borders as multiplicities that require a range of concepts to grasp their changing cultural, political, symbolic, and material facets and functions (Paasi 1998; Rumford 2006a; Sohn 2016; Walters 2002, 2006b).

As the sociologist Georg Simmel (2009 [1908]) declared, a border must be understood "not [as] a spatial fact with sociological effects, but [as] a sociological reality that is formed spatially" (p. 551). In a related move, Étienne Balibar (2002) argued that "to mark out a border is precisely, to define a territory, to delimit it, and so to register the identity of that territory, or confer one upon it. Conversely, however, to define or identify in general is nothing other than to trace a border, to assign boundaries or borders" (p. 76). What is often abstractly presented as a singular line on a map can only be made possible and enacted by the bundling of actors, regulations, standards, practices, and technologies that mark or define. In other words, borders are multiple—invoking different meanings, exerting control in different ways, and structuring their politics through an array of actors, technologies, and practices. Borders understood as polymorphous sites involve processes of de- and reterritorialization; they articulate and are formed by the complex relationships between mobility, security, law enforcement, and territory.

It is no surprise that the multidisciplinary field of border studies grew rapidly in the early 1990s after the demise of one of the most notorious border architectures in history—the iron curtain. It found its agenda in, and against, popularized ideas such as a borderless world and political deterritorialization. Accordingly, the *Ashgate Research Companion to Border Studies* introduces the field by noting that after the fall of the Berlin Wall, "[i]n summary, borders are still ubiquitous, are manifested in diverse ways, and have various functions and roles" (Wastl-Walter 2011, 2).[4] Since then, a variety of terms have sought to grasp the diverse manifestations, shifts, and roles of borders, including "borderscapes", "borderlands", and "border regimes". As Hess and Kasparek (2017) argue, border studies "emphasize the transformation of the border from a demarcation line surrounding national territory to a ubiquitous, techno-social, deterritorialised apparatus or regime producing geographical stretched borderscapes" (p. 59). Such notions conceptually destabilize borders' presumed fixity and linearity and expose the multiple conflictual determinations of the border—that is, the frictions and struggles that equally participate in their unstable constitution and contribute to political and social order. Borders have thus undergone processes of delocalization, through which border functions can lead to practices of remote control and preemptive governance (Bigo and Guild

2005; Broeders and Hampshire 2013; Guiraudon and Lahav 2000; Schulze Wessel 2015; Vaughan-Williams 2008).[5]

A key component in summarizing some of the core transformations of borders is the biopolitical turn. It articulates the "multiplicity and multiplication of biopolitical technologies" for the management of mobility and migration (Aradau and Tazzioli 2020, 201).[6] This term invokes, perhaps most clearly, the shift in the state's primary concern with territory to that of population—initially analyzed in Michel Foucault's seminal lectures on governmentality and biopolitics (2009).[7] Critical border and migration scholars have employed these insights to analyze the institution of the border—admittedly, an institution that in itself has hardly been a concern for Foucault (Walters 2010). This meant scrutinizing the distinct techniques and mechanisms of borders, which aim to include and exclude an "indefinite series of mobile elements" that originate *outside* the field of surveillance: "carts, travelers, thieves, disease, tourists, migrants, criminals" (Feldman 2011b, 381). While much of the literature has predominantly focused on the Global North, its verdict is that the principle of biopolitics has supplemented (but not replaced) the principle of geopolitics: borders now operate through spatially dispersed and temporally varied tactics of control, semantics, policies, laws, and technical architectures (see, for example, Leese 2016; Olwig et al. 2019; Salter 2013; Scheel 2020; Schwertl 2018; Szary and Giraut 2015; Tazzioli 2020b; van Baar 2017; Walters 2002). Concerned primarily with the profitable circulation of populations, borders can enact various techniques of exclusion, facilitation, detainment, acceleration, or incarceration. In summary, as Matthew Longo (2017) aptly summarizes, borders today "cannot merely be 'tall,' they must also be 'wide' and 'layered'" (p. 56).

Borders and technology

Without a doubt, from the beginning, the rise of large-scale databases and the commitment and deployment of digital technologies has enabled and intensified the biopolitical turn. The interdisciplinary scholarship detailed above has gone to great lengths to unpack the actors, discourses, facets, and functions that carry out today's increasingly digitally mediated border controls. Just like borders, as Dijstelbloem (2021) notes, technologies "inform—and limit—how societies are governed and can be imagined to be governed" (p. 9).

The growing production, collection, and storage of data seek to capture and trace the movement and institutional trajectories of populations, ideally enabling a new form of hyper-documentation, by which "each piece of data is linked to other data, and ultimately to a risk profile" (Salter 2006a, 47). This governmental desire is articulated by the introduction of various forms of biometric identification, the digitization of asylum and visa procedures, the creation of traveler watch lists or blacklists, and other related mechanisms that track mobility.

What is maybe most striking is how these practices of digital bordering illustrate the shift away from the national-territorial model of the sovereign border to the increasingly transnational or even supranational character of mobility control. The EU's recent centralization of the databases shared by its member states is one of the most prominent examples among many others across the globe. The Schengen space is conventionally characterized by the single market project and the formal abolition of internal borders between states. Since the beginning, however, Schengen states have cooperated in the realm of (border) security. This has led scholars to claim that European forms of border control and surveillance have gradually shifted toward forms of transnational policing (Feldman 2019; Walters 2006a), based primarily on the gradual construction of digital infrastructures that allow authorities to collect, process, and share what they define as security-relevant information.

As Papadopoulos, Stephenson, and Tsianos have suggested, in Schengen Europe

> [t]he most common manifestation of the border is not to be found along the geographical border line [...] but rather in digital records on laptops belonging to the border police; in the visa records of European embassies in Moscow, Istanbul, Accra or Tripoli; in the checkpoints of Heathrow, Tegel, Paris Charles de Gaulle or Mytilini Odysseas Elytis airports; in the German central register of asylum seekers [...]; in the online entries of the Schengen Information System (SIS), where the data on persons denied entry to the Schengen area is administered; in the Eurodac [...], where the fingerprints of asylum seekers and apprehended illegalized migrants are stored. (Papadopoulos, Stephenson, and Tsianos 2008, 176)

Databases might best articulate how the digitization of borders in Europe has involved the deployment of infrastructures across geographical and virtual space. Policy officials thus speak of the growing use of centralized large-scale IT systems as a transforming technology landscape in Europe, especially in the last decade (field note, OSCE Conference, 10–11 April 2019). With the establishment of eu-LISA in 2012, a single agency now administers databases such as the second generation of the Schengen Information System (SIS II), the fingerprint system Eurodac, and the Visa Information System (VIS). eu-LISA is also developing new systems, such as the Entry/Exit System (EES), the European Travel Information and Authorisation System (ETIAS), the European Criminal Record Information System for Third-Country Nationals (ECRIS-TCN), and interoperability to connect these systems.[8]

The increase in the literature on border and migration control through digital means is responsible for the proliferation of terms that seem to describe similar, but not identical, phenomena. For example, scholars have studied "digital borders" (Broeders 2007; Chouliaraki and Georgiou 2022; Glouftsios 2019; Trauttmansdorff 2017), "technological borders" (Dijstelbloem and Meijer 2011), and "socio-digital borders" (König 2016). All three terms refer to building large-scale IT systems that involve data-sharing practices between states to control migration. Another influential term is Louise Amoore's "biometric border" (Amoore 2006; Muller 2011), defined as the "portable border par excellence, carried by mobile bodies at the very same time as it is deployed to divide bodies at international boundaries, airports, railway stations, on subways or city streets, in the office or the neighbourhood" (Amoore 2006, 338). With this definition, Amoore underscored the diffuse character of biometric control in the contemporary regimes of mobility management, in which facial images, iris scans, and fingerprints seek to establish a migrant's "embodied identity" (van der Ploeg 2000). In less specific ways, the notions of "mobile borders" (Szary and Giraut 2015) or Côté-Boucher's (2008) "diffuse border" imply the various delocalized and spatially diffused characteristics of borders and their biometric reinforcement. In the same vein, scholars have deployed the idea of the "virtual border" (Zureik and Salter 2006, 1) and the related concept of "bio-informatic border security" (Vukov and Sheller 2013) to mark the shift in borders away from physical or territorial boundaries. Pötzsch's (2015) idea of the emergence of the "iBorder" likewise signals the exercise of "informational power" that digital technologies seemingly enable, as does Rygiel's (2011) politics of "e-borders" (see also Allen and Vollmer 2018). Finally, we add the term "liquid borders" (Moraña 2021) to this growing list of signifiers. The idea of liquidity not only points to the dispersed nature of borders but, importantly, also acknowledges the element of porousness that haunts every border, no matter how technologized it appears.[9]

It is important to note that some of these labels are not merely academic or activist concepts; they have sometimes been introduced by politicians, officials, or industrial actors who, contrary to the literature, strongly promote the deployment of digital borders. In this regard, "smart border" stands out as a term that has strongly shaped the discourse and practice of border and migration management policy. The terminology of smartness has strategically served industry actors, officials, national delegates, and experts in fostering distinct but coexisting visions and meanings of border security. Accordingly, smart borders have come under special academic scrutiny (see Chapter 4).

There is no inherent problem in using these terms except that they can cause the unintended effect of creating a rather artificial dichotomy between the digital and the physical, the virtual and the material aspects of borders. This dichotomy would prevent us from examining one of the book's core objects of study, namely the distinct ways in which technologies, devices, artefacts, and the so-called virtual space are shaped by social, cultural, economic, and political worlds and always enacted through actors, their narratives and performances. The "virtual world" thus emerges as an outcome of dispersed and multiple practices as well as of imagination and discourse. The role of social scientists, so to speak, is to account for the ways in which digital artefacts and devices are materially implicated in performing the social. In other words, we will be attuned to practices of imagining, assembling, and performing digital or virtual borders. As much as the biopolitical turn shifts the analytical gaze away from the border as a demarcating line, we must be attuned to the multiple enactments of borders and border security that take place prior to or after their deployment on territories—that is, in the concrete spaces in which digital borders become not only imagined, designed, and assembled but also administered, maintained, and repaired. This book thus aims to insert itself into the contributions that have started to analyze not only the biopolitics of digitally mediated borders and its implications on migration governance but also the laborious imaginative and infrastructural work carried out by actors to design and enact them.

The technopolitics of infrastructure

Imagination and infrastructure are two notions in scholarship on borders and migration that often seem to point in opposite directions. Imagination points to the blurry realm of fantasy, ideology, the abstract and the symbolic. Infrastructure, at least according to its original understanding, is commonly associated with physicality, material substance, or substrate (Carse 2016). Conceptually speaking, this book will connect these two notions to better understand the inner-workings and operations of the border regime and the meaning of contemporary border (in)security in Europe.

From an infrastructural perspective, border control does not seem to enforce an ever-present and all-seeing panoptic grip on mobility and digital borders do not simply appear as the durable, robust artefacts they are often portrayed to be. Instead, they are provisional, incomplete patchwork that require enormous amounts of harmonization and standardization—a constant concern for the actors involved in the governance of migration and part of the painstaking labour that must go into assembling, maintaining, and extending the spaces of security.[10] Large-scale databases in the border regime thus serve as powerful enablers of networked control, but they are also revealed as highly fragile entities, with their ever-growing capacity for knowledge circulation undermined by technical failures and breakdowns (see Chapter 3).

Infrastructures moreover complicate the politically popular representations of borders as walls and fences as they embody the different governmental logics of curbing, preventing, sorting, but also facilitating and circulating mobilities—whether they be people, capital, commodities, or information. Foucault's elaborations on apparatuses of security (2009) strongly evoke the infrastructural qualities necessary to produce particular types of knowledge and orchestrate the organization and optimization of circulation, sort out what is perceived as dangerous, and classify "good" and "bad" elements (pp. 31–32).[11] According to Brian Larkin, technological infrastructures enact governmental rationalities because they provide the underlying "networks that facilitate the flow of goods, people, or ideas and allow for their exchange over space" (Larkin 2013, 328). Infrastructure supports and stabilizes security apparatuses by guaranteeing, and thus often naturalizing, their operations of management, regulation, and control. They are fundamental for silently responding to a core puzzle of modern governmentality: "*How* should things circulate or not circulate?" (Foucault 2009, 65; emphasis added).

Border infrastructures arrange social, political, legal, and technical elements to form a larger, powerful network for the governance of mobilities. Science and technology studies scholars have therefore suggested that borders could be understood *as infrastructure* (Dijstelbloem 2021; Noori 2022; Pollozek and Passoth 2019). This heuristic lens perceives them as emergent sociotechnical arrangements of both human and nonhuman elements that turn into mediators. In other words, they enable

> *interactions* among actors, institutions, and technologies that constitute borders generate *changes* that affect the constituting elements, from which new relationships and entities emerge. [… T]hey include the circulation of all kinds of information, knowledge, and techniques. […] Combining the functions of managing passenger flows, checking goods, and regulating migration at the airport leads to new connections and disconnections among the actors, institutions, and technologies that execute these tasks. (Dijstelbloem 2021, 5; italics in the original)

During this book, I will continuously return to two core aspects that are essential for my investigation of digital border infrastructure. First, digital infrastructure must be permanently refined, monitored, maintained, and repaired in order to create the preconditions for data to be produced, circulated, and shared—in short, to create the material conditions to govern mobility via classifying and sorting procedures. This means that there is a wide array of infrastructuring work at play—construction, fixing and cleaning communication networks, coordination, monitoring, and prevention, and with that work comes a whole actor-network of technicians, employees, officers, and experts. This work is usually conducted in the mostly "invisible background" of information systems and can often be found in what Susan Leigh Star once described as "traces left behind by coders, designers, and users of systems" (Star 1999, 385). Maintenance and repair work invisibilize infrastructures as they ensure their continued taken-for-grantedness and normalized use, which produces the powerful effects of order. Maintenance and repair should thus be taken as integral parts of the technopolitics of borders and investigated as subject to the political negotiations, controversies, and social struggles that shape the making of (digital) borders.[12]

It would be misleading to locate infrastructural power only in the invisible, sustaining background work of infrastructures. Infrastructures, as Larkin notes, "are not just technical objects but also operate on the level of fantasy and desire. They encode the dreams of individuals and societies and are the vehicles whereby those fantasies are transmitted and made emotionally real" (Larkin 2013, 333). The second core aspect in this book, therefore, concerns the symbolic dimensions of infrastructures as metapragmatic objects—as "signs of themselves, deployed in particular circulatory regimes to establish sets of effects" (p. 336). A still rather neglected aspect in the vast literature on apparatuses and biopolitics (of borders), collective imagination plays a crucial role because it can shape and sustain what constitutes the values, ideas, and futures with which borders and mobile populations are governed.

Collective imagination is, in other words, an inevitable agent of the security apparatus' own reproduction under conditions of general uncertainty. It informs the selection of threats and dangers that must be identified and prevented; it constructs and affects possible futures that must be rendered knowable (to be governed).[13] Both imagination and infrastructure, future visions and their material inscriptions, play crucial parts in the governmental logics of security apparatuses. The collective values and promises of societies and polities are thus not simply and only scripted into infrastructure through the silent and invisible work of maintenance. All too often, they are (publicly) staged and performed through and with infrastructure or gradually realized through infrastructural initiatives. Scientists, technicians, and engineers pursue imagined social purposes; however, they are also always nurtured and intertwined with practices of researching, manufacturing, and developing techno-scientific artefacts. These practices encode broader ideals, promises, and desires.[14]

The power of imagination

The collective forms of sociotechnical imagination—the distinct imaginative capacities of groups, the mobilization of visionary powers, the ability to craft visions of technological futures—occupy a privileged place in this book's understanding of the making of borders and their digital infrastructures. Imaginations direct our attention to more subtle and mundane compositions that nevertheless lie at the heart of the border regime: they articulate the logic and rationale of governance, encode the principles of inclusion and exclusion, and inform the policies that must render migration a digitized, actionable, and governable object. These dynamics are inseparable from the border regime's ongoing violence and militarized activities against migrants and refugees, for example, in the Mediterranean Sea—perhaps one of the most visible and brutal articulations of the formation of European borders that has resulted in a huge number of deaths.[15] In comparison, the build-up and maintenance of the EU's digital border infrastructure seem to be less appalling and somewhat more silent or invisible. However, these practices form part of the same regime and are built upon the same logic. Large-scale databases are based on societies' principles and mechanisms of inclusion and exclusion and impact migrants' experiences at the border. They have also been widely normalized as indispensable components of border control and unchallenged guarantors of security in today's migration management. To paraphrase Bruno Latour's famous dictum (1993), (digital) infrastructure is the politics of bordering pursued by other means.

Engaging in collective imagination is thus a profoundly political act that must be accounted for in Europe's border regime. It accompanies the construction, maintenance, and justification of digital borders and their envisioned futures. Social scientists have long attempted to come to terms with imagination's potentially world-configuring impact—crystalizing it in fiction, metaphors, ideologies, and many other forms. Scholars such as Benedict Anderson, Cornelius Castoriadis, or Charles Taylor insisted on the role of social imagination as a key to solving the puzzle of the historical emergence and persistence of phenomena such as nations and nationalism. The imaginary potential of the nation, as Castoriadis noted, can appear more enduring than all other realities although often deemed highly irrational and unreliable (1990, 255). Anderson's (1991) study of nationalism likewise revolved around the question of how the nation could emerge as an enduring and sovereign entity, a provider of horizontal comradeship that would repeatedly demand immense human sacrifice. In other words, imagined political communities testify to the existence of a shared mental life that articulates itself in invented traditions and standardized narration of histories, acquiring the power to sustain and legitimize order (see also Hobsbawm and Ranger 1983; Renan 1990).

Building on this tradition, science and technology studies have developed a rich conceptual repertoire to investigate how desires, hopes, and promises (as well as the imagined threats, risks, and perils) are reflected in scientific, technological, and infrastructural innovations. Collective imagination constitutes what Ezrahi calls "the masonry of political world-making" (quoted in Jasanoff 2015, 12). Ezrahi (2012) identified the power of imagination in social and political life as a central building block of political orientations and systems of democracy. Turning to this ordering work of imagination means investigating a particular form of power in making and sustaining digital borders. It concerns the understudied region "between imagination and action, between discourse and decision, and between inchoate public opinion and instrumental state policy" (Jasanoff and Kim 2009, 123).

The notion of the "imaginary" can capture this ideational, often diffuse and emotionally charged, but also homogenizing construct that binds people together and produces shared systems of meaning and identity. As Claudia Strauss (2006) argues, the decisive question in the study of imagination concerns the relationship between individual and collective imagination, a recurring theme that she traces back to Marx's theses on ideology and commodity fetishism. Strauss finds that *"imaginaries"* need to "have a concrete location in material objects, institutions, and practices" to become collectivized in the first place (p. 325).[16] Imaginaries are always required when societies collectively establish and sustain political systems: they are brought into being by "fictions, metaphors, ideas, images, or conceptions that acquire the power to regulate and shape political behavior and institutions in a particular society" (Ezrahi 2012, 3).

Collective imagination thus concerns the crucial affective realm of politics, the field of ideas, norms, values, and culture through which groups collectively strive towards possible futures.[17] Jasanoff and Kim's well-known collection of investigations into the power of sociotechnical imaginaries (Jasanoff and Kim 2009, 2013, 2015) defines imaginaries as the "collectively held, institutionally stabilized, and publicly performed visions of desirable futures, animated by shared understandings of forms of social life and social order attainable through, and supportive of, advances in science and technology" (2015a, 4).[18] The term "sociotechnical" denotes the entanglement of technoscientific trajectories with political power, social morality, and institutional hierarchies. Imaginaries can thereby shape (and strengthen) the relationship between individuals, societies, and states once they become naturalized and are made hegemonic. Political power relies upon these performances and affirmations of imaginaries that are potentially mobilized by a myriad of collectives. Shared norms, cultural values, and collective futures are ritually produced, thereby assembling and characterizing entire political cultures (Berezin 1997).[19]

There has been a long-standing discussion in science and technology studies on how to locate the actors and determine the reservoirs of power that enable the design, stabilization, and distribution of shared future visions (Bayer and Felt 2019; Felt 2015, 2017; Hilgartner 2015; Jasanoff 2015b). It requires us to be attentive to communities or social worlds as well as to the material structures involved in their production and dissemination. The gradual extension of visions of the future is hardly ever a linear or natural process; it is contingent on the individuals, collectives, narratives, and performances and usually confronted by various obstacles, contestation, or failures. Rival visions and dissent may occur on one imaginary's path to extension or durability. However, once imaginaries become integrated into the practices of governance, they can dominate the political worlds of groups and become increasingly difficult to be replaced with alternative visions of the public good or societal progress. We need to zoom into the performances of larger visions as well as the myriad of small scales of social, epistemic, and material practices to observe how the wider networks of actors, discourse, policies, and technologies engage in the making of imaginaries.

Of particular interest for this study of the eu-LISA Agency in the digital border regime will be Stephen Hilgartner's concept of "vanguard visions" (2015), which defines visions of progress and desirable futures that still need to be collectivized in order to determine the broader relationship between society, politics, and technoscience. Vanguard visions of the future must be repeatedly performed and disseminated, before becoming stabilized and ultimately translated into imaginaries. Again, such processes of collectivization and normalization are far from self-evident; they are deeply engrained in, and contingent on, numerous cultural, social, and material practices that require deeper scrutiny. Social actors need to develop their resources, capacities, and instruments to carry out acts of assemblage and rehearsal as a community.

As we will see, eu-LISA is an excellent case to study how social groups acquire the material and organizational resources not only to promote but also to rehearse and, to a certain degree, stabilize their visions of future borders. Multiple ideas or visions among different communities may be at play and even in contention; however, it is the uneven distribution of performative power in the EU border regime that allows for filtering, combining, repackaging, and standardizing certain narratives and framings (while suppressing others). Often, this power can align a vaster, heterogeneous actor network consisting of officials, national delegates, experts, and industry representatives to support and disseminate these visions. In this way, collective imagination can be explored as a powerful driver of enacting this "outrageous and heterogeneous collage" (Law 1991, 18), appearing as what is commonly referred to as the European management of borders and migration.

The eu-LISA Agency: exploring an empirical laboratory

As social researchers of science and technology, the choice of where to focus our attention in exploring the digitization of the border regime and how to unpack the so-called virtual world of borders cannot be an arbitrary one. I have chosen to feature the eu-LISA Agency as the main actor in this endeavour. As a relatively unknown organization that has easily been overlooked in the literature, this actor is becoming increasingly relevant for understanding the contemporary dynamics in the border regime. Legally established in 2011 by Regulation (EU) No. 1077/2011, eu-LISA is responsible for administering and developing the main centralized databases related to the governance of migration in the Schengen space. It is also considered an institutional body that can actively promote and advance digital technologies as a "key success factor for the implementation of the Union's policies in the area of justice, security and freedom" (eu-LISA 2014, 1). Following its establishment, eu-LISA was tasked with the day-to-day management of three existing IT systems, the SIS II, VIS, and Eurodac. Even at that time, however, the development of new databases was already anticipated. Member states and their representatives were generally expecting EU border management and asylum policies to become so-called "IT-driven businesses". Therefore, the Agency's creation was also a response to policy makers' anticipations for the further digitization of the border regime. Since then, eu-LISA has continued to grow and, at the time of writing, employs a workforce of approximately 400 staff members.[20] In 2018, eu-LISA was granted an expanded official mandate, strengthening the Agency's standing and expanding its sphere of responsibility (EU 2018a). To summarize, eu-LISA received the legislative tools to roll out interoperability among databases, modernize and create new IT systems, and provide increased know-how and ad hoc assistance to EU member states. Furthermore, the new mandate allowed the Agency to expand its capabilities, evolving into a so-called "centre of excellence", a sort of proactive, entrepreneurial policy actor influencing the landscape of digital innovation within the realm of border and migration management (see also Chapter 2).

It might be tempting to consider eu-LISA's astonishing growth and its expanding digital infrastructure over the last decade as the result of what Morozov (2013) has called "solutionism"—a belief and a means of framing social and political problems in ways that invite (digital) technologies to solve them. The border regime's databases have appeared to offer natural solutions to officials and policy makers—and they have consistently found consensus among EU institutions and national governments. As in eu-LISA's statement cited in the beginning of this book, the digital or virtual world is both prescribed as a solution and portrayed as a necessary result of quasi-autonomous developments that shapes social transformation—a deterministic paradigm that typically accompanies solutionism. At the same time, EU policy makers repeatedly refer to databases and digital technologies as governmental responses to what they perceive as pre-political developments compelling them to take action.

However, eu-LISA's formation was not simply the inevitable outcome in a course of events; various alternatives were discussed in the offices in Brussels. One idea was to centralize the existing databases under the umbrella of the European Commission—an approach that would have required a massive increase in the Commission's human and financial resources. Moreover, member states had reservations about empowering the Commission in the delicate domains of migration and border security, leading them to ultimately conclude that a new European agency would be an alternative that was easier to control. To steer the Agency in the right direction, member states installed a management board comprising representatives of both nation-states and EU institutions. The emergence of eu-LISA can thus be seen as an example of what Sabel and Zeitlin (2010) refer to as experimentalist EU governance: the absence of an overarching institutional authority that enforces rigid, uniform goals and rules in favour of one that provides an institutional space that allows national and supranational administrative elites enough room to navigate and negotiate their interests.

This perspective makes eu-LISA a unique lens through which to observe the manifold practices in the digitization of the border regime that normalize mass dataveillance as a seemingly legitimate and indispensable form of mobility governance. Studying the Agency and its activities means grasping its role as a single institutional body in the border regime—a "vanguard" that represents, tests, and validates values, forms of expertise, knowledge, and justifications. At the same time, eu-LISA provides an opportunity to investigate the acephalous interactions among heterogeneous actors that participate in this digitization process and collectively engage in policy enactments or infrastructural maintenance work. Policy officials, bureaucrats and delegates, industry representatives, experts, and technicians from national governments and agencies are all involved in rehearsing and stabilizing imaginaries, aligning policies, and normalizing border dataveillance. The Agency serves as a focal point where all these diverse actors frequently assemble—where infrastructural practice and collective imagination coalesce. The Agency's operations also span multiple sites, revealing the geographically distributed character of its activities: the operational seat and data centre can be found in Strasbourg (France), its official headquarters in Tallinn (Estonia), a backup or business continuity site is situated in a mountain bunker near Sankt Johann in Austria's Pongau region, and a small liaison office in Brussels (Belgium), the capital of the EU.

This peculiar tension of examining the eu-LISA Agency as single and multiple will be present throughout the book. I do not intend to resolve this tension; I suggest rather drawing on it as an analytically productive element. To this end, I propose to reflect on the Agency through the metaphor of an "empirical laboratory" that is constructed to navigate the phenomenon in question—the digital transformation of the European border regime. eu-LISA should thereby not be seen here as simply another case study—a convenient means of recycling preexisting concepts and theories. Instead, the case suggests a more experimental, empirical approach that can capture multiplicity—(digital) formations, activities, products, artefacts, and dynamics in the digital border regime—while delimiting the territory of the empirical field. This approach assists us in distinguishing a case's inside from its outside, in getting to know our terrain step by step, and applying a certain degree of flexibility in the choice of which actors, policies, technologies, and situations to observe. We may recall Helga Nowotny's (1994) instructive characterization of how sociologists of science became interested in the complex territory of the laboratory: they began to unpack "the activities of the scientists, their technical practice in handling apparatus, [and] in measuring and checking natural processes [...]. The sociologists of science further encountered what was entered and written down. Notes and diagrams of all kinds, photographs and pictures which are produced with the aid of information technologies" (p. 76).

eu–LISA then appears from two perspectives, which I believe are both valid. On the one hand, the Agency exists as an institutionally formed body with distinct tasks, services, and activities in the EU. From this perspective, the book offers a story about an increasingly significant participant in the Schengen laboratory of border and migration control, whose political power and influence on shaping Europe's borders differ significantly from those of the EU's formal political institutions. It is the Agency's imaginative acts and performances, coupled with their commitment to a "politics of service" (Maguire 2023), which makes this case a captivating illustration of how agencies shape the European governance of borders. On the other hand, eu–LISA will prove to be a prism through which the wider dynamics and controversies in the creation and maintenance of digital border infrastructures can be made visible. It allows us to trace the interactions within this network comprising a multitude of elements—actors, imaginaries, practices, and technologies—that bind together this digital border regime and concurrently expose its inherent fragility.

In terms of method, my study has required an ethnographic approach that is interested in practice and routine (Silverman 2006), which allowed engaging with a mixed set of materials to explore how eu–LISA articulates, represents, and intervenes in making digital borders. To negotiate access and shift focus by following new data when they become available, I drew on a variety of supporting empirical sources—from official documents, presentations, visuals, and newspaper articles to email correspondence and informal, interpersonal exchange. Making meticulous fieldnotes and analyzing them throughout the research process, particularly during the early stages of seeking access, was a crucial technique that revealed many features of the social environments that eu–LISA creates and inhabits (Delamont 2007).

Mainly between 2018 and 2021, I observed a series of events with eu–LISA, including the OSCE conference "ID@Borders and the Future of Travel" in Vienna (April 2019), an eu–LISA industry roundtable in Bucharest (April 2019), as well as the Agency's annual conference, its evening event for participants, and the ensuing industry roundtable in Tallinn (October

2019). The COVID-19 pandemic forced organizers to switch into online formats, which allowed me to participate in another series of virtual events, including a conference organized by the technology company Vision-Box, as well as the eu-LISA conference and subsequent industry roundtable in 2020. In most situations, eu-LISA, the Commission, national representatives, and industry players shared the stage to present their agendas and products to establish digital borders in Europe. Furthermore, I conducted field visits to the Agency's headquarters in Tallinn, its liaison office in Brussels, and its operational centre in Strasbourg.[21]

Observational research activities and field visits were essential components for my analysis. Inspired by Annelise Riles (2000), fieldwork at the events and policy meetings brought a wide array of material and artefacts into view that I otherwise would not have gathered. These networks of conferences, roundtables, policy meetings in the border regime serve as crucial and standardized sites of knowledge production and essential spaces where future borders are imagined. They are "field configuring events" (Garud 2008). They produce a series of ethnographic artefacts that enable the proliferation of ideas, values, imaginations, and other types of knowledge, such as reports or presentations, and foster the routinized exchange of contacts. From each of the visits and observations, I was able to construct extensive field reports including field notes, photos, PowerPoint slides, videos, and informal conversations. Events moreover demonstrated the dispersed and multi-sited character of not only the digital border, but also the eu-LISA Agency, and, by extension, the apparatus of border and migration management.[22] Accordingly, field work and participant observation required me to conduct research at multiple sites, as the happenings and official activities stretched across the territory of the EU, including Romania (the then Presidency of the Council of the EU), Estonia and France (the Agency's host countries), Belgium or Austria (hosting additional representations of the Agency).

To investigate eu-LISA effectively, it was necessary to employ the tools of multi-sited ethnography (Marcus 1995). It is important to emphasize that conducting multi-site research does not necessarily oblige the participant-observer to make the specific geographical locations and their practices the primary subjects of study. Instead, as Feldman suggests (2011a), it requires researchers to acknowledge the organization of the (digital) border regime as a relational composition of multiple actors, practices, policies, futures, and technologies. In this manner, the researcher can elucidate practices and routines that are "present in multiple locations but [...] not of any particular location" (Feldman 2011a, 33). Ethnographic observation must therefore operate beyond locality and concentrate on the dynamics of relations.

Within this approach, interviews and more informal conversations were major empirical sets of sources and crucial inscriptions of narrative production (Czarniawska 2004). The narratives and stories told during interview situations were opportunities to make sense of social realities, biographical trajectories, and the wider actor network in which the interviewee is embedded. Interviews have been important ways of eliciting and analyzing the diverse repertoires and devices of narration as they are mobilized and resorted to by the interviewees—heavily depending on their professional practice and position.[23] A key technique in this regard was to apply an exponential, non-discriminatory snowball sampling to identify the network of individuals involved in the policy making or administration of relevant border databases (either on the European or national level), and of those representing national or European interests in the respective working groups of eu-LISA. This provided me with important hints about the manifold social arenas at eu-LISA, the ways in which advisory and working groups operate, and the social and material character in which supranational cooperation takes place in the EU.

As in any snowball sampling, there can be no guarantee of accurate representation, and not all respondents provided contact details of acquainted professionals or colleagues. Nonetheless, this technique allowed me to collect interview material that was not limited to the experiences and perceptions of experts formally representing eu-LISA or the Commission—the study's core focus. Instead, the sampling encompassed a broader informal group of actors with profound knowledge of policies and technologies of digital borders, including officials from institutions such as the Secretariat of EU Council, national programme managers in eu-LISA working groups or on the Agency's management board, individuals engaged in the European Parliament or the Committee on Civil Liberties, Justice and Home Affairs (LIBE), experts acting informally for the EC, or representatives of EU institutions with different forms of critical expertise on digital borders, such as of the European Data Protection Supervisor (EDPS) or the Fundamental Rights Agency (FRA).

Main arguments in this book

Which sociotechnical imaginations of borders and their futures have become enmeshed in the build-up of digital border infrastructure in Europe? And how are these imaginations assembled, performed, and stabilized in the border regime? In the ensuing chapters, this book will explore these questions by following the practices of collective imagination in the infrastructural making of Europe's digital border regime.

eu-LISA often brands itself as the "Schengen information engine"; however, upon closer inspection in this book, we will be cautioned against accepting such mechanistic (and seemingly innocent) rhetoric of an engine that delivers "raw" information on travelers and migrants. Instead, we will begin to see how eu-LISA's digital infrastructure is not simply a backstage tool in bordering Europe but generates visible effects. The central argument I am pursuing is that the expanding digital border infrastructure is a vehicle of collective visions, dreams, and promises of future border in/security. Through the prism of eu-LISA, collective imagination features prominently in the formation of epistemologies, values, knowledges, and representations that produce and legitimize digital EU borders. Ultimately, however, these visions create strategically simplified and sanitized understandings of border control. They express a governmental desire to manage abstract digitized "migrant objects" in experimental ways rather than assume responsibility for the realities of migration and the everyday violence that stems from crossing the EU's highly securitized borders.

This argument will be upheld across the different themes covered in the book chapters, which centre on the various infrastructural projects and policies, the labour of crafting, performing, and legitimizing them at eu-LISA, or the solutionist-driven ideologies that these projects and policies pursue. The book's chapters also display the vast range of imaginative and infrastructural labour that eu-LISA as this "Schengen engine" implicates. Between chapters, I provide empirical vignettes ("Interludes") with reflections, personal impressions of fieldwork, notes on methodology, or empirical challenges. They should offer the reader a firsthand account of doing research in the digital border regime. Illustrating concrete episodes of fieldwork, I find them particularly advantageous for conveying some of the important personal reflections that undergird more theoretical arguments in the chapters.

Chapters 2 and 3 will delve into the institutional organization of the Agency as a multiple and single actor. They carry us to the sites at which collective imagination and infrastructural work are performed. Chapter 2 probes into the Agency's role as a vanguard in designing the sociotechnical imaginary of digital transformation while aligning a wider actor network to support and sustain this imaginary. It demonstrates how this vision of a transformation has been carefully crafted, collectivized, and materialized through embracing an experimental approach to making digital border infrastructure in Europe.

Chapter 3 analyzes how eu-LISA stages ideas and visions of Europe and Europeanhood through the diverse work of infrastructuring. It examines acts of frontstaging and backstaging that present a fragmented composition of border infrastructure as a promise of united collectivity, coherence, and European integration.

Chapters 4 and 5 investigate two essential sites at which actors, databases, visions, and narratives are assembled in the making of new digital borders. Chapter 4 analyses the project of creating smart borders in Europe. It focuses on their distinct epistemology, enabled through modes of collaboration and narrative repertoires deployed at events, conferences, and roundtables.

The chapter seeks to understand how abstract and logistical visions of (smart) borders strategically detach us from the concrete realities and social implications of cross-border mobility.

Chapter 5 discusses the making of interoperability. It examines this policy's creation as a "necessary fiction" (Ezrahi 2012), which translates a contested, technical idea into a powerful political programme. This fiction can enact various solutionist ways of seeing and speaking about borders, steering collective discourse and behaviour in the management of European migration.

Chapter 6 summarizes some of the core arguments and implications put forward in this book—pondering on the powers and perils of imagining future borders. It suggests rejecting the predominant visions of digital borders and their futures and fundamentally rerouting them to focus on responsibility and accountability for human beings and their diverse forms of mobility.

Finally, Chapter 7, a short postscript, addresses the repercussions of two developments—the use of Artificial Intelligence and the COVID-19 pandemic, and their likely impact on transforming border infrastructures in the future.

First Interlude: Doing Research From Within the Border Regime

Field research involves different experiences of approaching and learning the empirical territory, replete with difficulties, frustrations, and idiosyncrasies. As a researcher, sometimes you do not reach your goal by the shortest route, but through detours, aberrations, and breaks. To bridge this Introduction and the ensuing chapters in the book, I propose here to acknowledge some of the pausing moments that emerged during empirical research and prompted reflection on the complex positionality of a researcher within the border regime, the conditions of access that must be negotiated, as well as the risks and limitations inherent in this type of research. At these junctures, memo writing and research diaries have proven to be indispensable tools to enact what John Law calls method assemblages (2004), connecting various sensitizing concepts, observations, methodological orientations, and analytical strategies, but also preserve the principles of openness, non-closure, and multiplicity within the realm of research practice. At times, these moments resembled the observation of doing science in its early stages by Ludwik Fleck, a physician and biologist: "amazement, a searching for similarities, trial by experiment, retraction as well as hope and disappointment. Feeling, will, and intellect all function together as an indivisible unit. The research worker gropes but everything recedes, and nowhere is there a firm support […]. Every formulation melts away at the next test" (1981 [1935], 94). Research on the "social" is predominantly characterized by its procedural and iterative nature, and it includes spontaneous and opposing observations that challenge a researcher's presumptions, prejudices, or prepared hypotheses. As Law (2004) argues, social scientific method must grapple with mess. Social scientists should account for the messy realities they encounter rather than sanitize and simplify empirical worlds by forcing them into neatly preconceived boxes of social theory.

In practice, this often poses a challenge, and it certainly presented challenges during my research on the eu-LISA Agency and the development of new digital borders. It was crucial, for instance, to systematically consider the contingent local and social conditions of field access as well as the diverse gate-keeping methods employed by Agency professionals in the border regime. In my particular case, obtaining access was not solely reliant on the willingness of established contacts, but instead had to be negotiated throughout numerous email conversations and requests directed to various officials, each of whom may have pursued their own vested interests in my research. For example, I observed interlocutors within the Agency strategizing about ways (regardless of their level of seriousness) to potentially leverage social scientific research to the Agency's benefit or advantage. Additionally, it is noteworthy that my efforts to establish contact through direct, personal communication with individuals might be considered unconventional when dealing with an official EU border security agency. Nevertheless, this was facilitated by the fact that the Agency was still a relatively young organization and had not yet fully completed formalized or standardized protocols for engaging with social researchers. This meant that were no rigidly controlled channels of communication, formal permissions, or strict access controls over its staff members. Like any Agency, eu-LISA has found itself entangled in institutional competition, struggling for visibility and resources within the EU, a situation that has also affected its accessibility. As one representative pointed out, "I'm not criticizing, but I'm saying it's much […] easier to say, 'let's give 10.000 border guards to Frontex.' Because this [will] impact the public opinion: 'look, we are doing something!' But if you look at eu-LISA, you do what? [… P]ut someone behind a computer?" One can only speculate whether these circumstances have eased access to some of the Agency's members and events, even though the overall research accessibility to the Agency remains complicated—as is typical in the realm of security actors and institutions (Bosma, De Goede, and Pallister-Wilkins 2020; Klimburg-Witjes, Leese, and Trauttmansdorff 2022).

Conducting research and collecting data in (border) security contexts often occur in secured or sensitive environments, leading to significant ethical implications for social scientific research. An obvious case can be made for articulating one's own position clearly vis-à-vis officials and other research participants, for example by explicitly outlining study objectives, intentions, and directions. Additionally, research, not only in security contexts, often requires utmost confidentiality when handling collected data, such as interview material, transcripts, or audio files, through processes of anonymization and safe storage. At the same time, adhering to standard research practices and meeting formal requirements in environments of security and secrecy can be challenging, if not entirely unattainable, even when trying to obtain simple forms of consent.

However, there is another delicate aspect that relates to one's own movement and activity within such security settings, like those involving a border agency: it requires the researcher to provide personal data (either voluntary or involuntary) in exchange for collecting empirical data.

The act of providing information can have significant disempowering consequences—a fact well recognized by scholars in borders studies. In relatively conventional and seemingly innocuous scenarios, this involved disclosing personal information such as one's name, nationality, and address to gain access to eu-LISA events. On another occasion, I found myself having to submit passport copies and my fingerprints to enter one of eu-LISA's facilities—without knowing about the potential whereabouts of these data. In these circumstances, there is often little time available to make an informed decision and ponder its ethical implications for the research being conducted. What remains is a firsthand encounter with a security culture in which the routine usage of biometric fingerprinting appears entirely normal. Clearly, such experiences give rise to questions regarding the limited scope and meaning of the concept of informed consent within highly securitized, biometric environments more broadly.

Then there is what we often casually refer to as the broader context in which my ethnographically oriented research was situated. A significant portion of this book was composed while I was at an Italian university, in a country where the former Italian Minister of Interior (and, at the time of writing, Minister of Infrastructure and Transport) was undergoing trial on charges of deprivation of liberty and abuse of authority. In 2019, he had issued an order to deny the "Sea Watch 3", a vessel that had rescued 53 migrants off the Libyan coast, entry into Italian waters. When, after more than two weeks at open sea in critical conditions, the ship decided to enter the port of Lampedusa, an Italian patrol boat unsuccessfully attempted to block its entry. The captain of the patrol boat was arrested, and the ship was seized. The then Minister of the Interior accused its captain and the crew of being "criminals" who had committed an "act of war" (D'Alessio 2021).

Other contextual factors at play included Poland's imposition of a state of emergency along its border with Belarus, a military-sealed zone extending three kilometres that denied access to everyone, including journalists, nongovernmental organizations, and other civil society actors. The EU and Poland accused Belarus of using migrants as a "weapon", luring them with false promises onto EU territory and engaging in hybrid warfare—forcibly pushing back migrants and leaving them trapped in a deadly border area. These are just two examples that illustrate an increasingly violent and deadly border regime, where seemingly exceptional cases of violence against basic human rights, push backs, and the denial of asylum rights become normalized—alongside the criminalization of rescue and help and the militarization of border control. Furthermore, Russia's invasion of Ukraine, which began on 24 February 2022, has caused millions of people to seek protection in EU countries. While EU member states have made a significant decision to open their borders to provide temporary protection of displaced individuals from Ukraine, their doors remain largely closed for non-Ukrainian nationals, underscoring the inherently racist underpinnings of the border regime.

My research took place in locations that, on the surface, seem remote or disconnected from these instances of crime and human tragedy. However, it is essential to recognize that they are embedded in the same border regime, which aims to control human mobility and prevent the entry to those deemed undesirable. Most policy events or conferences I attended as a researcher were primarily focused on enhancing the effectiveness of border and migration control. Needless to say, it is imperative to acknowledge the violent consequences that accompany these efforts to maintain the "effectiveness" of this regime.

At the same time, my seeming disconnect or distance at these conferences and events was interesting. More generally, it requires a researcher to be mindful of how they can gain insights into the gradual making of a digitized border regime and the directions into which their gaze is guided. For instance, comprehending the mechanics of digital bordering first and foremost necessitates knowledge of a language that is specialized, abstract, and expert-driven. The clearest indicator of this is maybe the omnipresent use of acronyms, manifest in the social and political arenas of the border regime. How to communicate and write about digital borders, including the use of their specific linguistic terminology, becomes a delicate matter. Engaging with key actors, their behaviours, and their discourses means not only understanding how they think and speak, but also, perhaps even more delicate, learning and adopting to think and speak like them. Acronyms are an obvious example for embracing and internalizing this specialized language, as they provide a sense of mastery over highly complex and legally intricate technologies and regulatory systems. Carol Cohn (1987a, 1987b) highlighted in her influential work on nuclear language by defence intellectuals that "[a] more subtle […] element of learning the language is that, when you speak it, you feel in control" (1987b, 704). This seems unavoidably present also in the technical, bland language employed by the policy makers and designers of digital borders. It is a language that effectively black-boxes or avoids human reference in the machinery of digital borders (see Chapter 4). Any study aimed at unravelling the inner operations of the digital border regime carries this risk of perpetuating and normalizing its language and underlying logics. I do not believe that there is a one-sitz-fits-all-solution to this problem, such as avoiding acronyms whenever possible. My own position is instead that it is imperative to listen to this professionalized discourse and narratives and understand how they contribute to what I, along with Cohn, refer to as "technostrategic effects" that enter the imaginaries of border security. Ultimately, it is up to the reader to judge whether I have appropriately addressed this concern in my writing on the powers and perils of imagining future digital borders.

As a result, the themes in this book will analytically prioritize aspects resembling the inner workings of the digital border regime. This has its obvious limitations as it does not incorporate the essential perspective of migration and migrants' autonomous acts and subjectivities. Autonomy of migration approaches argue that borders should be explored by privileging (the viewpoints of) mobility and migration, as these always precede the logics, developments, and operations of borders (see, for example, De Genova 2017; Mezzadra 2011; Scheel 2013; Tsianos and Karakayali 2010). Although this work does not fully embrace this approach, it is crucial to acknowledge that the absence of such perspectives constitutes a significant gap. This book cannot include the concrete situational encounters of bordering, which would lend more significance to these perspectives. At the same time, however, this does not imply that the contemporary injustices, violence, and oppression in present-day border regimes go unnoticed. Nonetheless, it leaves my research endeavours with modest intentions: I aim to shed light onto the sociopolitical character, ongoing viability, and persistent fragility of the European border regime through conducting research on collective imagination and digital infrastructuring from within. I write this story in a spirit that aligns with Rose's adept description of an author's partial grasp, which recognizes

> what little one grasps and the great gulf of ignorance which that partial grasp reveals. [... F]or to satisfy the demand that one might write without ignorance would not only make writing impossible; it would also deny that encounter with the unknown that carries with it the possibility, however slim, of contributing to a difference. (Rose 1999, 13–14)

2

The Imaginary
of Digital Transformation

The registering, processing, and storing of migrant data have proliferated and transformed the landscape of border control in Europe.[1] This chapter describes how IT systems have become an integral part of the discursive and material infrastructures of the border regime in the EU, and how these hold the complex logics and the imaginaries of control in place. As the digital infrastructures of borders are built, they "become spaces of bordering practices in their own right" (Walters 2009, 495). This is aptly demonstrated by the decades-long, legal and technological expansion of biometric IT systems such as the Eurodac system, the centralized fingerprint database for asylum seekers, or the Visa Information System, which stores and crosschecks the biometric identities of visa applicants. In official terms, the EU seeks to manage migration by continuously improving "the Union's data management architecture for border management and security" (EU 2019a, 1), which is based on the promise of constructing new databases, such as the centralized Entry/Exit System (EES), and promoting interoperability between databases, for example, through an underlying common identity repository of biometric templates.[2] The continuous build-up and expansion of transnational databases and the practices they involve not only testify to a digital solutionism behind contemporary processes of rebordering but can also be seen as part of the "reaction formations" to cross-border mobility (De Genova 2017a, 5)—a process we describe as the digital infrastructuring of borders.

This chapter also moves away for a moment from focusing on the heavy investment in databases and related IT infrastructures to reconfigure borders and instead begins to investigate collective visions of border (in)security as key actors within these developments. In doing so, we will specifically look at the role of eu-LISA—the responsible body for developing and building IT systems, which aims to "provide continuous monitoring of infrastructure, services and systems" (eu-LISA 2015a, 8). Being interested in the imaginative dimension of this technological project, specific attention will be devoted to how databases and related infrastructures encode and translate future visions of (in)security and social order. In other words, the chapter will examine the interplay between collective imagination and processes of digital infrastructuring. It will direct our attention to eu-LISA's construction and rehearsal of a sociotechnical imaginary of digital transformation, which aims to stabilize both the shared vision of border (in)security and the related infrastructure.

Drawing on the work of Stephen Hilgartner (2015), the chapter analyzes the efforts of eu-LISA in trying to implement what Hilgartner called a "vanguard vision" of the sociotechnological problem at stake. Furthermore, we will follow the work done to transform it into a widely shared and institutionally stabilized sociotechnical imaginary, which is actualized through the emerging digital infrastructure. Unpacking the making of this imaginary will allow us to understand why and how the visions of certain futures seem to prevail over others and, most importantly, become politically normalized and powerful—even though officials and experts oftentimes refer to the actual construction and operation of databases/digital infrastructures as yet fragile and uncertain.

The chapter's analysis contributes to the body of scholarship at the intersection of migration and border studies, on the one hand, and science and technology studies (STS), on the other. These studies have explored the various processes of infrastructuring to bring out the often invisible, laborious, and taken-for-granted work needed for the creation and maintenance of contemporary borders. We might call this turn a heuristic shift to studying how actors, institutions, and technologies "move migrants within specific infrastructural frames" (Lin et al. 2017, 169) and become part of an increasingly logistified management of migration (Altenried et al. 2018; Mezzadra 2017). A shared emphasis among scholars has been directed towards the emergence and proliferation of techno-material devices and practices that enact migrations in and to Europe (Leese, Noori, and Scheel 2022; Scheel, Ruppert, and Ustek-Spilda 2019). The digitization of border and migration management has also been examined as the formation of an "administrative ecology" (Dijstelbloem and Broeders 2015), calling for an investigation of the hidden scripts of a violent border regime. Migrations are brought into being and rendered governable through practices of inscription and visualization (Dijstelbloem, van Reekum, and Schinkel 2017; Follis 2017; Pezzani and Heller 2019; van Reekum 2019). At the same time, infrastructures "reveal and […] perform broader legislative, political and administrative transformations in the European bureaucratic order" (Pelizza 2020, 263). In other words, border and migration control infrastructures are co-produced with the sociopolitical orderings of Europe (Pelizza 2020; Pollozek and Passoth 2019).

However, what these studies have given less attention to is the powerful role of sociotechnical visions, which forms the core contribution of this chapter's analysis. To this end, the chapter will first outline a conceptual approach to borders as sites of experimentation, and then proceed with the empirical analysis for this chapter.

First, we will have to revisit the making of eu-LISA as a relatively young institution in the EU border regime and how it enables its member states to centralize a growing digital infrastructure of borders. Through orchestrating relations between various actors in the EU border regime, the Agency has positioned itself as a vanguard in forging and rehearsing a particular vision of reconfiguring borders by digital means. Secondly, we will delve into the practices of narration and visualization that construct a particular future imaginary to be realized through the "digital transformation". Third, the chapter will examine when and how this imaginary is rehearsed to align new actors with each other. In doing so, the Agency adopts an experimental approach, gradually developing and testing potential options, and thereby working towards the imaginary's stabilization.

Conceptualizing EU borders as sites of experimentation

To capture the heterogeneous bordering processes in Europe, the notion of the "regime" has been used to describe the "multitude of actors whose practices relate to each other, without, however, being ordered in the form of a central logic or rationality" (Tsianos and Karakayali 2010, 375). Scholars have more recently argued that digital infrastructures have become key sites and arenas for the interplay and contestation between state and nonstate actors, (im)mobilities, and various regulatory practices in the border regime (Amelung et al. 2020; Lin et al. 2017; Pelizza 2020; Pollozek 2020). The distributed character of infrastructures has directed their attention to the multiple and dispersed operations of control through which borders enact and maintain their "double function of politics at a distance and virtual data collection" (Tsianos and Karakayali 2010, 374).

However, to understand the distinct experimental character through which these digital borders are currently developed, deployed, and policed, it seems valuable to employ the notion of the "laboratory" as a sensitizing framework. This notion has traditionally been used as a metaphor to describe Schengen as a "testbed" for European integration and transnational cooperation between security actors to govern mobile populations (Hess and Kasparek 2017, 60; Zaiotti 2011, 74–75). In this context, we may consider the introduction and expansion of a large-scale digital infrastructure as the laboratorization of the Schengen Area (allowing free movement of people), effectively transforming borders into sites of experimentation. According to

Karin Knorr Cetina (1999), the laboratory is conceived as a space in which objects can be manipulated and reconfigured so that "they match with an appropriately altered social order" (p. 44). However, experimentation has also been increasingly carried out beyond the classical laboratory, and we have witnessed the emergence of concepts such as "living labs", "real-world laboratories", and "society as a laboratory" (Guggenheim 2012; Van De Poel, Mehos, and Asveld 2017). This is in line with Engels, Wentland, and Pfotenhauer's (2019) argument that, currently, "it is society *as well as* technology that are subject to experimentation and testing" (p. 3, emphasis in original).

This chapter's understanding of the border laboratory follows Guggenheim's definition (2012) that characterizes the laboratory not as a physical, fully controlled territory but as space of experimentality that aims to bring under control the data and objects it seeks to manage. The laboratory is thereby essentially a "procedure that often results in a space with the properties to separate controlled inside from uncontrolled outside" (p. 101). Not only do borders move into the laboratory (Bourne, Johnson, and Lisle 2015), but the Schengen space as a laboratory "must be permanently brought into being, and it must be imagined and practiced" (Felt 2017, 153). The introduction of large-scale infrastructures in the border regime must therefore be imagined and gradually implemented to establish this space of experimentality. Take, for example, this statement of a senior official in the EU: "Now, the real test is with the development of new systems. And we have to see how that works out" (Interview 13, 2019). This official does not understand and anticipate the build-up of IT systems in the border regime to be an infrangible project with stable and transparent outcomes. Instead, he implies that uncertainty and instability might be gradually reduced through a process of experimentation. In that sense, experimentation turns infrastructures into emerging sites for engaging with and producing "new worlds" (Jensen and Morita 2015, 85) and the limits thereof. It is a procedure that performs what Callon, Lascoumes, and Barthe (2009) call "laboratorization", a continual and "interminable undertaking, always starting up again" (p. 67).

What is central to the (experimental) process of infrastructuring, as this chapter will argue throughout, is how it is imagined and performed and by whom. How can infrastructures become those "emblematic reflections and representations of particular social or political agendas" (Aarden 2017, 754)? Following Jasanoff and Kim's framework of sociotechnical imaginaries (2009; 2015), we will trace the "collectivized visions of social order and (in)security" that are promoted as "attainable through, and supportive of, advances in science and technology" (Jasanoff 2015a, 15). As Jasanoff contends, designs of the future, articulated as collective acts of imagination, operate as "a crucial reservoir of power and action [that] lodges in the hearts and minds of human agents and institutions" (p. 17). Driven by the promises of science and technology, future visions of border (in)security are disseminated to become "integrated into the discourses and practices of governance" (Jasanoff 2015b, 329). The strength of this framework lies in its capacity to explain how a particular technological trajectory within the border regime is related to the construction and gradual domination of certain visions of order and progress—through advances in digital technology.

Imaginaries have been associated predominantly with the modern nation-state that orchestrated the co-production of visions of science and technology with national policies, regulations, and institutions. However, forging and advancing imaginaries are frequently carried out by smaller collectives, such as institutions or corporate actors that may operate on the transnational level (Sadowski and Bendor 2019; Schiølin 2020). Pickersgill (2011) uses the case of neuroscience and law to show how imaginaries of transnational collectives (other than states) can be constitutive of, and simultaneously produced by, anticipatory and normative discourses that either develop and promote, or limit and restrict, certain engagements and ways of thinking. Institutional actors can secure their ascent and positions of power if they possess the means and resources to assemble and stabilize imaginaries, that is, to homogenize the visions of collectives and gradually silence alternatives. In this context, Hilgartner (2015) speaks about vanguards who portray themselves as the chosen harbingers of change by promoting bold or progressivist visions yet to be stabilized or embraced by larger political or social collectives.

The study of eu-LISA is a case in point. The chapter will illustrate the Agency as a European vanguard that assembles, rehearses, and stabilizes the sociotechnical imaginary of digital transformation. Although its representatives tend to emphasize the technocratic character of this Agency, their shared imaginations routinely focus on the digital infrastructure of borders, turning it into a vehicle "whereby those fantasies are transmitted and made emotionally real" (Larkin 2013, 333). By examining the emergence, projects, and activities of this European institution, we can further delve into the gradual formation and rehearsal of a specific vision of future borders, its underpinning norms and values, and the process of its materialization.

Connecting these two lines of thinking—infrastructural experimentation and collective imagination—the Schengen borders will be investigated as sites of infrastructural experimentation and allow us to trace how an imaginary can obtain agency in shaping technological change, becoming scripted "into the hard edifices of matter and practices" (Jasanoff 2015b, 323).

"Not just an IT system": the eu-LISA Agency as vanguard

Following its legal formation in 2011, the eu-LISA Agency has grown into a central node within the EU border regime. Although the Agency administers and develops six relevant large-scale databases related to the governance of borders and migration today, there are still few academic contributions that account for the distinctive role of this institutional actor and its practices. Bigo (2014), for example, mentions that the Agency represents a regrouping of software engineers and technicians and institutionalizes a perception of borders as "something to be analysed as points of entry and exit, connected through computerized networks that gather and analyse the traces of travelers" (p. 217). Another notable exception is also Tsianos and Kuster's (2016a) article on "the power of big data within the emerging European IT agency", which conceptualizes eu-LISA as a "technological zone" that ultimately intensifies surveillance through its expansionist and technocratic character, striving for the "optimization of technical process solutions, advanced data convertibility, and the excess of data" (p. 240). In a similar fashion, Glouftsios (2021) analyzes eu-LISA's mundane technological work to make visible how maintenance and repair "sustains the power to govern international mobility by digital means" (p. 457).

While it is certainly worth acknowledging the significance of its technocratic character, I suggest examining eu-LISA also as a central agent in imagining and anticipating a vision of border (in)security that should be materialized through its (experimental) practices. This will allow us to see how the Agency operates as a hybrid institutional space in which various epistemic communities interact and various futures of borders are anticipated and negotiated. As one Agency representative paraphrased it, eu-LISA is "an Agency that ensures many things" (Interview 3, 2018).

In the EU's emblematic regulatory jargon, Regulation No. 1077/2011 sets forth the rationale for establishing the Agency: "With a view to achieving synergies, it is necessary to provide for the operational management of large-scale IT systems in a single entity, benefitting from economies of scale, creating critical mass and ensuring the highest possible utilization rate of capital and human resources" (EU 2011, 2). The creation of the Agency is here explained as a rational and cost-sensitive step to efficiently govern the expected expansion of large-scale IT systems in the so-called area of justice, security, and freedom. At the same time, this story conceals the rather complex and diverging interests and contestations involved in the making of this institution, which involved the rearranging of knowledge patterns and governmental negotiations vis-à-vis techno-scientific developments.

The European Commission's continuous aspirations of Europeanizing the agenda of border security through centralized IT systems, such as the Visa Information System and Eurodac, have always been met with some scepticism by EU member states. EU states therefore did not embrace the prospect of a larger border infrastructure project becoming part of the Commission's domain, as it would have meant boosting the Commission's resources and thus its institutional power over the sensitive agenda of migration and borders. The increasing extension of borders into the virtual realm of databases thus turned European IT systems into sites of institutional struggles for sovereignty and power. Consequently, one national interviewee emphasized, "this is the member states' data. So, we are owning the data, which is important, so it is still, [...] let's call it communication towards the member states [...] that this is our Agency" (Interview 24, 2019). EU agencies are not simply the European Commission's little helpers but are often compromise solutions that epitomize the experimentalist framework of EU governance (Sabel and Zeitlin 2010). Established as an agency, eu–LISA has thus allowed to shift the necessary technical, human, and financial resources to a "European" body in better control of member states. A management board with representatives of the member states and the Commission was installed to oversee "the effective and coherent delivery of the eu–LISA vision" (eu–LISA 2022a). Accordingly, the Agency must also ensure it "continuously align[s] the capabilities of technology with the evolving needs of Member States" (eu–LISA 2017a, 4).[3]

This brief account of the negotiated establishment of the Agency also explains its relative institutional autonomy, which enables it to advance some of its own agenda within broader objectives of EU border and migration policy. At the same time, it gives member states a sense of centralized control over the transnational IT systems. Nonetheless, this chapter takes a step further by asserting that the Agency has established itself as a vanguard, formulating and acting "to realize particular sociotechnical visions of the future that have yet to be accepted by wider collectives" (Hilgartner 2015, 34). Consequently, eu–LISA should be regarded as an institution-in-the-making—one that solidifies and legitimizes an expanding transnational dataveillance landscape in the EU border laboratory. Hence, it becomes important to dissect its narratives through which ideological and normative elements become enmeshed with future visions of border (in)security and its material infrastructure.

Narrating the transformation: inevitability, unidirectionality, and crisis

Three core narrative elements repeatedly emerged in the conversations with senior officials and higher representatives of eu–LISA and in their public appearances at official events. At times, they clash with individual statements made by national experts and practitioners at the Agency, which tend to highlight its strictly executive mandate. Nonetheless, the Agency actually appears as a vanguard by imagining and anticipating a particular future, creating a moral economy around it, and discursively setting "the conditions of possibility for action in the present, in which the future is inhabited in the present" (Adams, Murphy, and Clarke 2009, 249). These narrations are frequently combined in the concept of "digital transformation", which articulates an abstract future horizon and echoes broader contemporary imaginaries such as the "digital revolution". At the same time, it signals the Agency's desire for change and the promise to actualize change through its infrastructural practices.

The first narrative element relates to the inevitable and totalizing character of digital transformation to bring into being our secure future. Techno-optimist sentiment prevails in this narrative, but the meaning of inevitability also disempowers social actors, framing them as exposed to and not agents of technological change. They are passengers without the capacity to steer: "One of the things I constantly repeat in different fora, […] indeed, today we see [a] very major transformation of border management and internal security" (Interview 1, 2018). Another high-ranked EU official claims likewise: "We are witnessing a deep transformation as a fast process of convergence" (field note, eu-LISA conference, 16 October 2019). As such statements are omnipresent, they together discursively affirm and reproduce inevitability and situate the future in the here and now. It is a quasi-compulsory vision calling for immediate action in the present. During an eu-LISA event, one of the presenters argued, "You are starting this journey whether you want it or not" (field note, eu-LISA Industry Roundtable, 24 April 2019). The policy fields of border control, migration management, and internal security are framed as converging pieces fully determined by the "whole"—they become, inevitably, elements of the same "bigger and unique journey" (field note, eu-LISA Industry Roundtable, 17 October 2019). This "digital journey", in which everyone is perceived to be a voluntary or an involuntary passenger, conditions the scope and rationale of the Agency's interventions: "We step into the future and invest into the future, that is what we do today" (field note, eu-LISA Industry Roundtable, 24 April 2019), whereas "all these expenses, if you like, are in fact investments for the future of all" (Interview 3, 2018). Rendering the transformation inevitable in the name of a secure future frames the Agency's building and expansion of a digital border infrastructure as a mandatory intervention.

The second core element constructed through narration and visualization is unidirectionality. It provides another powerful resource for officials to endow digital transformation with authoritative determination. For instance, during an official presentation, the Agency would symbolize unidirectionality by a linear arrow (see Figure 2.1). The arrow signals the integration of both time and technology into one clearly directed progression, leading to a fully virtualized space. The caption a "shift from physical to virtual" plainly invokes the notion that we find ourselves on a trajectory of change, on "a cumulative journey […] from now to then" (Appadurai 2013, 223). In a conversation, a senior official explained that the transformation's "most obvious aspect, of course, is movement from the physical to the virtual

Figure 2.1: "Transformation", a slide presented at the ID@Borders conference (April 2019) by eu–LISA

Source: © eu–LISA

world, which means that today, border management and internal security, migration management, all those areas are totally dependent [...] from the data and information available" (Interview 1, 2018).

While these representations remind us of neoliberal dreams of data-driven, seamless global networks and flows in contemporary capitalism, they also appear to render invisible the physicality of border environments, migrant bodies, barriers, queues, and checks by shifting them to a virtualized space. This image promises to detach human mobility from its very physical and local situatedness and render it into data streams and data points that are visible and actionable in a laboratory-like environment operating on a seemingly global scale. Conceptualizing the transformation as a unidirectional shift from "physical to virtual" neglects not only the human dimension of such transformation, but also the many collateral realities (Law 2015) that are created and that migrants have to confront. The virtualized laboratory articulates a desire to obtain one particular mode of authorized seeing (Jasanoff 2017), that is, a "view from beyond", that conceals any frictions between human mobility and border control. The lab then seeks to dissolve the boundaries between the site and object of experimentation, translating both border settings and migratory human subjects into data that ought to be channeled and calibrated.

The third recurrent narrative element identified is the double sense of urgency and insecurity, repeatedly conjured by a future that is couched not only in progressivist notions but also in visions of crisis and undesirable threats. For instance, eu-LISA's (2017a) public strategy implies that its activities seek to avoid the "dramatic consequences on the future of Europe" if Europe reveals itself of being "too open and therefore exposed to the effects of globalization" (p. 7). More generally, the concept of crisis is routinely invoked to render necessary the continuous build-up and implementation of large-scale IT systems. As one Agency official argued, "we experience in Europe a lot of immigration and financial crises, two crises at the same time, especially with immigration and war around the Mediterranean. [... Y]ou will see that indeed, the situation [...] we experienced the last three, four years augmented, if you like, the need for the systems" (Interview 3, 2018).

The "digital transformation" presents a project that secures European order against a future that is pictured as potentially undesirable and dangerous. The invocation of "crisis" both naturalizes and affirms challenges to social order while calling to solve them via a technological fix. As a permanent diagnosis, as Schinkel (2015) defines Walter Benjamin's conceptualization of crisis, it appears "in the form of a crisis-recovery, of a crisis-as-opportunity and therefore at best of an affirmative critique" (p. 44). The transformation imaginary therefore engenders a crisis/order combination that, at the same time, perpetuates the illusion of techno-scientific progress.

eu–LISA's sociotechnical imaginary is assembled by means of a specific set of narrations and visualizations that portray the digital transformation as inevitable, unidirectional, and urgently needed. These elements may not be exceptional and resemble similar tropes in large-scale technological projects or innovation; however, they gain credibility and compose this imaginary only through specific, situated narrative performances. They allow the Agency to portray itself as a vanguard with almost eschatological potential. One official argued, "we are the people who materialize the needs of the European citizens […]. We are the people who make their concerns […] or their wishes reality, through technology" (Interview 3, 2018).

The invocation of the "European citizens" and their desires that must be directly realized by the Agency's techno-material intervention implies that its vanguard role does not require conventional democratic legitimacy. It seems to be substituted by the Agency's role as a harbinger and frontrunner in driving the transformation—"this very fast process of convergence between border management, internal security and migration management" (Interview 1 with EU official, 2018). The sense of urgency is important to the evocation of an exceptional space in which the Agency wants to offer a disciplining guidance and epistemic orientation, demanding compliance with techno-centric transformations promising security for the future. At the same time, it limits the discursive space in which this future could be called into question, marginalizing alternative visions or framing them as destabilizing.

Embedding and rehearsing the transformation imaginary

Aligning Actors—Turning a vision into a shared imaginary
In the institutional machinery in this Schengen border-laboratory, eu–LISA's function as a "knowledge hub" should provide an arena in which different actors and communities can engage in collective acts of imagination. At the Agency's official events, this sometimes can happen in overemphatic ways, for instance, when the audience is called upon to acknowledge the "power of thought and imagination to create something", and Abraham Lincoln is quoted as saying "the best way to predict the future is to actually create it" (eu–LISA 2019a).

Conferences, industry roundtables, and other forums are spaces in which to circulate discourses or problematizations of "smart" or "new" technologies among a variety of policy delegates, technical experts, industry representatives, and national bureaucrats in the police and migration sectors. These professionals use these meetings to communicate as "peers" in the border regime, speak about potential future challenges, and foresee and anticipate change (Interview 17, 2019). As Feldman (2014) crucially observed, the protocols of such ritualized meetings "ossify" social patterns that create the "epistemological condition for policy knowledge, and a discourse through which migration can be described as a particular kind of problem" (p. 49). These gatherings then also engage professionals and delegates in particular future-making practices and give them the feeling of speaking a common language (see also Chapter 4).

The ostentatious, anticipatory orientation toward the future testifies here to the important role of building aspirational regimes and transnational communities for digitally infrastructuring borders (Wienroth 2018). Participants must embark on the almost impossible task of creating a shared epistemological space in which they can discuss a "European" understanding of digital borders. This sense is expressed, for instance, by one of the participants who was interviewed:

> [T]here is a very big difference [in] understanding what this all means. [… W]e have different actors: ministerial actors, there are agencies, there are different agencies, there are ICT people, there are people working with the national legislation. And it's very hard, […] to form a common understanding of what's happening and what is needed on the national level. So, these seminars, […] it's actually distributing information to everybody. (Interview 26 with a member state representative, 2019)

Despite these apparent challenges, meetings allow the Agency to align other actors and rehearse the transformation imaginary in a setting inhabited by a wide range of European security professionals and commercial stakeholders. A high-ranked official, for example, appeals to "the industry to join in this broader project, in this bigger and unique journey" (field notes, eu-LISA Industry Roundtable, 17 October 2019). eu-LISA therefore constitutes the "territory" in which technological promises and futures are collectively framed and promoted. Beyond policy meetings and conferences, the Agency seeks to enrol actors by publishing in quarterly publications such as *Border Management Today*, which likewise address the broader epistemic communities of security and IT professionals.[4] Here, the buzzwords and slogans are pitched, in repetitive style, to illustrate the contours of the imaginary: "the digital transformation of border management in the EU and globally will continue at high pace in the coming years" (Garkov 2020, 29). "Stakeholders", such as "carriers, passengers, airport and seaport operators and other relevant actors", need to be integrated into the process of "redesign[ing] of business models at the borders" (Garkov 2020, 29) and aligned with this vision. Therefore, the alignment of a growing number of diverse actors must be achieved to stabilize eu-LISA's sociotechnical imaginary and to fully unfold the power of its material realization—the IT infrastructure of border control.

A process of experimentation

In the EU border regime, the transformation imaginary is furthermore embedded in concrete practices and activities, assembling the material infrastructure, the meaning it should acquire, and the normative values that promise to preserve order. Understood as "practices of experimentation" with and through the gradual infrastructuring of borders, they illustrate how futures are not simply imagined collectively in a vacuum but rehearsed in specific contexts and integrated into, and thus stabilized through, concrete artefacts and projects. Experimentation is here conceived not as a sudden, large-scale social experiment, but as a continuous, staged process driven forward by agencies such as eu-LISA that subject EU borders to a regime of testing. The Agency promotes and performs these experimental practices as preferred modes of assembling technologies, databases, institutional and human actors, and futures, through either large-scale IT projects or its hybrid agenda of research and development.

A good example is the so-called Smart Borders Package, proposed as "the next steps in border management" (EC 2008). Initially, it contained a set of legislative proposals that planned to biometrically register and store all non-EU citizens' entries into and exits from the Schengen territory in an Entry/Exit System. Sontowski (2018) demonstrates how smart borders have evolved as a contentiously debated project repeatedly brought to the brink of failure. A key turn in these controversies has been the involvement of eu-LISA, which was tasked with establishing "a unique and large-scale EU pilot" (eu-LISA 2015b, 3). The pilot branded the project as "testing the borders of the future" to anticipate the "significant transformation" that the border management of the EU would undergo. The Agency conducted the pilot in collaboration with the consultancy PricewaterhouseCoopers to explore how "we make the external border a reality [...] in this European question of borders", according to one consultant (Interview 5 with private consultant, 2019). In 12 EU member states the pilot tested the enrolment procedures of biometric registering and identification, that is, various amounts and combinations of fingerprints, facial images, and iris scans, of third-country nationals at 18 border crossing points. Casting biometric (re)bordering into the language of testing became an instrument to confront vocal opposition against new smart borders, especially in the European Parliament, where the roll-out of biometrics on this scale was criticized as disproportionate, ineffective, and expensive. Through its involvement and subsequently released technical reports, eu-LISA aimed to produce "(counter)evidence" (Sontowski 2018, 2739), which also envisioned smart borders to be a realizable goal on a linear trajectory that is propelled by experimental activities such as research and testing.[5] The reports of the pilot visualized these experimental activities as cornerstones in the construction of smart borders (see Figure 2.2). They seem to enrol various actors, such as consultancies, vendors, member state experts, representatives of the EC, and technicians, into this gradual process of realizing a large-scale IT system—a move that is hoped to support the imaginary of transformation to materialize.

The second example is the large-scale project of interoperability that is being developed by the Agency (see also Chapter 5). Interoperability's widely debated legal framework was adopted in 2019 to render possible the rearrangement of the infrastructural architecture of EU borders by interconnecting all databases used in the management of migration and borders (EU 2019a, 2019b). The interoperability project strives to technically converge databases that have previously been operating separately on principles of data protection, thus pooling and repurposing sensitive personal data of third-country nationals. While this new technical architecture is intriguing for various reasons, as we will explore later, this chapter is mainly interested in reflecting on it as an additional moment in the gradual process of infrastructural experimentation. Its mechanisms and actual effectiveness are often described as complex, precarious, and uncertain, that is, as a test. One interviewee explained, "that's going to be a big test; [...] there is no other way to do it. [... Y]ou need an Agency to do it, and now we have to see what comes out" (Interview 13 with EU official, 2019).

The infrastructural project is here conceptualized as an experimental process that can only gradually reduce uncertainty and complexity in the border regime (Van De Poel, Mehos, and Asveld 2017). In a feasibility study on interoperability as the "future architecture" (eu-LISA 2019b), the Agency furthermore argues: "Given the significant changes to come, it is critical that new developments and evolutions currently being planned and even under way proceed with full knowledge of the intended future state" (p. 5). Testing activities are seen as means not only to acquire "full knowledge" about any IT system but also to broadly rehearse and thus gradually stabilize the imaginary of digital transformation as the solution to future problems. Documentation and reporting, more generally, play an important role in rehearsing the sociotechnical imaginary in different contexts, which in turn allows the Agency both to distribute the relevant knowledge and to navigate moments of friction or contestation.

A third example of this experimentality relates to the Agency's goal and its declared intention in its new mandate to evolve into a centre of excellence and node of research and development within the border regime (EU 2018a). As one Agency official argued, the agency assumes "a completely new role in terms of research. [...] We have also reinforcement in terms of pilot projects, proofs of concept, testing. So, basically more and more the role of eu-LISA is there, it's clear, kind of" (Interview 28, 2019). The

Figure 2.2: Indicative timeline for the establishment of smart borders

First feasibility study and impact assessment	Initial Legislative proposal	Technical Study	Testing *Preparation*	Testing *Execution and Reporting*	Modified legislative proposal	Development of system	Going live of system
2008-13	2013	2014 Mar – Oct	2014-15 Sep – Feb	2015 Mar – Nov	2016	2017-20	2020

Source: eu-LISA (2015b)

mandate endows the Agency with the ability to increasingly carry out activities that bring to life, according to another interviewee, "a knowledge hub by default" (Interview 25 with EU official, 2019), that is, research, individual pilots, and prototypes of bordering devices (EU 2018a, Articles 14–16). Again, enhancing experimental activities is perceived and promoted by the Agency as a "contribution growing over time as the pace of change quickens" (eu-LISA 2022b). The Agency is promoted as a site where ideas, values, norms, and future visions are again and again assembled in moments of infrastructural experimentation.

Conclusion

This chapter aimed to carefully unpack the making of the sociotechnical imaginary of digital transformation to illustrate how visions become collectivized and transformed into powerful agents in infrastructuring borders and the transnational regime of migration control. It argued that the materiality of technologies and the devices of rebordering are not the only issues that need closer attention when studying border regimes. As in the case of eu-LISA, dissecting and analyzing the visionary dimensions of infrastructuring helps to understand how collective imagination opens up or closes down sociotechnical realizations, tacitly governing the realm of the possible and contributing to the mounting normalization and public acceptance of border dataveillance. The Agency mobilizes the performative power of the imaginary—one that envisions an inevitable, unidirectional, and urgently needed digital transformation for ensuring border security. It also brings together a diverse set of actors and practices under the banner of this infrastructuring project. This permits the Agency to present itself as a harbinger of compulsory change and its activities as legitimate means to realize the imaginary. This concept of the transformation contains the promise of gradual and unidirectional change, through which digital solutions arrive in almost arbitrary forms—whether they relate to the coordination, interconnection, implementation, or the automatization of border control. The transformation imaginary thus contributes to naturalizing a deeply held solutionism that proposes (future) techno-fixes to fundamentally social and political problems (Morozov 2013).

Moreover, the imaginary gives rise to a space of experimentality where human subjects seem to be exposed to numerous technological and social interventions with unclear outcomes. The EU's Schengen Area transforms into a "laboratory" where the governance of human mobility is portrayed as detached from physical bodies and border environments. It portrays the complex governance of mobility as securely manageable in a flattened world of calibrated and aligned data streams.

Although the collection of data related to mobile subjects presents complex and multifaceted challenges, the imaginary and the associated process of laboratorization embody the powerful concept of simplification, supporting the illusion of making humans and their mobility "behave as in the research laboratory" (Callon, Lascoumes, and Barthe 2009, 65). Simplification implies the idea of "infrastructuring people", an undertaking that, in reality, involves an exceedingly complex process. Here, however, the process is envisioned as a straightforward two-stage procedure. In the first step, IT-assisted bordering practices would transform humans into data sets, turning them into IT-readable identities and, in theory, classify them in distinct categories. Subsequently, simplification then promises to facilitate digital-ordering practices like sorting and selecting.

Consequently, simplification seeks to black-box the intricate local and temporal conditions of bordering, which bodies encounter and occasionally resist. The quest for this techno-scientific manipulation in the conditioning of mobility echoes Shiv Visvanathan's characterization of the *laboratory state* (1997). It produces the "hyper-objectification" of migrants (Feldman 2011b, 389) through which people, rather than being encountered as qualitative subjects, are transformed into and managed as abstract, quantitative, and calculable objects based on the digitized fragments of their identity.

Moreover, European institutional actors promote and portray Schengen border interventions as techno-scientifically certain, accurate, and reliable, whereas the potential errors and inaccuracies that frequently occur during data entry and processing remain challenging to subject to public scrutiny. Thus, making mobility conform to the lab tends to not only foster a growing indifference toward migratory human beings, but also ignore the social consequences deriving from inaccuracies and mistakes in digital bordering processes.

In essence, the imaginary that this chapter has scrutinized raises novel and pressing questions pertaining to responsibility and accountability. It invites us to acknowledge, first and foremost to recognize, eu-LISA as a responsible agent, not only envisioning and supporting the implementation of this digital border regime, but also determining what kinds of actions with regard to migrants are delegated and to whom. It requires us to relocate the places where these seemingly abstract actions (of digital infrastructuring) materialize in space and time, and to then gain a better understanding of how responsibilities are distributed and where or by whom power and authority is exercised. In other words, how can we better identify and make visible the distribution of responsibility and accountability, which seem to be ambiguously allocated across this transnational border regime? Questions of this nature are increasingly crucial to maintain this increasingly dominant imaginary of the digital transformation, and the resulting borderscapes of exclusions, open to scrutiny and contestation.

The upcoming chapters delve into additional performative aspects of infrastructuring work. Specifically, they will describe and scrutinize the performative acts of infrastructuring, wherein representatives, experts, and technicians from the Agency publicly formulate ideas of Europe or European identity and link them to the digital borders. In Chapters 4 and 5, I will revisit some of the consequences arising from abstraction and simplification.

Second Interlude: Three Empirical Vignettes

1. A visit to the agency

In 2018, the German daily Süddeutsche Zeitung reported on an EU Agency known only to nerds and police officers.[1] The article painted eu-LISA as a strong contender for "the most obscure Agency" within the EU. It suggested that the Agency had built a somewhat questionable reputation by managing vast databases of personal information discreetly, operating largely behind the scenes and away from public scrutiny or transparent governance.

Before embarking on my journey to Tallinn, Estonia, to see eu-LISA's headquarters (HQ), I had already read this article. Although I had received an invitation to attend its annual conference held at Tallinn's Hilton Hotel—an

Figure 2.3: eu-LISA's HQ in Tallinn, Estonia

Figure 2.4: eu-LISA's HQ and the old Seaplane Harbour (in the back left)

ostentatious, ritzy place in the city—I encountered some difficulties in scheduling a meeting with my contact. They explained that the timing was not ideal for a visit due to the extensive preparation required to accommodate various stakeholders, industrial tech companies and member state delegates. To see the new HQ of the Agency nevertheless, I opted for a bus ride to the Lennusadam station, situated in the Kalamaja district (the "Fish House district"). This small coastal area along Tallinn Bay owed its name to the city's former fishing harbour. Kalamaja itself holds a significant place in the city's infrastructural history, having witnessed the construction of factories when the railroad connection between Tallinn and Petersburg was established, bringing in an influx of workers into the city. Today, the neighbourhood is predominantly inhabited by Estonian bohemians.

eu-LISA's HQ are located next to two historical buildings, both popular tourist attractions. The first is the notorious abandoned Patarei Prison, often categorized as a lost place of dark tourism. This prison, with a grim history, served various roles, including barracks, a high-security facility, and political prison during both Soviet times and the Nazi occupation. The second attraction is the Lennusadam, the Seaplane Harbour, an old hangar building. This building now hosts the Estonian Maritime Museum, featuring large-scale replicas of a World War I seaplane and a submarine, as well as an extensive collection of old weapons.

Lennusadam also serves as a venue for eu-LISA's official evening events. Right next to it stands eu-LISA's brand-new HQ. The entrance gate, much like the entire structure itself, is fortified with high-security measures. Three flags symbolize Estonia, the eu-LISA Agency, and the European Union— subtle reminders of Europe's presence that both visitors and passersby can identify. Surrounding the property are security fences; some room has been left for a potential expansion of the compound in the future.

The architectural design of the building resembles a hyper-modern glass cube. Situated amid the environment of Kalamaja and adjacent to these two strange historical places, it appears as spectacular as it is enigmatic and obscure, seemingly out of place in its surroundings. It almost stands as a testament to its own reputation suggested in the newspaper article: located next to the open sea, the cube is encircled by high protective fences and surveillance cameras. Made of glass windows, the building does not appear transparent or welcoming but opaque, especially when viewed from a distance.

2. A promotional video on the construction of the HQ

What is the origin of this building? On eu-LISA's official YouTube channel, which has around 500 subscribers (in April 2023), one can find short videos featuring the training the Agency offers to member states, promotion videos about "interoperability to achieve a safer Europe", recorded speeches by the Executive Director on "Europe Day", or highlights of eu-LISA conferences. While these videos are, of course, primarily promotional in nature, they also serve to showcase the Agency's status as an official organization and are produced as a gesture of transparency for an anonymous (online) public.

There is one video that has particularly piqued my curiosity: it documents the ground-breaking ceremony of eu-LISA's new HQ.[2] The video, titled "Cornerstone Laying Ceremony", employs drone footage to offer a bird's eye view of the construction site, capturing the picturesque seacoast and, notably, what I later identified as Lennusadam and Patarei Prison visible in the background. More significantly, the video chronicles a visit to the future site of eu-LISA's HQ by some key figures, including some of the Agency's staff, its former Director Krum Garkov, the Mayor of Northern Tallinn, and the Estonian Minister of the Interior. Dressed in white safety helmets, the participants have a uniformed appearance that oddly matches their business attire.

This video of the event and the activities undertaken at the site convey several possible representational and symbolic meanings. It serves as a promotion of the Agency's emergence and growth, symbolized by the construction of its new office. The video skillfully constructs a narrative by showing clips of prepared speeches and emphasizing the symbolic act of laying the cornerstone, which includes the placement of a time capsule into the concrete. It assembles familiar discursive elements that imbue significant meaning to the cornerstone-laying ceremony.

In one part of the video, we can witness the then Estonian minister, standing at the construction site, celebrating it as a "really, really great moment" and offering congratulations to the Agency, which "already [had] a great history in Estonia". He goes on,

> setting a cornerstone for a new head office for eu-LISA is not only a cornerstone for eu-LISA; we can also say that it's a cornerstone for [the] digitalization of [the] security of [the] European Union. I hope that in the future more and more new startings of different databases in the European Union will be started from this house.

Next, Garkov takes the stage, reflecting on how "it all began", underscoring the Agency's increased significance: "eu-LISA is one of the foundations of [the] Schengen Area, one of the foundations [of] border management, internal security, and migration management in Europe […]. We found a very good home here in Estonia, in Tallinn." This "new home", as the YouTube description adds, will "provide our staff with a modern working environment to successfully perform our tasks as required by the continually progressing digital era".

In all the speeches, main buzzwords such as "digital transformation" are consistently linked to Europe and its border (in)security. At the same time, they are also firmly rooted in Estonia's national self-image of a digital state, digital society, or digital economy—signifiers that are prominently displayed in various public spaces, including Tallinn's airport. Upon arrival, large letters greet travelers with the title "the world's most digitally advanced society". Estonia is promoted as "e-Estonia", proudly bearing "the first digital country", and its groundbreaking "e-administration" is praised. These are the trendy components of a vocabulary that must design and cultivate a progressivist vision of Estonia as a European nation.

3. Another visit to the agency

My first visit to Strasbourg had been arranged by an eu-LISA officer, whom I will refer to as "Richard". I first met him during an industry roundtable event in the spring of 2019. Shortly thereafter, I embarked on a bus journey to eu-LISA, located in the calm suburb of Neuhof, roughly half an hour away from Strasbourg's historic centre.

During our interactions on the sidelines of the roundtable event, Richard praised Strasbourg as the "true capital of Europe", appreciating Strasbourg's historical commitment to reformist values and its enduring spirit as well as its strategic geographic location, situated between two European powers

Figure 2.5: Rue de Schengen in Strasbourg, the street behind eu-LISA data centre

and former rivals, Germany and France, which would now represent the economic heart and motor of the entire continent. He felt that it was the right place to be for an Agency such as eu-LISA.

When one strolls through Neuhof's petit-bourgeois rows of houses, it is difficult to imagine the presence of an IT centre here, especially one that contains the massive European collection of data, comprising biographic and document information, biometric fingerprints, and facial images of travelers, asylum seekers, and visa applicants. The streets of Neuhof carry the names of local artists and writers, but one particular street sign discreetly alludes to the EU's migration and border regime: "Rue de Schengen", situated just behind eu-LISA's data centre. In front of the data centre, on Rue de la Faisanderie, one can observe a transmission tower and lots of barbed wire, with signs indicating that this is a "area protégée".

When I arrived at the entrance gate, a security guard announced my presence via walkie-talkie. Richard emerged to greet me, as the centre had failed to register my name and identification. I had to submit a copy of my passport prior to my visit. Together, we proceeded to an entrance hall that resembled an airport security area. Upon receiving my visitor badge, an additional step remained—the capture of my fingerprints. With a smile, a woman behind a counter handed me a compact black fingerprinting device. Both Richard and the woman instructed me on the proper placement of my index finger on the device. Three attempts later, Richard jokingly remarked, "Well, in terms of your 'fingerprintability,' you've at least met one criterion to join the ranks of eu-LISA staff". We then continued

Figure 2.6: eu-LISA data centre in Strasbourg

Source: Süddeutsche Zeitung Content and Janis Brühl, © Süddeutsche Zeitung GmbH, München

through automated security gates, which resembled the typical rectangular frames at airports. Richard clarified "We do this fingerprinting because you could easily throw your badge over the fence into the grass at any time, and someone might pick it up. But, with your fingerprint, we now possess your unique identity."

In one of the meeting rooms within the centre, I conducted an interview with both Richard and his supervisor. After roughly an hour and a half of conversation, I expressed my interest in seeing the actual data centre. My request surprised them initially, but eventually Richard was tasked to grant me a brief glimpse. With somewhat nonchalant agreement, Richard walked me across the premises, leading us to another building. As we moved from room to room, every door we passed through had to be securely closed behind us to gain access to the next one.

A series of stairs and numerous corners later, Richard swung open the last door to a spacious basement—an air-conditioned room with rows of black and white racks, spaced approximately half a metre apart, most of them with blinking lights. Richard explained the composition of these racks: the older black racks mainly belonged to the SIS and Eurodac systems. Part of their duty involved maintaining these systems and transitioning them into white racks, signifying "updated" racks. Over time, the room should become populated with racks dedicated to future systems, including the Entry/Exit System, the European Travel Information and Authorization System, or the European Criminal Records Information System for Third-Country Nationals. Richard politely declined my request to take a picture, arguing "I mean you could take any random picture found on the internet when searching Google images of 'data centre'."

This was certainly true, as confirmed by the (above-mentioned) newspaper article in the German daily Süddeutsche Zeitung. The article features a photo of the racks and provides an accurate description of its environment: a somewhat unremarkable basement filled with equipment, the constant hum of air conditioners maintaining the correct temperature, and nearly identical racks flashing rhythmically. Pointing to various locations, Richard indicated, "Eurodac here, the Visa Information System there, the Schengen Information System over there ...." Our visit was coming to an end. I thought of the newspaper article which posed a thought-provoking question, leaving the reader and myself, standing in eu-LISA's basement, pondering, "Who gains access, and who is excluded [...] decisions seemingly all based solely on these black and white racks?"[3]

3

Assembling a Fractional Europe

In the vignettes above, I have described three different scenes from my fieldwork. The first vignette chronicles a visit to eu-LISA's headquarters in Tallinn, where regular gatherings with national delegates, officials, Agency personnel, and industry stakeholders take place. As previously mentioned, Estonia is the official location of eu-LISA, making it the official EU Agency representation. This vignette offered a brief glimpse into the local setting where this IT systems Agency is situated. The second vignette narrates a specific event or occurrence at the Agency: the official inauguration of its new headquarters, which is captured in a video. As we will see, events hold significant relevance for the Agency, and eu-LISA is actively involved in various types of events. They can also shed light on how specific performances take place, the use of dramaturgical elements, and the types of audiences that are addressed. The third vignette describes my visit to the Agency's operational centre, where the mundane work of administration and data maintenance tasks are carried out.

In this chapter, I explore eu-LISA's management of IT systems and infrastructures as sites at which Europe is supposed to materialize. As historians of science and technology have argued, infrastructures have emerged as the "backbone" of European integration because their material composition and qualities "form the physical basis for transnational flows of people, goods and services" (Badenoch and Fickers 2010a, 2). This perspective has also been applied to explain the gradual construction (and expansion) of the Schengen space, which, by progressively dismantling internal borders among its member state nations, has profoundly shaped the governance of mobility across the continent. More specifically, the 1985 agreement between France, Germany, Belgium, Luxembourg and the Netherlands to establish the Schengen Area relied on what they termed "compensatory measures" for abolishing border controls between their countries. Among these compensatory measures was the first generation of the Schengen Information System (SIS), designed to facilitate the exchange of data among national security authorities regarding individuals and objects classified as potential risks. The SIS would later undergo significant transformation and expand into an extensive surveillance tool (Brouwer 2008; van Munster 2009).

The SIS marked the first transnational database that became part of a larger, evolving digital infrastructure, which has redefined the European border and its connection to nation-states, giving rise to what Walters (2002) called a European space of transnational mobility governance "despite the continued existence of different national economic and social systems" (p. 569). Schengen can thus be seen as a manifestation of "infrastructural Europeanism" (Schipper and Schot 2011)—the process through which infrastructures constitute "material backbones for the emergence of new transnational communities and societies" (p. 249).

By exploring eu-LISA's database management, I examine how the concept of border (in)security becomes a matter of infrastructure. More specifically, and drawing inspiration from Star and Ruhleder (1996, 112), I ask *when*, and under which circumstances, (digital) border security is conceived and constructed as a distinctly European infrastructure. I therefore turn to the imaginations and visions of Europeanhood or European identity that are linked to the digital infrastructure governing borders.

eu-LISA serves as my focal point lens for this investigation. The Agency's role may "sometimes not [be] so well understood at first sight", as one Agency official admitted, but ultimately eu-LISA is the "Agency that prevents, if something [...] happen[s], that Schengen will end immediately" (Interview 12, 2019). My primary focus is thus on the Agency's efforts in "infrastructuring", which Walters (2011) defines as the "difficult and painstaking labour that goes into assembling, maintaining or extending [...] new spaces of security" (p. 54), such as the European space of border security. I am particularly interested in the difficult investments and practices essential for ensuring the continuity of information exchange over time. These are elements that the broader imaginaries of technological transformation typically fail to acknowledge. As we witnessed in Chapter 2, the imaginary of digital transformation rather reinforces the idea that society and politics must adapt rapidly and inevitably to technology-driven change.

The concept of infrastructuring, on the contrary, suggest looking at transformations from a praxeological standpoint. It privileges the process in infrastructure rather than the product, and explores the entanglements of social, imaginative and material activities that constitute infrastructure.[1] Moreover, it requires us to be attentive to both the "conceptual plasticity and the undeniable materiality" of infrastructures (Carse 2016, 35). In other words, it represents a co-productive perspective that considers the material practices (that easily fade from view when focusing on higher order concepts and promises) as well as the imaginations, ideologies or visions that are continuously encoded in the interconnectedness, standards and networks of infrastructures. Although many studies of infrastructure tend to prioritize the techno-material aspects today (even if they emphasize the hybrid character of human and nonhuman actants), it is essential to recall Larkin's significant argument that infrastructures invariably "operate on multiple levels concurrently. They execute technical functions [...] by mediating exchange over distance and binding people and things into complex heterogeneous systems and by operating as entextualized forms that have relative autonomy from the technical function" (Larkin 2013, 335–336). To delve into eu-LISA's infrastructuring work for creating and maintaining digital borders, we must examine how the Agency contributes to ensuring cooperation among the various authorities responsible for operating borders (involving, for instance, the complex and technical means to connect border crossing points, police stations and consulates). This concerns the methods employed in the processing and sharing of traveler data, which ultimately become an integral component of the multiple mechanisms used to select and filter mobility.

A small note of caution: this chapter is not so much interested in assessing whether eu-LISA is an effective and successful agent in European integration, enabling the smooth and seamless administration of the Schengen space. Instead, I attempt to explore what Larkin (2013) called "entextualization", a process through which complex, heterogeneous networks appear to emerge as coherent European infrastructure. I draw from the work of Stephen Hilgartner (2000) to develop an understanding of infrastructuring as a performative technique of frontstaging and backstaging. Infrastructuring thus encompasses the practices that distribute what is sensible and perceptible and which aspects and characteristics of infrastructure are made invisible or concealed. In other words, we need to view eu-LISA not only as a conventional service supplier in the business of IT, but as an entity that actively performs the digital border infrastructure, something inextricably linked to material and historical contexts.

To explore these dimensions, I have already introduced the Agency's two primary locations through ethnographic vignettes of my visits. The subsequent sections aim to explain the management and performance of digital border infrastructure through material, social and imaginative means. In the final section of this chapter, I will discuss my findings in the context of the infrastructural making of Europe. Drawing on insights of John Law, I will reflect on how the eu-LISA case enables us to see the emergence of fractional Europe, performed as both multiple and singular, appearing as a coherent whole while simultaneously being dispersed and decentred.

Performing the digital infrastructure of Europe's borders

Events: presenting digital infrastructure "on stage"

> Performance, the enactment of the poetic function, is a highly reflexive mode of communication. (Bauman and Briggs 1990, 73)

In his description of iron construction, Walter Benjamin (2002 [1982]) stated that iron was destined to serve the architecture of the future. Contemplating railroad construction, he observed that "technological production, at the beginning, was in the grip of dreams. (Not architecture alone but all technology is, at certain stages, evidence of a collective dream.)" (p. 152). However, we must scrutinize where and when collective desires and political dreams are made accessible, and how they are performed and mediated to an audience.

These questions prompt us to reflect on events that allow us to capture what Hilgartner (2000) (in reference to Goffman) terms the techniques of "frontstaging" and "backstaging" when organizations seek to stage and invoke their (technoscientific) authority. Events, such as the inauguration ceremony described in the vignette, offer ideal opportunities for deploying techniques of performing infrastructure. STS scholars have focused on events as occurrences that can "bring multiple elements and levels of infrastructures into view and reconfirm and/or reorganize the relations between them" (Badenoch and Fickers 2010a, 13–14). Horst and Michael (2011) contend that an event is an "actual occasion comprised of the coming together of numerous entities that are social and material, human and non-human, macro and micro, cognitive and affective, available and unavailable to consciousness" (p. 286). In this sense, front- and backstaging can be understood techniques that delineate, shape and mediatize this convergence of entities for (imagined) audiences. In other words, they emphasize specific entities, making them more visible and articulate, while backgrounding others and rendering them less accessible. They produce the entextualized forms and qualities of infrastructure.

Viewed from this perspective, the video of the eu-LISA inauguration ceremony played a role in generating forms of mediated participation for an (anonymous online) audience, allowing them to become part of a collective performance of the infrastructure (a form of participation that would be entirely inaccessible through individual visits to the eu-LISA headquarters). The inauguration event had to articulate and make visible a European moment (however vaguely defined) that placed spotlight on the Agency as its essential infrastructural agent for European border security. At this moment, the "eventing" of infrastructure (Badenoch and Fickers 2010a) positioned the Agency as a spokesperson for Europe and staged its authority over the digital border infrastructure and its presumed security assurances.

While the inauguration ceremony on eu-LISA's YouTube channel serves as a particularly illustrative example, similar patterns of mediatization take place at the Agency's annual conferences, roundtable discussions, and other policy gatherings, often organized in extravagant settings and sometimes livestreamed on the Agency's public channel. These events incorporate dramaturgical elements that offer observers and audiences a shared experience: they communicate the digital border infrastructure as an emergent, significant and unified object under the Agency's responsibility and governance.

Events may exhibit ritualistic elements and a repetitive, standardized discourse concerning migration "problems" and border control challenges. However, they are also specific performances of the digital border infrastructure that engage observers and participants in the construction of political identity and a sense of European selfhood. As Rao (2001) suggests, they are "ubiquitous strategies of claim making that link diverse participants together into a collective performance" (p. 266). Accordingly, it is common to observe the frequent use of the plural pronoun "we" when discussing imperatives for action, such as "we are not going to build that alone", "we need", "we must" or "we now can". Furthermore, during one annual conference, a presenter not only emphasized how the future build-up of new databases was consolidated under the institutional umbrella of eu-LISA but also metaphorized it as a European response to "Eurosceptics" and a reason for "EUphoria" (field note, eu-LISA Conference, 16 October 2019). During conference breaks, video screens displayed various promotional videos about "the big job of maintaining EU borders", with a voice-over reminding participants about the "huge and important job requiring seamless operation between large and complex infrastructures involving IT systems across many European countries".[2]

Events showcase infrastructure and its management on stage; they enable eu-LISA to demonstrate its infrastructural power through performance. These events portray the establishment and administration of digital border infrastructure as the main site of Europe's materialization. This has to be accomplished through two primary acts of frontstaging. First, infrastructural events foreground the apparent presence of a cohesive political community, even though, in reality, it comprises diverse audiences, actor groups and professional communities. In this sense, experts and representatives of smaller and less powerful nation-states feel integrated into the Agency's main professional terrain, which is effectively presented as European. The mere recognition that one is invited to an active and mediated participation in a ritualized performance (similar to the concept of a rotating EU presidency) instills a certain sense of membership or belonging that is crucial for constructing collective political identity.[3]

Furthermore, infrastructural events allow to synthesize and, at the same time, obscure differing interests and varying interpretations; they present *semantic coherence* despite the presence of multiple meanings associated with infrastructural configurations. While eu-LISA (and other institutional actors of the EU) emphasize European collectivity at their events, the inauguration ceremony for the new headquarters had in fact also displayed partially competing, or ambiguous, interpretations. Estonian officials, for example, leveraged eu-LISA's role as an institution overseeing transnational databases in order to foreground national interests and nurture Estonia's image as a digital state or "e-society". Additionally, Estonia's efforts to bring the Agency to Tallinn upon its establishment were even more obvious. During that time, a representative of the Estonian Ministry of the Interior stated: "We are not interested in bringing just any kind of Agency to Estonia. 'IT' is what we, Estonians, all understand and what we appreciate. It is part of our national image" (Estonian World, 23 April 2013).[4] During events, such divergent and contradictory implications can either be concealed or skillfully conjoined to accommodate multiple interests and purposes. In simpler terms, an infrastructural event can create a sense of unity out of multiplicity.[5]

Wrestling with the installed base

In the previous section, I illustrated how elements of the digital border infrastructure are performed through frontstaging. Events enable actors to engage in the symbolic or mythical construction of European collectivity. However, this process necessitates relegating any ambiguities, contradictions or contentions regarding infrastructure's sociomaterial construction and institutional histories to the background. What is presented as a single

Figure 3.1: A livestreamed speech by eu-LISA's former Executive Director at the annual conference of eu-LISA (2019), with the flags of Estonia, the EU, and eu-LISA in the back

European character actually relies on a diverse and collective construct. Nevertheless, this cohesion is maintained through the existence of material and organizational structures closely related to what has been described as the "installed base" from which any infrastructure's "strengths and limitations" are inherited (Star 1999, 382). In the case of eu-LISA, the ability to attain the position of a spokesperson demands not only entering the stage with a coherent and seemingly unified voice, but also backstaging other elements. In fact, backstaging acts should be viewed as techniques that "hold the history of spaces and places at a distance but in reserve, at once acknowledging their presence and not allowing them into the narrative" (Badenoch 2010, 56).[6]

eu-LISA's geographical dispersion across the continent is a revealing example: its headquarters is located in Tallinn, its operational data centre in Strasbourg, its backup site in Austria's Pongau region. This constellation is the result of past organizational trajectories, political arrangements and compromises. Initially, Estonian authorities were disappointed that not a single database was physically located in Tallinn, a detail deliberately omitted from the speeches during the cornerstone laying ceremony. When eu-LISA was created in 2011, its mandate included taking over the management of existing systems like the SIS and Eurodac, which were previously based in different places and operated by different actors. However, once the Agency was launched, French officials ultimately refused to relocate the SIS from their national territory. The decision to retain command over this transnational database of migration control and border security, rather than transferring it into the hands of a new member state, was intended to convey a political message and underscore France's geopolitical significance in Europe (Interview 24 with member state representative, 2019). Unlike Tallinn, Strasbourg was perceived as a secure location within NATO-surveilled airspace, providing critical security infrastructure and maintaining a sufficient distance from Tallinn's neighbouring geopolitical adversary, the Russian Federation.

Since its creation, the development and management of the digital border infrastructure within eu-LISA has been the subject of political negotiations and power struggles between states. These negotiations eventually led to the organizational division of the Agency into having distinct seats: an operational centre (Strasbourg) and an official headquarters (Tallinn). It was imperative for eu-LISA's operations to remain in Strasbourg, as this was where French authorities had previously administered the SIS. Furthermore, IT systems such as the VIS and Eurodac were either created in or transferred to Strasbourg. Moreover, former (French) personnel who had overseen the SIS could now be seamlessly integrated into the new administrative structure, now formally under the auspices of a European Agency.[7]

Similarly, member states negotiated the location of the backup site for eu-LISA's databases. They ultimately decided to establish this site within a mountain near Sankt Johann in Austria, which was a former bunker facility secured by the Austrian military from the Cold War era. The site had already been chosen as the backup location for the new generation of the SIS (known as SIS II). During the EU's deliberations on potential backup site locations for eu-LISA's databases, Austrian authorities competed with a proposal from Finnish officials, who proposed a site near the Arctic Circle. Eventually, the Austrian mountain was selected due to its geographical distance to Strasbourg and its preexisting military infrastructure (Interview 7 with member state representative, 2019).[8]

These examples highlight the contingent interconnection of geographical, historical and organizational arrangements that have shaped the institution of eu-LISA as well as its administration of its digital border infrastructure. They also demonstrate that infrastructural Europeanization is rarely a smooth integration process orchestrated by a united political front or community. Instead, it is a complex undertaking influenced by multiple material, social and political factors, such as the competition between Schengen states and aspiring members, national and geopolitical interests, organizational and material structures, and compromises between all these elements. We may refer to this as the preinstalled base, which has been subject to national competition and controversy and contributes to its inherited weaknesses. Dividing the Agency into three geographical, organizational sites, for example, has had considerable logistical and budgetary implications for both eu-LISA and EU member states.

In summary, events serve as both opportunities and tools of communication that bring together materiality, values, meaning and identity. Through mediation and coordination of these elements, they showcase Europe "on stage". Therefore, events do not represent Europe as it exists, but instead contribute to "the mythical construction of the mediated centre (Europe) at its most intense" (Badenoch and Fickers 2010a, 14). Events present digital border infrastructures as if grown de novo, backstaging their negotiated material characteristics and compromises and breaking away from the inertia of their installed base. Front- and backstaging, performed for various audiences, appear as the techniques through which digital border infrastructure must be made visible as distinctly European.

Infrastructural breakdown and failure: conjuring organic visions

In order to introduce eu-LISA's data centre, we need to move away from the staged events or event-driven activities to the routine, technical tasks involving IT systems, carried out daily by eu-LISA staff at the Agency's operational site in Strasbourg. Despite this seemingly mundane environment, as we will explore, the Agency's officials and experts still partake in both back- and frontstaging, engaging in a particular performance of infrastructure, and thus also in the formation of (non-)audiences.

Confronting the inherent unreliability of infrastructure

[F]ailure is key. That said, disconnection is only possible if connection, or the possibility of connection, is present, if a system of forces can be formed. (Graham and Thrift, 2007, 7)

[Y]ou know, it sounds so clean and easy, but, you know, rarely in reality are things that clean and easy. (Interview 23 with member of the European Parliament, 2019)

While not particularly spectacular, eu-LISA's operational centre is highly secured and accessible only to authorized personnel; no events are organized here. Instead, technicians, experts and engineers operate the transnational, centralized digital border systems. This work is so routinized that it can be challenging to articulate at times. Unlike in Tallinn, there is no theatrical display when these officers emphasize the technological detail and professional routines required to carry out their tasks and duties. Much of their expertise is acquired through hands-on experience and knowledge is gained through job practice. These activities may occasionally seem mundane and unexciting, but they demand a profound understanding of information technology and database systems.

A representative, when describing these operational and backup centres, remarked: "It is very difficult to describe because there is no particular scheme to follow, but […] well, as mentioned, it is such a diverse or multifaceted work […] every day brings something different, you know?" (Interview 7, 2019). Agency staff draw attention to the dynamic infrastructural life of IT systems that requires continuous reconstruction and renewal to sustain the day-to-day functioning of digital borders. Infrastructural life, in other words, demands constant and proactive maintenance, a 24/7 service that involves monitoring network connections to anticipate sometimes perplexing system behaviours. An Application Management Unit should ensure first-level support, examine the electronic operations of systems, and resolve problems with various applications that may obstruct the flow of data: "You create volumes to prevent data queuing, you watch the screens to ensure the searches […] can take place, the transactions […] can take place as well. […] You ensure that everything operates as it should" (Interview 27 with EU official, 2019).

By describing these activities as "iterative repair", Glouftsios (2021) accurately characterizes the infrastructural tasks performed at eu-LISA. From the perspective of eu-LISA engineers, repair work is an integral component of their everyday responsibilities, a prerequisite for responding to the ongoing disruptions and disconnections within different parts of the systems. Another key set of activities relates to reactive measures in response to breakdown and failure, which are almost infrastructural features of infrastructures that technicians are trained to handle. These activities have produced an entire lexicon of technical terms that describe the multifaceted work of engineers: adjusting configurations, changing firewalls, modifying the status of communication networks, replacing hard disks, and intricate and resource-intensive practices like troubleshooting, bug fixing and incident handling.

> We have network engineers [and] system engineers on site that take care of troubleshooting. I don't know, let's say the network is down, it doesn't function anymore, or [...] some server is down, and they need to repair. You know, if one server is down, it means that, if there are four in a cluster, the other three will take the load, but not forever. I mean, it can't work forever, so you need to eventually repair the server that is done. So, this is what we are doing [...], in [the] case of troubleshooting an incident. (Interview 27, 2019)

Maintenance and repair work must also encompass severe incidents and less common but more challenging scenarios that are difficult to resolve. An officer at eu-LISA shared various examples of such situations. These included instances where hard disks and power adapters needed replacements but were missing or defective, or new components had to be inserted but require the shutdown of entire applications.

In the backup bunker situated in the remote Pongau region of Austria, there exists a nearly identical systems duplication known as the "warm standby". In critical situations that could severely impact the active site in Strasbourg, a detailed procedure allows for the transition of operations to the backup site in approximately 20 minutes, to enable the uninterrupted processing of data between border passage points across Europe: "whenever there is a failure [...] on the system, so the system is down, you need to switch to the other site manually, or, take over manually from the other site from St. Johann" (Interview 27, 2019).[9] The bunker in Sankt Johann im Pongau also serves to ensure that the EU border regime's digital function continues to operate in the event of a more severe disaster, such as prolonged regional power cuts or, as one officer at eu-LISA envisioned, an explosion at the Fessenheim nuclear plant located 80 kilometres from Strasbourg.

These depictions provided at eu-LISA's data centre make it evident that managing the digital infrastructure of borders primarily revolves around monitoring service and responding to tracking incidents, bugs, breakdowns and failures. This can be aptly referred to as the essential backstaging operations that maintain the computational power and interconnecting capacity for data processing across the continent. "Correction and adaptation", as Glouftsios (2021) terms it, emerge as essential modes of backstaging that are upheld through the continued administration of digital border infrastructures.

Another important aspect of backstaging operations is standardization. For eu-LISA, data must be stored and processed by adhering to specific uniform procedures. As Andrew Barry (2006) argued, connection and data practice standards allow the establishment of infrastructural zones that create the transnational governance of mobility across distant geographical locations and through the involvement of multiple actors and institutions. Consequently, the objective of monitoring is not only the detection of potential bugs or failures but also includes the regulation of aberrant behaviour in the practices and operations of member states. In this regard, eu-LISA exercises a form of governance partly by identifying and taking action against dysfunctional national networks.

> We pursue [...] active monitoring of the network connection, active monitoring of the behavior of systems in order to promptly intervene [...] and to recognize cases of malfunction, [if] something's fishy. We observe also—to the extent it is visible, and to a certain degree this is the case—whether there are obvious malfunctioning issues originating from member states. (Interview 14, 2019)

In this instance, standardization is a process primarily accomplished by detecting and investigating aberrations or otherwise malfunctions that become visible on the screen in Strasbourg. These indications suggest that the malfunctions occurred not at the central level but rather at a local level within a member state:

> [I]n the case of interruptions [...] or obvious deviations from the standard behavior of the local system, [we] get in touch with the colleagues and say, "we note here that you are no longer receiving reports from us. [...] [On our end], data is queuing more and more— check out what's happening on your side!" (Interview 14, 2019)

Furthermore, duplicates of the systems are specifically designed to simulate network breakdowns in joint exercises. These exercise scenarios are intended to train and discipline member states in order to coordinate and follow standardized protocols.

The Agency's efforts to oversee, trace and standardize operational procedures also point to a more pressing concern in the management of the digital infrastructure of borders: poor data quality is considered a core impediment to achieving uniform standards. The quality of data largely depends on the local conditions, environments and actors involved in registering and identifying people and inputting their data into the systems. Data quality amplifies technicians and engineers' sense of having to grapple with an inherent unreliability of the digital infrastructure. eu-LISA employees and engineers have limited room for action in this regard because standardization initiatives primarily involve giving "feedback about issues that may not be apparent to them [national authorities]; but through centralized monitoring, we can indicate to them what the potential issue might be before it [be]comes a significant issue" (Interview 4, 2018).

Nevertheless, data quality is predominantly reliant on the information imported into the systems, and the process of data clearing has gained a notoriously bad reputation in existing IT systems (FRA 2018; field note, eu-LISA Industry Roundtable, 3–5 November 2020).[10] Another representative, working at the backup site, argued that despite eu-LISA's claim of improving data quality, their options are in fact quite limited. He emphasized that what ultimately counts as fundamental principle is "garbage in, garbage out"—"if you enter bad data, you have no choice but to work with them!" (Interview 7 with member state representative, 2019).[11]

Le cœur numérique/the digital heart: keeping the body alive

eu-LISA's service-oriented work is dominated by the inherent unreliability of infrastructural networks and the fragility of data flows. Addressing these challenges requires the continuous mobilization of substantial financial, technical and human resources. This is a key factor why infrastructure produces entire work cultures of repair for which maintainers and responders are urgently needed, for instance, for upkeeping the transnational apparatus of border security (Bellanova and Glouftsios 2022a; Glouftsios 2021; Graham and Thrift 2007).

Accordingly, eu-LISA faces a key challenge, not only focusing on traditional budgetary advantages (in the competitive arena of EU agencies), but also grappling with the difficulty in recruiting technicians and engineers to serve as maintenance and repair personnel. As one official in Tallinn explained, most challenges are "resource-based, maybe budget-based, and when I say resource, [I mean] also expertise. If we can attract enough expertise as to have enough resources to work into the same direction, that would be good" (Interview 27, 2019). Another official expressed a more pessimistic outlook: "I can only hope that they [eu-LISA] do not only get new tasks but that they get sufficient money, and that they can recruit technicians, good technicians" (Interview 9 with EU official, 2019).[12]

The everyday conditions and operational procedures at Strasbourg's data centre give rise to what Karin Knorr Cetina (2009) has termed "synthetic situations". Synthetic situations are defined by response presences that require continuous monitoring, intensity and preparedness, and they directly stem from infrastructural unreliability. I propose to see these responses as recurrent instances of backstaging that push back against interruptions, incidents, deviations and breakdowns. These responses are not only epiphenomena of the Agency's work but constitute its central position in the border regime; as one official argued: "It makes plain our position as [an] Agency and why Europe invests in these huge efforts" (Interview 14, 2019).[13] At the same time, the backstaging efforts undertaken by technicians and engineers at the Agency perform *audience work*. They relegate unreliability to the background behind scenes and create a peculiar non-audience: the professionals, border guards and end users who must remain unaffected and undisturbed by the inherent unreliability of the digital border infrastructure.

In turn, their active involvement in backstaging provides engineers and technical experts with a profound sense of duty for upholding *order*: their responsibility is to preserve and display order, a direct result of the tedious and behind-the-scenes efforts to ensure network connectivity and linking bordering spaces through data. To illustrate, one of my interlocutors at eu-LISA poignantly metaphorized the data centre as the place where the EU's "living organism" is nurtured and sustained:

> If you like, you can imagine an operating data center of this size, of this order, in principle like a living organism. There, the body constantly exchanges [...] cells, but it is nonetheless the same human being. But all micro-components of such a system are subjected to a permanent exchange of renewal, either technical renewal or pure replacement of what has already been there before. (Interview 14, 2019)

Drawing parallels between their work tasks and the constant exchange of somatic cells and, as another interviewee added, the "permanent process of renewal and renovation", eu-LISA engineers and experts evoke a utopian aspiration and attribute a broader sociopolitical significance to infrastructure.

Elsewhere, similar corporal analogies are employed by eu-LISA representatives to imagine and illustrate the Agency's data centre as the digital heart of the Schengen space (see Figure 3.2 below).[14] These corporal analogies and organic metaphors serve to render visible what might otherwise remain incomprehensible or seemingly hidden—that is, the connection between data flows and (the establishment of) social order, between material infrastructure and the governing polity, between technologies and the formation of Schengen with its market and free movement. These metaphors are not simply decorative elements of speech; they serve as "fundamental linguistic and cognitive tools or thinking about the world and acting on the world" (McLeod and Nerlich 2017, 2).

However, these metaphors are also ready-made tools to invisibilize what would usually come to the fore: disruptions, breakdowns and irregularities in network connectivity. These organic visions stand in stark contrast to the mundane environment and daily grind of Strasbourg's data centre and its operations. Instead, they conjure up a seemingly vibrant and stable European connectivity, shielded from unreliable technology and the fragmented array of local practices that relegate supply chains and data streams to the background. These metaphors portray the Agency's work of infrastructuring, material networks and technical connectivity in ways that directly link them to the imagination of a European community and a collective order.

Using biological concepts and metaphors for infrastructures has a long history, as Richard Sennett's account of emerging modern city spaces demonstrates. New urban infrastructures, such as Hausmann's street maps of Paris or the construction of the London Underground, are depicted as veins and arteries that provide the modern city with vitality and order (Sennett 1996, 401–414; van Laak 2001). In similar ways, eu-LISA's infrastructuring work is likened to a biological organism, characterized not by stasis but constant movement and flux. As the interlocutor from eu-LISA claimed: "There is never a status quo, where [you] would simply [... wrap] your arms around and hold tight—there is a permanent process of renewal, exactly like our living organism" (Interview 14, 2019). Yet, while Sennett's analogies involve the movement of people as the underlying driver

Figure 3.2: Screenshot of eu-LISA's announcement of its anniversary conference (October 2022) in Tallinn, Estonia

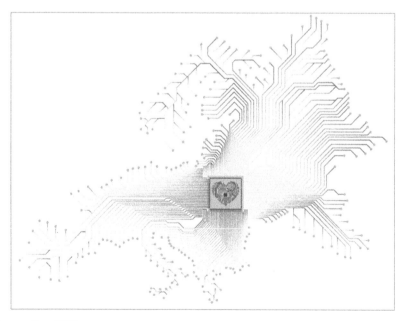

Source: © eu-LISA

and defining feature of the city and its evolving modern order, eu-LISA's organism is fed by the *circulation of data*—or data doubles that facilitate, accelerate, regulate or disrupt the movement of groups of people.

Ultimately, front- and backstaging efforts aim to establish a specific *presence-absence* of digital infrastructure, where infrastructural operations must reside in the naturalized invisible background, grappling with unreliabilities and carrying out monitoring, standardization, response and repair. The eu-LISA Agency's vision of a harmonious connection between its infrastructure and European governance is propelled by an illusive objective of complete transparency. Despite the strikingly erratic and incoherent character of infrastructuring, characterized by backstaging a series of incidents, interrupting events, imperfect operations, collective order is once again imagined as organic, stable, seamless and coherent— much akin to the functioning of a human organism.

A case of fractional Europe

This chapter has explored various approaches to infrastructuring as a specific means of frontstaging and backstaging work. In the ethnographic vignettes told previously, I introduced the primary sites where this work is taking place. Subsequently, I analyzed how events bring to the forefront ideas of Europeanhood and European community that are associated with building and administering digital border infrastructure. I then detailed the activities related to monitoring, maintenance, repair and standardization practices carried out at the eu-LISA data centre, which backstaged and concealed infrastructural failures, disruptions and tensions in the systems.

A significant part of eu-LISA's infrastructural work, therefore, is to promote the normalized and uninterrupted use of IT systems and their communication networks, ideally with the ultimate goal to achieve a "deep taken-for-grantedness" of digital infrastructure (Graham and Thrift 2007, 8). This is not beyond dispute, as one official explains: "[B]ecause we do this work in the background, lots of people forget. So, this is the main problem, the lack of visibility that we have on the daily work [...]." In a way, official events must supplement this image and aim "to pass the message, to say what [...] the implications are [of this Agency's work]" (Interview 12, 2019).

The metaphor of the organism is a striking example of not only how technicians, officers and engineers make sense of their own work but also how they use this imagery as a tool for thinking and acting—for a "politics of service" (Maguire 2023)—in the digital border regime. Border infrastructure is presented as enabling the life of a larger collective, providing it with material connectivity and digital flows. Much like our own bodies, it claims to sustain our lives without us being aware of the ceaseless organic processes within our bodies—the exchange of cells, the continuous circulation of blood through our veins.

As one of our main actors in this chapter claimed, the result of eu-LISA's backstaging efforts is that their operations are "in principle invisible. Well, obviously, you can maybe see that there is dandruff on the jacket, but otherwise you don't recognize it" (Interview 14, 2019). But what else should remain hidden? The biological metaphors to depict a single unified whole must not only visualize a seemingly natural collective body, maintained through permanent circulation and exchange of data. They also conceal from where, and from whom, data flows and circulation are extracted and generated. However, research on border and migration technologies has extensively documented how data circulation is inextricably intertwined with the (racialized) techniques of making populations legible (Amelung, Granja, and Machado 2020; M'charek, Schramm, and Skinner 2014; Pelizza 2020).

Bordering encompasses a range of practices, such as digital registration, identification, visualization, and classification, which enact migrants as others. These practices are integral parts of the infrastructural arrangements that simultaneously constitute and enact the contested entity called "Europe". Such enactment of Europe is inherently multiple, enabled when mobile individuals are transformed as non-Europeans into "European-legible" populations. eu-LISA's analogy of a living organism and its vision of a collective body thus both conceal and rely upon what Annalisa Pelizza described as the "processing of alterity" (2020), that is the translation and enactment of migrants as data objects, rendered legible and processable for authorities.

The findings of this chapter draw our attentions to the imaginative aspects and capacities involved in the project of creating populations as legible objects of government—once referred to as a "central problem of statecraft" (Scott 1998, 2). We can contextualize eu-LISA and its infrastructuring practices within the broader context of European integration and infrastructural Europeanism—both of which are shaped by the sociotechnical processes of bordering. European integration, in this context, is far from a straightforward and linear political process but rather an "emergent outcome of a process of linking and delinking of infrastructures, as well as the circulation and appropriation of artefacts, systems and knowledge" (Misa and Schot 2005, 1).[15] Our analysis of eu-LISA's front- and backstaging work has revealed that both imagination and materiality play crucial roles in this "laboratory of infrastructural collectivity" (Opitz and Tellmann 2015a, 172). Europe must be envisioned, staged and represented as cohesive, unified and singular precisely because infrastructure, like borders, is always a patchwork, fragmented, partial and multiple. Events must bind together a dispersed set of agents, tools and technologies to present Europe as a coherent entity; organic visions of collectivity are staged against the unpredictable, complex and technical character of maintenance and repair work.

John Law (2002) offers us a more valuable metaphor than body analogies for capturing the entanglement of both the imaginative and the material in making and managing digital infrastructure. He suggests that "fractional coherence" articulates how an object (in Law's case, an aircraft) "comes in different versions […] And yet these various versions also interfere with one another and shuffle themselves together to make a single aircraft" (pp. 2–3). In other words, unity and coherence cannot exist without fractionality.

In this sense, the chapter has aimed to illustrate the making of a "fractional Europe"—a Europe pieced together and disrupted through ongoing acts of front- and backstaging the various elements of border infrastructure. Just as eu-LISA's institutional history and organizational trajectories have proven, the Agency itself remains inherently fractional. Its power to consistently appear on the scene as a European spokesperson is rooted in its capacity to carefully shuffle and create unity, coherence and order from multiplicity, chaos and disarray. As we have observed, any success here can only be partial; coherence can never be a stable phenomenon. The boundary between what's visible in the front and invisible in the back, between audience and non-audience, the balance between order and chaos must be constantly redrawn. Europe, in this sense, remains fractional.

Third Interlude: Another Vignette—The Golden Age?

October 2019: The evening reception on the sidelines of "The New Information Architecture as a Driver for Efficiency and Effectiveness in Internal Security" conference was held at the Seaplane Harbour Museum in Tallinn. Three buses were arranged to take the conference attendees from the Hilton Hotel, where the conference took place, to the museum situated next to eu-LISA's headquarters. I found myself seated next to a younger businessman during the bus ride, and our conversation, typical of such events, quickly turned to the introduction of his company's product line: automated borders, smart corridors, facial recognition technology, and especially effective fingerprint scanning systems. He proudly emphasized that their products could complete necessary background checks "in just a few seconds", promising a smooth and speedy bordering processes. His company's portfolio did not differ much from those of other vendors present at the conference. In fact, many industrial players were promoting similar products and were heavily focused on the marketing potential for things like "paperless strategies" and "seamless traveling experiences".

As the crowd disembarked from the bus and walked up to the museum, businesspeople and other participants continued their conversations about topics such as "identity programs", the "identity management business" or the "border continuum".

The Seaplane Harbour Museum, a former military hangar, is a feature in any Tallinn tourist guide. It hosts a World War I exhibition focused on submarines, naval artillery and sea mines. While attending the evening event, I wondered who within the Agency had selected this odd location and pondered the reasons behind their choice. Was it because of its proximity to the Agency? Perhaps the Agency wanted to provide international guests with an opportunity to explore a nearby tourist attraction? Before the reception officially started, attendees were given a tour of the exhibition, including a walk along the deck of one of the submarines exhibited in the hangar. "James", a national delegate and one of the official speakers at the conference, took the time to explain some of the weaponry's historical context and the deployments of these massive old submarines. In his previous career, James had served in his country's military, later becoming a border guard, and eventually working for his interior ministry.

The Agency had organized a buffet and a band for the reception. It also announced that the scheduled welcome speech by the executive director at that time, Krum Garkov, had to be cancelled at the last minute due to other obligations. James, who was accompanying me at the buffet, expressed his upset at what to him appeared to be a rather undiplomatic act. It sparked a broader discussion critiquing EU agencies and their handling of European digital border initiatives. Generally, James had doubts about the prospects and feasibility of EU's new centralized databases, commonly referred to by everyone at the conference as Europe's smart borders. With sarcasm, he went on to characterize EU conferences as highly proficient in offering attendees lavish meals and posh hotels. Such events, he implied, primarily align with the agendas of senior officials and their respective agencies in the EU while perfectly articulating the EU's excessive bureaucratic nature. The sarcastic attitude he displayed when discussing policy meetings and the smart border initiatives aimed to reflect his ability to voice his own individual thoughts, conveying what he "really thinks".

The exchange brought to mind observations by anthropologist Gregory Feldman, who noticed that policy environments are typically far removed from many of the everyday realities of their participants, including their roles within national bureaucracies, their local contexts, and the day-to-day

Figure 3.3: Conference setting at eu-LISA's annual conference (2019) at Tallinn, Estonia

Source: © eu-LISA, photo credit: Sven Tupits

challenges they encounter. Delegates participate in these international meetings while simultaneously complaining about their impersonal atmosphere and the predetermined outcomes. As Feldman explains, participants "may creatively do their jobs, but they are not present as particular speaking subjects" (2014, 49).

Similarly, during my conversation, James's use of sarcasm struck me as a way to react to his perception of losing his individual agency. James seemed to welcome my presence as an outsider, someone to whom he could reveal insights beyond the shallow surfaces of the polished evening reception. He pointed to various interconnected aspects of the meetings and events we were attending, as well as critical comments he made in his previous speech that an outsider might not have fully grasped. Subsequently, he introduced me to a compatriot who worked in a business consultancy and had suddenly joined us at the buffet. James hinted at the massive financial investments in IT for border control purposes and amusingly remarked, "Well, in general, for us border guards and for you consultancies, it's just the golden age!"

4

Crafting the Epistemology
of Smart Borders

The preceding vignette recounts my attendance at an eu–LISA event held on the margins of two larger events, where new ideas and concepts for border technology, databases and their interoperability were presented, discussed and negotiated. One was the Agency's annual conference that announced the "New Information Architecture", while the other was an industry roundtable. I use this vignette and draw upon my observations from both events as points of departure for the chapter's empirical and analytical focus on the project of "smartening" border management in Europe.

The literature on smart borders often associates two key features with smart borders. The first one is broader and conceptual: smart borders are frequently seen as exemplifying the evolving nature of digitally mediated bordering processes, becoming increasingly fluid and dispersed. Dijstelbloem and Broeders (2015) describe this as the proliferation of procedures and practices that establish a web of relations between "databases, fingerprints, migrants' bodies, directives, policy documents, European and national bureaucracies, and so forth" (p. 27). The smart border is now commonly perceived as "a diffuse one physically extending both beyond and inside its geopolitical location, and involving a multiplicity of sites for the surveillance of movement" (Amoore, Marmura, and Salter 2008, 99; see also Côté-Boucher 2008).

The second characteristic is more empirical: the designs and the operations of smart borders typically involve an increasingly diverse array of stakeholders (beyond the state), particularly from industrial sectors interested in "smartening" the border. For example, an eu–LISA representative described this as the "modern way of operating", adding that "I don't even know [...] how many hundreds of persons we are cooperating [with] in the industry" (Interview 28, 2019).[1] Most scholars refer to these two general characteristics when analyzing the different roles, functionalities, rationalities, and challenges associated with smart borders as part of the broader digitization of migration control regimes and the changing character of borders themselves.[2]

In this chapter, I am less interested in a diagnostic assessment or critique of the smart border project. Instead, I delve into the necessary and painstakingly laborious social and epistemic efforts involved in making smart borders, efforts that are regularly carried out at conferences, meetings, roundtables and events like the one described in the vignette. Smart borders emerge here also as an epistemological project that shapes how bordering processes can be known, represented and discussed. I use the notion of epistemology by drawing on Jasanoff's (2005) concept of "civic epistemologies" to describe how culturally specific ways of knowing science and technology play out in political debates and decision-making around technology. Civic epistemology refers to a culture of "how political communities know things in common" (p. 250) and encompasses "institutionalized practices by which members of a given society test and deploy knowledge claims used as a basis for making collective choices" (p. 255). Unlike Jasanoff's concept (which is typically employed in comparative studies), I do not imply the involvement of a national or even European citizenry on whose behalf public knowledge is performed and authorized in response to technoscientific developments. Instead, my analysis centres on eu-LISA's conferences and roundtables as arenas in which "knowledge is presented, tested, verified, and put to use" (p. 258). At these sites of infrastructural experimentation, a particular epistemological framework establishes the credibility and legitimacy of how digital borders should be developed and deployed. This epistemology is not predominantly defined by formal rules and regulations, but rather through a *distinct political culture and practice*, characterized by institutionalized conditions, modes of interaction and collective approaches of testing, envisioning and demonstrating knowledge and representations of borders. Examining these conditions can shed a light on how smart borders become increasingly normalized and how they perpetuate the idealized promises associated with the concept of smart borders.

To understand how this epistemology is crafted, I begin by describing the standardized conditions present in these eu-LISA arenas, which create a ritualized atmosphere conducive to events, a sort of "clubbability", favouring and fostering a particular epistemic orientation among participants. Next, I elaborate on how smart borders operate as a boundary object, allowing heterogeneous actors to articulate incommensurable but coexisting visions and interests within the context of the same smart border project. Following this, I explore the repertoire of logistical language around smart borders, which frames how borders and border crossings must be problematized and how challenges must be addressed. In the final section of this chapter, I expand on some of the conclusions and implications of this epistemology of smart borders. I argue that it nurtures forms of knowing, representing and speaking about borders and migration that are not only solution-oriented but also "technostrategic" (Cohn 1987a). It must signal a mastery over technical complexity and provides epistemic keys to a world in which borders and migration are managed at a distance, thus sidestepping the complex realities and violence associated with border control in Europe.

Before delving into this analysis, however, I will clarify the connection between the European so-called smart borders initiative and the new databases that are currently in development at eu-LISA.

Digital embracement: new databases for smartening the border

The notion of "smartness" has always served as a repository of multiple meanings, emerging as a ubiquitous and adaptable term in a wide range of innovation-driven projects and policies, from smart cities and smart homes to smart health and smart borders. Within the EU border regime, Jeandesboz (2016b) highlights that smartening is a process of "multiple translations and enrolments through which the technical side of dataveillance – platforms, automated gates, matching systems, and so forth – has become associated with the processes of policymaking" (p. 292). Despite the complexity of this notion, there are two prominent large-scale systems that will form the backbone of smart borders, promising to generate new knowledge about travelers and their movements: the Entry/Exit System (EES) and the European Travel Information and Authorization System (ETIAS).[3]

The first system, the EES, will require all short-stay travelers, regardless of their visa status, to register their identity information. Third-country nationals or travelers from countries outside the EU will be required to register not only biographical data and travel information but also provide five fingerprints and a facial image. Moreover, this system will retain data concerning the duration of their stay within any Schengen member state and automatically notify national authorities if a traveler exceeds the authorized stay of 90 days in case no exit has been recorded.

The purpose of this system is to cross-reference the data with the Visa Information System, aiming to identify so-called "visa overstayers". The EES thus addresses a long-standing concern shared by Schengen member states. Over the years, they have incrementally aligned and tightened their visa policies, which has led to third-country nationals facing an increasingly restrictive legal environment that leaves them with no options for legally staying in the EU. The result is that individuals most often arrive in Europe with a valid visa, exceed their authorized stay, and end up categorized as irregular or illegal migrants.[4]

The second database is the ETIAS, designed to store data on persons who typically do not require visas to enter Schengen states. A primary objective of this system is to ensure that travelers obtain authorization before embarking on their journey to a Schengen state on regular terms, effectively enabling authorities to scrutinize and potentially deny transit or entry to a person whose travel might pose "a security, illegal immigration or high epidemic risk" (EU 2018b, L236/1). This will require travelers to complete an online application, providing details related to their identity, travel documents, places of residence and contact information. A significant part of the ETIAS regulatory framework concerns the establishment of a watchlist that would filter those classified as risk—in other words, creating a "connection between data in an application file and information related to individuals" (L236/5). The system's overarching goal, therefore, is to preemptively screen and assess travelers to Europe, sharing strong similarities with the US ESTA (Electronic System for Travel Authority) and Australia's ETA (Electronic Travel Authority).[5]

As these databases equip member state authorities with the tools to further digitize mobility control, they continue to enhance what Torpey (1998) describes as the "embracement" of mobile populations moving across or within the borders of Schengen states.[6] This digital embracement is perhaps most visibly articulated in the replacement of manual passport stamping with the electronic registration of travelers' entry and exit, which aims to provide border and visa authorities with more comprehensive information about an individual's travel history. It is also evident in the wider restrictions pursued by respective legal regulations, specifically the establishment (and prevention) of what constitutes "irregular migration and to facilitate the management of migration flows" (EU 2017, 327/22). Consider, for instance, the remarks of an EU official who reflected on the advantages of these new systems in creating personal travel histories:

> It [… is] a very important component. If you can make sure that a visa applicant has had [a] couple of Schengen visas in the past years, it's a signal that he is trustworthy, and he is reliable, and he didn't overstay […]. Of course, on the other hand, if you can see that there were previous refusals, that's also an indication that the application should be thoroughly checked. So, this database helps a lot, because what happened [with] what we had before with the Visa Information System, the consular officers relied on indications on the passport as such. Of course, you can visually see that there were Schengen visas issued beforehand; before, a visa sticker is in the passport. But what if the applicant had a new passport? Then you lose this information. (Interview 9, 2019)

In summary, the EES and ETIAS seek to create new types of information through bordering procedures at various sites; they connect them with data from other systems and attempt to reduce opportunities for migrants to reappropriate mobility (Scheel 2017). These databases therefore seek to enable mobility control to become further detached from (Schengen's) territorial boundaries while increasing its remote operations (Salter 2006b; Zolberg 2003). Peter Adey (2012) aptly captures the rationale of dataveillance that informs smart borders and their associated IT systems, the EES and ETIAS: it "[draws] upon the resources of information networks between states. It pushes and pulls at these flows just as it modulates the mixtures of people and things. Some are sent packing and others eased through" (p. 20).

The ritualistic conditions for imagining smart futures

Even though the smartification of borders is closely linked to the development of the EES and ETIAS, its social promise tends to be fairly detached from the concrete technical functionalities of these systems—much like so many promises associated with emerging infrastructure projects. Smartness invokes a more general "wager on the future—a strategic belief that smartness will operate" (Sadowski and Bendor 2019, 548). As Sadowski and Bendor argue, such a wager is encouraged by the strategic belief that smartness can respond "to present conditions and entrenched existing political economies while also paving the way to a thriving, prosperous future" (pp. 547–548). The smart borders project, therefore, not only aligns with and rehearses the wider imaginary of technological transformation but also builds on multiple tropes and narratives of smart futures. These are consistently and repeatedly featured in presentations and discussions at conferences, industry roundtables and policy meetings within the border regime. As we have observed, they are "field configuring events" (Garud 2008) where politics, security, technology and business intersect most publicly.

Annelise Riles (2000), drawing on her ethnographic work at UN conferences, finds that (transnational) meetings operate as particular "forums[;] they 'mobilize,' they '[set] in motion a process,' they generate publicity, and most of all they draw in a wide variety of participants. Yet the purpose of this flurry of rather processual oriented activity is always described in wider instrumental terms" (p. 13). Likewise, the events I attended punctuate a configuring network of actors and participants and link their activities and interests against the backdrop of a seemingly wider "problem" that discursively connects migration, security, and technology. These elements are bound together by the participants' virtues, behaviours, visions and narratives, which create the conditions for the making of smart futures and the digital borders envisioned to realize them. In these settings, "[p]eople and their virtues *matter*", as Steven Shapin (2008) notes elsewhere, "and that mattering is absolutely central to the rationally calculative worlds where late modern finance meets technoscience" (p. 270; italics in the original). In a similar vein, we turn our attention to the ritualized patterns of behaviour, values and interactions of conference and roundtable participants, shedding a light on some of the inner workings of the EU border regime.

Formality and clubbability

In a comprehensive report, Lemberg-Pedersen, Hansen, and Halpern describe one of the key purposes of eu-LISA events:

> At the Roundtables, it [is] possible for industrial actors to liaise with government representatives and communicate their preferences and suggested solutions to the development of IT systems. Roundtables, as well as conferences, are important sites for the industry in order to influence the policies and choices of technological solutions underpinning the large-scale information systems. (Lemberg-Pedersen, Hansen, and Halpern 2020, 66)

Since its establishment in 2012, the eu-LISA Agency has established itself as an integral member of a larger network that convenes regularly, not only at its own meetings but also at international conferences, business venues, fairs and promotional exhibitions. Part of the Agency's agenda involves developing a knowledge hub, which goes beyond merely creating a gateway for the industry. The Agency participates in multiple meetings where one must interact with "external parties to build up knowledge and exchange that knowledge", as a representative stated (Interview 4, 2018). These "external parties" encompass a diverse array of actors within a network that spans across the continent (and also, partly, the world), comprising governmental and industrial representatives, financiers, brokers, IT companies and enterprises (such as Secunet, IDEMIA, InGROUP, Jenetric, Gemalto, and Gatekeeper Security), implementers, transport companies (such as Lufthansa and SITA), security professionals and border guards from different nation-states.[7] These events serve as platforms to bring these actors together and play a crucial role in the global factoring, legitimization and proliferation of security in today's world.

An intriguing characteristic of these events is their standardized settings and environments. As "James" sarcastically noted in the vignette earlier, meetings can appear highly repetitive when attended frequently (as delegates usually must do); they tend to yield rather thin and predictable outcomes with little impact or consequences for operational activities on the ground. The formalistic procedures at these events are executed in a uniform manner—for instance, the almost interchangeable lists of opening and closing speakers, arranged according to hierarchical bureaucratic ranks; repetitive speeches by government officials who read from prepared talking points with feigned enthusiasm, highlighting the solemn atmosphere, the "excellent organization", the "huge significance" of the meeting, or the "historic" crossroads. At the same time, these procedures establish a repetitive framework for amplifying the connected themes of migration, security and technology. Often, these events have a moderator with limited knowledge of the conference topics, who attempts to link familiar ideas from the speeches and discussions and guides the audience throughout the day.[8] The artificial formality of the setting arises from substantial social and financial investments made to create a standardized framework to which participants can collectively refer. This pertains not only to the repetitive speeches and similar agendas but also to the choice of high-end, internationally recognizable locations, such as the Hilton Hotel in Tallinn or the Radisson Blu Hotel in Bucharest.

At the same time, these events cultivate what Steven Shapin (2008) describes as a sense of "clubbability" (p. 270). Clubbability results from the events' "compression of time and the intensity of interactions across boundaries" (Garud 2008, 1084). It makes the virtues of familiar people recognizable and is, as a result, crucial for establishing one's orientation towards, and judgment in the worlds of, technoscience, finance and security. At different sites and in different venues, participants recognize each other, their encounters become familiar, and their greetings are exchanged as a matter of routine. The behaviour and communication of participants become more casual, and conversations can easily be picked where they were left off in a previous encounter.

A case in point is the "ID@Borders and the Future of Travel" conference, which was hosted by the OSCE and the UK-based non-governmental organization "Biometrics Institute". It took place at the esteemed Hofburg Palace in Vienna in 2019 and it prominently featured eu-LISA alongside the European Commission on the main panel, where they presented the overarching policy framework and expectations for the development of new smart borders. The sessions offered "Platinum" and "Gold" sponsorship opportunities, enabling organizations to secure their positions alongside high-level speakers from governmental agencies like INTERPOL and eu-LISA. This event provided companies with the platform to introduce and promote their products and to nurture relationships with delegates of nation-states and regional organizations.

Meetings like "ID@Borders and the Future of Travel" consciously exhibit bourgeois etiquette and typically present a fairly male-dominated environment, embodying the Silicon Valley-style culture of the security industry, where management skills and behaviour are considered as significant as expertise in security technology.[9] Ultimately, clubbability, combined with the contrasting formal framework of events, often results in environments that appear highly ritualistic, with some of these rituals even being ironically imitated. Rituality, in other words, provides a convenient way to express the clubbability of participants. For example, at the "ID@Borders" conference at the Hofburg palace, participants had to engage in a playful competition to exchange as many business cards as possible for the sake of "proper networking" and to fulfil the "real" purpose of the event (field note, OSCE Conference, 10–11 April 2019). The act of business card exchanging, a nearly universal ritual in the business world, here took on an ironic twist to imitate familiar behavioural patterns, evoking a shared sense of belonging among the participants' same "club".[10]

Ritual behaviours and proceedings, in this sense, serve to communicate familiarity with form (Berezin 1997, 250). They create particular standardized patterns of communication and lead participants to jointly "confer and negotiate the meaning of a significant event" (Feldman 2014, 49). They define the points of association and cultivate an environment of familiarity, allowing to express clubbability. The drawback of fostering such homogenized, collective rules of behaviour and discourse is that it occasionally leads to participants experiencing boredom and monotony (as seen in James's case in our vignette). As Feldman (2014) aptly pointed out, "communicative standards get institutionalized and rituals take on, if not affective powers, then at least the hegemony of bourgeois manners. […] It yields a homogenizing effect so often seen in bourgeois politesse that tends to bore those consumed by it more so than animate them as unique individuals" (p. 49).

Conferences and events in the EU border regime are formalized sites of border policy making. They create a recognizable, entrepreneurial world in which rituals and clubbability conceal the lack of actual (social or cultural) associations between their participants. By compressing time and space, they disrupt the usual temporal rhythms of everyday (bordering) work that participants are usually involved in. Instead, these events encourage them to shift their focus away from the local and complex realities of migration and mobility and direct their attention to what must be achievable in a technoscientific future. It is in this sense that such meetings become powerful tools of political communication and imagination. They provide the epistemological conditions for collectively envisioning future borders. Therefore, we now turn to the prevailing epistemic orientation in these meetings, which is not about collective reflection—understood as a meaningful way of sharing, understanding and learning from experience to inform and develop further practice—but instead anticipation.

The urge to anticipate

Anticipation, according to Adams, Murphy, and Clarke (2009), can be perceived as both an epistemic orientation and a "moral imperative, a will to anticipate" the future (p. 254). As such, it opens a space—in the name of what lies ahead—to act in the present. By serving as a temporal orientation, it not only directs and moulds knowledge toward speculative forecast and prediction, it also acts on the present as the realm of potentiality, mobilizing what is presumably possible.

This ostentatious enthusiasm to anticipate and thus to envision the smart future of borders is a key virtue at these conferences. At the "ID@Borders" conference or eu-LISA industry roundtables, this prevailing epistemic orientation is often displayed in presentations, more than detailed descriptions of particular technologies or explanations of bordering tools and products. The conference presentations tend to focus on broader projections about the potential evolution of global mobility and tourism and what their substantial economic benefits could look like. These are the overarching themes against which commercial technological products must be promoted and substantiated as credible.

The urge to anticipate also conveys a sense of competitiveness and creativity. This is often invoked, for instance, by simplistic proverbs that are prominently featured on PowerPoint slides: "Technology, like art, is a soaring exercise of the human imagination" or "The only constant in the technology industry is change" (field note, OSCE Conference, 10–11 April 2019).[11] These superficial statements are accompanied by buzzwords like "cloud technology", "artificial intelligence", and "data analytics". Participants indulge in an almost mythical storytelling where the innovative products conjure up "borders without boundaries", or a "digital future [where] there is a role for everyone to play". Participants appear to be privileged figures riding the wave of an "amazing momentum in our history, in how we can make these sustainable paths in the future" (field note, OSCE Conference, 10–11 April 2019).

Nevertheless, at times even policy officials must feel that the Silicon Valley-inspired urge for anticipation should be restrained. During an industry roundtable organized by eu-LISA and the Romanian EU presidency, a senior agency representative cautioned the audience that, in reality, "the time for theoretical debate is over". His concern revolved around the fear that exaggerated techno-idealism could divert attention from critical practical matters "on the ground" that urgently demand focus on "align[ing] technology for the practices at borders" and "find[ing] practical and pragmatic solutions" (field note, eu-LISA Industry Roundtable, 24 April 2019).

Despite such occasional moments, we observe that the urge to anticipate remains a prevailing sentiment during discussions on the smart future of borders. As an epistemic orientation, anticipation exploits what Adams and colleagues call the "'sense' of the simultaneous uncertainty and inevitability of the future, usually manifest as entanglements of fear and hope" (2009, 249). Foreseeing, predicting and preparing for technoscientific futures emerges as one of the core features that ties these stakeholders—industry people, delegates, implementers, governmental experts, officials, border guards, brokers, and financiers—to a temporary, joint epistemic community.

A summary of eu-LISA's 2018 annual conference entitled "EU Borders—Getting Smarter Through Technology" echoes the significance of this imperative for the so-called stakeholder community:

> Engagement with the border guard community to enable their anticipation of future developments and their input during their development process will be key. The main conclusion drawn from the conference is that the future is already underway – the challenging digital journey that will completely change the outlook of the information architecture in the Justice and Home Affairs domain has already started. The goals can't be reached in isolation based on work by EU Agencies or Member States alone. We need to engage all the stakeholders including carriers, airports as well as land and sea border operators. (eu-LISA 2019c, 60)

Smart borders: a boundary object

> So, imagine how many procurement processes will be ongoing. It is maybe a thousand, because there are different systems, different member states. Also, there are the four [Schengen] associated countries, different levers and levels of technologies and there are national[ly] definitely different topics. (Interview 28 with member state representative, 2019)

As suggested by this quote, smartening borders in the European border regime is expressed on multiple scales and levels. It is a testimony to the growth of what some observers have referred to as the security or border industrial complex (Cooperate Europe Observatory 2021; Jones 2017; Smith 2019). Smart borders are frequently portrayed as an industrial product par excellence, the result of marketization strategies by private actors and consultancies, which have continuously sought to stimulate greater demand for border-related technologies and have shaped the border regime in accordance with their profit-driven interests.[12] Such diagnoses, however, run the risk of oversimplifying the border industrial complex by presenting it as a composite of two relatively stable camps of interest: private (market-driven) actors on one side and state actors on the other.

Instead, as we have observed, we are faced with a multitude of actors, practices and interests that intersect at eu-LISA meetings. Their challenge lies in finding ways to reconcile the different meanings of smart futures and future borders while collaboratively navigating the digital transformation of the border regime. Smart borders should therefore not be merely viewed as a product of industrial security companies; rather they should be seen as a boundary object that enables different communities of practice to craft their epistemology of digital borders. This can be achievable because these

Figure 4.1: "What's next?", a slide presented at the ID@Borders conference (April 2019) by eu-LISA

Note: Featuring mountains in the background, the slide offers a visual metaphor for the desired entrepreneurial anticipation of "what lies ahead".

Source: © eu-LISA

communities can continually "translate, negotiate, debate, triangulate, and simplify in order to work together" (Star and Griesemer 1989, 389).

"Smartness", with its emphasis to anticipate the future, its loose foundation rooted in two large-scale IT systems, and the idea of automating and platforming borders, invites actors to engage in joint epistemic labour aimed at reconciling coexisting meanings and interests. In the words of Star and Griesemer, smart borders can be described as

> plastic enough to adapt to local needs and the constraints of the several parties employing them, yet robust enough to maintain a common identity across sites. [...] They have different meanings in different social worlds but their structure is common enough to more than one world to make them recognizable, a means of translation. The creation and management of boundary objects is a key process in developing and maintaining coherence across intersecting social worlds. (Star and Griesemer 1989, 394)

This does not imply that the various groups and actors within the border industrial complex are striving for a consensus (see also Star 2010). Instead, they perform what Niewöhner (2015) characterizes as an experimental type of "co-laboration", a "transient, non-teleological joint epistemic work without the commitment to a shared outcome" (p. 236). Smart borders allow for the coexistence of diverse (and sometimes even incommensurable) interventions, interests and goals. They serve as particularly valuable objects of co-laboration in the transformation of borders (without the necessity of arriving at a traditional consensus).

As illustrated in the following sections, we can reconstruct (at least) three distinct meanings of how European smart borders could be enacted, whether displayed during conferences or emerging through the narratives of experts and officials: firstly, as a project for networking European-wide borders; secondly, as a site where a multifaceted European digital security market should manifest itself; and, thirdly, as tools to reconfigure state border control within the context of the global economy.

Networking European borders

To begin with, smart borders are conceptualized as a means to realize the idea of fully networked European borders.[13] While this vision is prominently endorsed by the EC and agency officials, it is only occasionally articulated by national delegates or experts. For instance, a national expert responsible for coordinating the implementation of the new databases in their country explained, "from a European perspective, the management of EU external borders as an interconnected one is still in its infancy. [...] [T]he way it is planned now, to my knowledge, has never existed before in the European area" (Interview 2, 2018). Smart borders then typically represent a central platform for materializing what Jensen and Richardson (2004) have termed the "European monotopia", a unified vision of European spatial development and integration.

This distinct spatial rationale persists within the ongoing efforts of the EU and its institutions to establish and maintain Europe as an "organized, ordered and totalized space of zero-friction and seamless logistic flows" (Jensen and Richardson 2004, 3). Consequently, smartening borders is here primarily envisioned as a particular method for (re-)organizing, and thus harmonizing border control. This perspective was emphasized by a senior official in the European Commission's unit for information systems for borders and security who claimed, "What we do is not technical at all. It's deeply political because it's really about how you organize your external borders, [and] why you organize them in such a way" (Interview 13, 2019).

EU officials and agency representatives repeatedly stress the need for border management to be reconfigured as a wider harmonized network of actors and practices beyond individual nation-states. For example, in an article published in the quarterly journal *Border Management Today*, former eu-LISA Director Krum Garkov stated: "Today border management is no longer a business only for government and border agencies. In the digital age, cooperation and information exchange is vital for efficient border management since the challenges and threats are beyond capacity of a single governmental agency or country to resolve them" (Garkov 2020, 29).

Moulding the formation of Europe, as pointed out by Andrew Barry (2001), entails not only the construction of common European laws and markets but also the formation of European objects and artefacts. In the context or our illustration, smart borders generate a hybrid bundle of transnational databases, bordering devices and practices that have the capacity to reorder and standardize bordering procedures across nations and their governing bodies (field note, OSCE Conference, 10–11 April 2019). This transnational "business", as Garkov describes it, further reinforces the spatial concept of a European monotopia—a fully networked space that appears to be in state of perpetual uncertainty and contention, not least because it is disjointed by deep-seated power struggles (Jensen and Richardson 2004, 69ff.). In its most visible forms, the debates surrounding European monotopia, along with its implicit assumption that individual European states can no longer adequately protect their borders, unfolds in the tensions between EU institutions and member state authorities (or their border personnel on the ground) as well as their disagreements concerning sovereignty. For instance, a national delegate at a conference, somewhat irritated, suggested:

> They want to harmonize border control. They want, I think, to make sure that border control through the whole of Europe is done in exactly the same way. […] I understand that for somebody whose job is to sit behind a desk in Brussels and not work with—let's say—these kinds of people and processes on [… a] daily basis, it looks strange that in Slovenia they are doing things differently than in Finland. (Interview 26, 2019)

In this scenario, enacting smart borders becomes a project aimed at networking European borders. It embodies an agenda that is frequently at odds with the daily operational concerns of national border authorities. Instead, it promotes the monotopic vision of Europe as a logistical, seamless space, attainable only through fully networked borders. Simultaneously, this vision reveals the disputes and conflicts around sovereignty and power, which permeate the interactions (and rivalries) between European institutions on the one side and national authorities on the other.

Creating a digital border security market

During a break between sessions at one of the conferences, a salesman from a private security company in eastern Europe told me, "It's up to me to build a market!" (field note, OSCE Conference, 10–11 April 2019). He perceived the making of smart borders as the focal point of a growing, multifaceted European market in digital border security. The creation of smart borders appeared to him as a lucrative, long-term prospect in which, through an array of negotiations, translations, research activities and adaptations, one could intervene to turn borders and control technologies into marketable commodities. Indeed, smart borders are tangible evidence of how companies and consultancies have increasingly gained legitimization and influenced rebordering activities within and beyond the European border regime.

However, private security companies and their business representatives are not the only actors embracing this vision of a transnational security market. eu-LISA officials occasionally describe the creation of this market as a "spillover effect" (Interview 28, 2019; field note, eu-LISA Conference, 16 October 2019). The spillover effect would infuse border management with market-oriented principles and values, including competition, public–private partnership, and innovation. Accordingly, one of my interlocutors within the Agency underscored, "for those systems [of the smart border], we want to be, you know, let's say, new and innovative. [...] So, this spillover goes to the need to be technologically up to date. It goes to the private sector companies and to the academia" (Interview 28, 2019).

Smartening borders amplifies both market supply and demand. The creation of border dataveillance databases, such as the EES and ETIAS, attract extensive budgeting activities on behalf of the EU. They benefit not only member states as customers searching for appropriate devices and infrastructure, but also the broad spectrum of suppliers, such as security enterprises and the "wide range of European IT companies who are providing different level[s of] hardware and software and who are providing services linked to them" (Interview 28, 2019). Lemberg-Pedersen and colleagues have documented in detail how the EU nurtures what they call a multifaceted "border control market" (Lemberg-Pedersen, Hansen, and Halpern 2020, 16). This includes not only the contracting of businesses in aerospace, defence and biometric security but also the mobilization of "a plethora of small and medium-sized businesses [...] who also reap smaller contracts concerning IT, housing, interpretation, health, cleaning, layout/ design, software, conference and meetings, consultancies, maritime or aviation services, office supplies or transportation" (p. 16).

Accordingly, at roundtable events, conferences or policy meetings, one can observe the presentation and visualization of a diverse range of devices, artefacts and services: flexible suitcases with portable fingerprint machines, portable cameras, and various screening and surveillance equipment. Notably, the EES generates a significant demand for what is advocated as necessary "mobile borders", which must biometrically capture movement and verify individuals while complying to European standards regarding biometric quality and storage capacity (field note, eu-LISA Conference, 16 October 2019).

Smart borders are thus envisioned as a way to expand the "multiplicity of sites where detectors and effectors interact with flows of people and goods" (Broeders and Hampshire 2013, 1207) and transform each potential detector and effector into a subject of marketing, adaptation and customized design. Smart borders, in other words, serve as a testbed for creating a European-wide, multisectoral market for digital border security. A national delegate expressed astonishment at the extensive scale at which the smartification of borders has been taken place: "These are super expensive systems, you know, the European procurement. It's always the best price [*laughing*]; these are ridiculous numbers, you know, if you compare them to national-level ICT projects. Add one or two zeros to them, so somebody is making lots of money with this" (Interview 26, 2019).

Reconfiguring control at the borders of the state

Furthermore, the smart borders initiative reveals how the formation of state borders is inextricably bound to its relationship with global security and the economy. Member state authorities exhibit a particular interest in smart borders because the timing of control has emerged as a pivotal factor in "[transforming] the relationship between economy and security at the border from a contradictory one into a productive one" (Leese 2016, 418).[14] In this context, mobility is primarily portrayed as a potential source of capital: during the COVID-19 pandemic, a representative of eu-LISA argued, "fifty million plus [...] third-country nationals crossing borders contributed to the EU GDP with 300 billion Euros". Consequently, any successful implementation of smart borders would have to take into account how Europe is "perceived from the rest of the world", which entails considering whether people experience long wait times at the border, the volume of travelers, and their contributions to the economy (field note, Visionbox online event, 30 September 2020). In this light, smartening borders is primarily driven by the economic interests of states, and fuelled by the promise of optimizing the temporal management of control and speeding up business flows through infrastructural setups such as automated identification and e-gates. Smart borders are here portrayed as a *reaction* to the pressures of the global economy—and subsequently offered as effective means to turn mobility into differentiated, profitable and frictionless flows.

Such visions, aspirations and demands, as scholars have frequently pointed out, do not result in the abolition of borders, but rather in their delocalization. Border control is translated into various spatial and temporal regimes, speeds, waiting periods and deportation practices (Murphy and

Maguire 2015, 172). Ideally, the traveler can be enroled, verified and cleared before they arrive at the state's territorial boundary. This principle of preclearance is exemplified in the objectives of the ETIAS regulation, which enables authorities to conduct preliminary checks on identities and match information with profiles on a watchlist. Control procedures are also temporally expanded *after* crossing a Schengen border—as outlined in the EES regulations. The entry and exit of travelers should not only be recorded but also automatically reported to authorities, alerting them to unregistered exits, which may then indicate a potential "overstay".

In conversations, debates or presentations, the concept of extending or making the border multifaceted appears time and again. This embodies an abstract and logistical idea of optimizing circulation by stretching control across both time and space. Bordering, as one Agency official anticipated, "doesn't all happen at a border checkpoint. In fact, in many cases, I think [...] they will be declaring information in advance, registering things on smartphones, et cetera, that then will be detected as they cross the border area." The interviewee also raised questions about the future of border controls, pondering, "do you have a follow-up when you cross the border? Where does the story end?" (Interview 4, 2018).

Ultimately, smartening entails here the enrolment of a myriad of carriers and transport companies as co-bordering actors, in what is termed the ecosystem of border management. Supported by the EES and ETIAS as the underlying backbone of border smartification, transport companies will be confronted with a number of legal, technical and financial obligations, for instance, the requirement to integrate technical specifications such as a "web service" to verify "whether third-country nationals holding a Schengen short-stay visa issued for one or two entries have already used the number of entries authorized by their visa" (EU 2017, 3). Additionally, ETIAS obliges air, sea, train and bus carriers to query the database via a "carrier gateway" that "provide[s] the carriers with an 'OK/NOT OK' answer" (EU 2018b, Article 45). As a result, smartening borders envisions multiple points where various types of private stakeholders can become incorporated into the mechanisms and practices of remote control (Zolberg 2006).

In this vision, making smart borders does not entail the material creation of networked European borders or reinvigorating a multisectoral market for digital border security. Instead, smart borders should serve as advanced instruments of remote control, effectively making countries co-bordering partners whose screening and filtering efforts benefit each other. Transport companies and carriers are here moreover imagined as what Zolberg (2006) would term ancillary border police at the behest of states.[15] The magnitude of these enrolments is seen as problematic only in terms of their complicated logistical implementation and challenges, as elaborated by this official: "I find it very hard to be fulfilled by this transport sector. [...] It's a heavy area because we are placing

Figure 4.2: "Stay Open, Stay Secure", a slide presented at the ID@Borders conference (April 2019) by eu-LISA

Source: © eu-LISA

[…] duties to have the software to check fingerprints, for example, and all the software to see the identity of the person" (Interview 28, 2019).[16] By dislocating the border and enroling private entities, smart borders are thus envisioned as tools that facilitate the reconfiguration of mobility control, structured around the twin imperatives of security and the economy (see Figure 4.2).

The logistical language of smart borders

Viewing smart borders as a boundary object helps us understand how different actors in the border regime perform joint epistemic work and maintain coherence in the pursuit of different goals and visions. These actors interpret "smartness" or "smartification" differently within the transformation of the border regime. Producing boundary objects thus serves as a crucial method of communication across dispersed groups. We now turn to another shared mode of communication: the abstract, rationalized linguistic repertoire that spans different goals and visions in smartening borders.

This specialized language is a vehicle for what some scholars have labelled the logistification of migration and borders (Altenried et al. 2017, 2018; Bojadžijev 2019; Mezzadra 2017). It both reflects and shapes how border management and cross-border movement are known, articulated and communicated. Moreover, as we will observe, this language operates in what Carol Cohn (1987a, 1987b) calls "technostrategic" terms. It seeks to promote a specific techno-solutionist mindset, strategically framing problems through the lens of logistical rationality. Hence, crafting the epistemology of digital borders is also a transformative process at the linguistic level, assembled and forged by officials, delegates, experts and specialists in the realm of migration management.

Acronyms: learning the language of migration and border management

One of the most remarkable aspects of the language of migration and border management is the omnipresent use of acronyms. When it comes to digital borders, acronyms are the exclusive way they are referred to and discussed. Acronyms dominate speech at every meeting and have become integrated in policy documents, statements and reports. Jeandesboz (2016b) has highlighted this peculiarity:

SIS. SIS II. EURODAC. VIS. PNR. EES. RTP. Each of these acronyms stands for a computerized system for the collection, exchange and analysis of data related to persons crossing the external borders of the EU. These acronyms have colonized EU policy documents, public statements of European officials and politicians, and increasingly scholarship on EU border security. (p. 292)

EES and ETIAS are just two of the most prominent acronyms used to denote the dataveillance systems underpinning smart borders.

Universally recognized among participants in conferences and similar events, acronyms offer a clear advantage: they form linguistic entities that can be spoken and written quickly, condense discussions, and deflect questions regarding their often complicated, bureaucratic names and titles. However, as Cohn (1987a) suggests, we should examine their potential purposes beyond the sheer principle of utility.[17] By reducing language only to what seems necessary, Cohn argues that acronyms limit "the communication to the initiated, leaving the rest both uncomprehending and voiceless in the debate" (p. 20). The use of acronyms within the context of border IT systems signals a form of membership in an exclusive circle possessing insider knowledge, a group where there is no need to elaborate on the overwhelmingly complex technological architecture, bureaucratic chasms and legal specificities of systems. Acronyms, and the language in which they are embedded, should instead be perceived as a way to "act as a form of abstraction, removing you from the reality behind the words" (p. 20). Similar to abstracted facts, acronyms no longer question their (future) use and purpose and leave behind their politically disputed past. They also serve as elements of a discourse nurtured by the epistemic approach of anticipation present at the border regime's events, as they invoke mastery over technical complexity and offer linguistic access to a world where borders and migration can be managed abstractly and at a distance.

It would therefore also be unwise to reduce smart borders to a simple euphemism, coined by a creative mind within a security company's marketing department. Much like other digital border terminology, including acronyms, smart borders represent a sanitized form of framing and speaking about borders. This terminology grants access to the visions and narratives of the various groups of policy makers, delegates, experts and representatives, thereby contributing to the creation of "common sense" and discursive sovereignty over digital bordering. By mastering this linguistic repertoire, one gradually gains the ability to avert from the messy, ambiguous and deeply technopolitical realities in the digitization, classification and categorization of human mobility. Sanitized abstraction embodies a particular governmental perspective: it helps to disassociate border management from the sociotechnical practices of border control and, in doing so, excludes those who are subjected to its violent manifestations and consequences from the conversation.

The proliferation of logistical terminology

Another component of this language revolves around the proliferation of notions within the smart borders initiative that are anchored in the rhetoric of logistics.[18] Reinhardt Jünemann, a prominent figure in industrial logistics in Germany, defines logistics as the responsibility of allocating "the right amount of accurate materials as logistical objects at the right place, of the right quality, at the right time, at the right cost" (in Altenried et al. 2017, 45; own translation). This articulates a distinct institutional fantasy that can also be found in the narratives of smart borders, where borders are increasingly described in terms of platforms and ecosystems. These concepts invoke the ideal allocation of tasks and information among stakeholders in a process that neatly organizes and classifies mobility: tracking a migrant's journey from beginning to end, orchestrating their profitable integration into economic sectors, and monitoring their return or potential deportation. Data, as one of the participants at "ID@Borders" claimed, thereby hold the promise of realizing this fantasy, "extending" the border control process: "[S]o how do you create that rich picture of what the border looks like[?]" (field note, OSCE Conference, 10–11 April 2019).

Terms like platform and ecosystem do not drop from the sky.[19] Instead, "platform" must convey a specific rationality that calls for new informational channels and the convergence of a hitherto fragmented architecture. Traveler identity must now be provided "just-in-time" or "to-the-point". Databases that were previously separated by legal boundaries become now at least semantically treated as "one single platform, one single picture" (field note, eu-LISA Industry Roundtable, 24 April 2019). Similarly, a delegate from the EC presented smart borders as "a platform for border management [...]; it is one unique system at the end of the day [...] for border guards to help and provide them with information" (field note, eu-LISA Industry Roundtable, 24 April 2019). The concept of the "IT platform", as another official suggested, must "facilitate and ensure the smooth operation of the Schengen Area" (Interview 9, 2019). This logistics-based approach aspires to manage human mobility in a manner similar to the circulation of economic goods and capital, envisioning its realization through the optimization of data streams.

A similar, frequently mobilized, notion is the "ecosystem" (of border and migration management).[20] For instance, a senior eu-LISA representative referred to the EES and ETIAS as "the heart or nucleus of the new 'ecosystem' for border management that we are building, which includes equipment and solutions for data and access of information" (field note, Visionbox online event, 30 September 2020). Once again, the digitization of mobility is linked to a logistical fantasy, according to which human mobility can be managed like commodity circulation through a virtually interconnected network of stakeholders. In the *Border Management Today* article cited earlier, Garkov also presented the "digital challenge at the borders" as something that can be addressed through the ever-expanding "eco system of devices and solutions":

> [O]nce [the new large-scale IT systems are] deployed, the ability of this new information architecture to deliver its anticipated policy objectives and operational benefits will depend largely on the quality of the data fed into it; and timely and efficient access to the information extracted from that data. For this reason, alongside it Europe has started the deployment of a new eco system of devices and solutions for acquisition of raw data and access to information for the purposes of border management. (Garkov 2020, 27)

In sum, the emergence of notions such as "platform" and "ecosystem" epitomizes the logistical fantasies expressed in the language of managing digital borders. Databases, and digital technologies in general, play central, promissory roles and must produce "timely and efficient access to information extracted from that data", as Garkov suggests. They may open up a broader imaginative horizon that resembles digital Taylorism, a rationalized "system of real-time control, feedback and correction" (Altenried 2019, 122). Logistical notions aim to invoke rationalization, standardization and recomposition through digital means. The underlying fantasy they promote revolves around a Taylorist division and control of information, where migration can ideally be managed just-in-time and to-the-point.

Logistical challenges: human elements

A third dimension in this paradigm relates to the framing of how the challenges of smart borders are perceived and described, for example in the presentations and discussions at the 2019 industry roundtable in Bucharest. During the roundtable, participants focused on the most effective methods of rolling out smart borders—that is, how the EES and ETIAS would be implemented across all member states. The discussions centred, among other topics, on the possible obstacles for this endeavour. An EU official, in their opening remarks, concluded with a question that directly addressed the industry, demanding its alignment with and support for the smart borders initiative: "Can [the] industry deliver towards member states and become part of [the] success story?" (field note, eu-LISA Industry Roundtable, 24 April 2019).

The meeting continued with presentations by various companies showcasing several technological devices that aimed at redesigning border procedures to operationalize the EES, for instance. Devices were typically imagined for deployment in paradigmatic logistical spaces where smart borders need to be materialized: airports, seaports, bus and train stations.[21] These sites presented the most significant challenges to the uninterrupted flows or the successful acceleration of circulating goods and people. The meeting centred on the management of these spaces, recognizing that the circulation could be potentially obstructed; here, flows and streams had to be acted upon and rendered seamless. The spaces were portrayed as intermediaries that could bring the logical visions into being or pose obstacles to their realization.

Thus, two persistent challenges arose during the meeting. One was identified as the complex infrastructural environment and the limited time available to transform such spaces into fully functional logistical zones. In this envisioned scenario, borders had to be configured into a "liminal zone between inside and outside space", as highlighted by geographer Deborah Cowen (2014, 82). Some national delegates expressed their concerns, primarily directed at the security and IT companies: "The real problem is the time. We have one year, only one year to acquire such devices [...]. You say we have to specify processes [...]. I don't see solutions here. [...] We need clear answers from the industry because we don't have time" (field note, eu-LISA Industry Roundtable, 24 April 2019). This criticism also reflected their frustration for having to adhere to a flawed schedule for the implementation of the databases.[22] It emphasized the arduous long-term investments required to revamp borders, especially in terms of their infrastructural environments. For example, the port was mentioned as a specifically difficult case, as illustrated by a document prepared for the meeting by eu-LISA's Working Group on ICT Solutions for External Borders:

> In many of these ports there is no physical infrastructure/buildings, no fixed control booths or equipment. In some instances, border guards/police have to drive several hours from the nearest police district location/station to reach the port. Sometimes the vessel does not come into port at the scheduled time, making planning for border authorities difficult. Border checks, as well as vessel and crew list controls, are often carried out on the ship or in the port, outside the physical facilities.
>
> Member States and Associated Countries have different weather conditions: in the north, temperatures can fall to below minus 30 degrees Celsius, and in the far north the days in the winter season have only few hours of daylight. In southern countries on the other hand, the heat and sunlight pose other challenges. (eu-LISA 2019d, 13)

It is evident that EU external borders represent here complex and hybrid assemblages of technological devices, data practices, physical spaces, transport artefacts, natural environments and weather and temperature conditions. The participants of the roundtable underscored the diverse range of material needs and challenges in reconfiguring borders, that is, introducing biometric identifiers to register entries and exits, and transforming them into the imagined environments of zero-friction and seamless logistic flows.

Another recurrent challenge was described as the human element. From a logistical perspective, humans were perceived as a central operational concern, both in terms of their agency as subjects utilizing technologies and operating databases, and as objects being targeted by bordering procedures. These challenges were operational, not primarily technological, because "the human element is always going to be there, and [it has] got to be taken care of, of course" (Interview 4 with EU official, 2018). Officials consistently claimed that "it is not only about IT", or that "technology is not the bottleneck". Instead, the human element was perceived as an inherently unruly category. For example, the end user (such as police or border guards) would need to accommodate and learn to adapt to new technological procedures and environments. "Smartening" the border would thus be associated with a significant investment in training border personnel to change their "mentality" and habits when operating borders (Interview 27 with EU official, 2019). The need for "change management", a concern repeatedly articulated, was evident in order to align police and border authorities with new, "smart" procedures. A similar viewpoint was expressed, in perhaps a less managerial manner, by a national delegate and regular participant in eu-LISA's roundtables:

> [T]here's a huge, huge [amount of] work from our side to get the data transformed into useful information for the end user. This is not old. For eu-LISA, this is just a technical project, but with border and police officers, it's not. It's not just technical, it's [a] social and even organizational project. You have to make them integrate this information […] with the tools that they are already familiar with, you have to give them the right information at the right time, you have to talk with them. We have to involve them in several interactions, and all this takes time. (Interview 17, 2019)

The human factor represents here a significant operational challenge in the project of smartening borders. In her article on industrial border representations, Maria Schwertl (2018) accurately suggests that borders have undergone a dual process of dehumanization: they invisibilize the human objects of border technologies (that is, border crossers) but also obscure the human subjects (that is, border guards operating bordering devices). Consequently, in most of the idealized representations of smart borders humans are notably absent. Concepts such as ecosystems and platforms are emblematic of this envisioned world, where experts and specialists seek to transform borders into nodes or chokepoints of logistical procedures and circulation. According to the logistical logic, these nodes must encompass both an extensive and intensive dimension (Altenried et al. 2017, 23). Smartification must extend the border by integrating a larger number of stakeholders into its operations; but it must also intensify the border by employing additional sensing and monitoring techniques to optimize measurement and calibration of movement.

The terminology surrounding smart borders can thus be viewed as a product and a vehicle of a logistical logic that shapes how we discuss and think about borders and cross-border movement. It conveys highly abstract and rationalized notions of how borders should function, often relegating human beings to a marginal or invisible status. Migrant subjects vanish from discourse, and border guards are portrayed as recalcitrant elements that hinder the realization of this logistical fantasy. The consequence of such abstraction is that human mobility is depicted as no different than the circulation of other objects and goods. This raises the suspicion that such linguistic repertoire serves as an "ideological patina" that does not really inform political decision-making, but rather hides the complex political reasons for developing smart borders (Cohn 1987a, 24). Far more often, logistical language is employed to strategically mask the sociopolitical nature and consequences for (cross-border) mobilities, effectively serving as a legitimization of smart borders as purely techno-operational solutions.

Figure 4.3: A flyer for eu-LISA's industry roundtable in 2019, depicting two parallel bridges crossing the sea

Note: This picture does not seem to be chosen arbitrarily; it consciously displays bridges as enablers of circulation and exemplary infrastructural devices of logistics. Humans are absent from this image.

Source: © eu-LISA

A concluding note on self-referentiality and strategic detachment

The analysis presented above explored the creation of smart borders as depicted at policy conferences, meetings and roundtables. Although connected to the material construction of two large-scale IT systems, smart borders also aim to reshape the knowledge and representation of borders, rooted in a particular political culture where various communities and actors within the border regime can interact and collaborate. I have attempted to articulate the epistemological conditions of policy conferences as specific sites that foster an entrepreneurial environment with somewhat loose but ritualized interactions among participants, along with a strong anticipatory mode of orientation toward (smart) futures. Additionally, I defined smart borders as a boundary object that can "mean different things in different worlds" (Star and Griesemer 1989, 388), enabling actors to work together experimentally while pursuing individual goals. Finally, an essential aspect in crafting this epistemology was identified as the logistical idiom that clouds smart borders.

To summarize, there are two main takeaways from understanding smart borders as an epistemological project. The first is that it establishes a form of ideological consistency in the decentralized domain of border and migration management. Clearly, consistency and coherence among heterogeneous actors is performed rather than actualized. Nevertheless, by disrupting the daily habits and rhythms of security professionals and border guards, coherence is forged through the constant self-referentiality on display during these meetings. As illustrated in our vignette featuring James, occasional boredom and monotony may be drawbacks, but ritualized events manage to keep the policy world firmly detached from the messier and more ambiguous empirical worlds and realities.

The second takeaway concerns the technostrategic effect that we have observed in relation to the language of logistics. According to Cohn, this effect gives individuals a sense of control and mastery, for instance over the complex digital border systems, but it also offers a sense of detachment, distance or even *escape*: this is not about individual consciousness but more about "the structural position the speakers of the language occupy and the perspective they get from that position [… that] puts them in the position of the planner, the user, the actor" (1987b, 706). The reality becomes "itself a world of abstractions" (1987a, 22).

This also applies to the conferences where participants employ the logistical language of smart borders that is supposed to manage mobility in terms of flows and streams at a distance—through the neat allocation of data among multiple stakeholders. Migration must be enacted as a calculative, abstract reality, as logistical populations—that is, consisting of "connect[ed] bodies, objects, affects, information, without subjects, without the formality of subjects" (Harney and Moten 2013, 92).

Crafting the epistemology of smart borders demonstrates how solutionist approaches promise to offer escape from the empirical realities of migration; escape however will never be entirely successful, because reality, as Latour (1987) reminds us, "is what resists" (p. 94). Nonetheless, the desire to escape is concerning enough, especially in light of the daily violence and human deaths that occur as migrants seek to overcome the border regime on their way to Europe. The epistemology of digital borders, crafted and shaped at policy conferences and meetings, is an epistemology of strategic detachment; it avoids these concerns rather than addressing them because they would promptly raise questions about responsibility and accountability for these deaths.

In the next chapter, I will shift my focus to observe how solutionism is further articulated and enacted in concrete policy making. My investigation will thereby revolve around the policy of interoperability, one of the latest attempts to construct and frame bordering problems and fix them, notably by mobilizing the powerful imaginative repertoire for fabricating yet another fiction.

Interoperability: Making a New Policy Fiction

Interoperability has emerged as a prominent buzzword in various arenas of digitization, particularly so where multiple information systems have been constructed and an increasing number of users have vested interests in access to respective data collections.[1] The notion of interoperability, however, sometimes appears to be exceptionally vague, as it can imply very different forms of data practices, infrastructural configurations, standardization procedures or institutional reorderings (Pelizza 2016a).

In this chapter, I address interoperability in the context of the EU's ongoing efforts to reshuffle digital border and migration control. As announced in the European Commission's *Strategy towards a fully functioning and resilient Schengen area*, interoperability seeks to achieve "one of the world's most technologically advanced border management systems" (EC 2021a, 7). This statement serves as a typical example of how interoperability has been promised as yet another building block for generating "complete, reliable and accurate information" (EC 2021a, 8) on migrants and their identities— a presumed silver bullet solution to the multiple challenges posed by the governance of migration and its infrastructures.

Policy officials often present the push for interoperability as a major paradigm shift in digitizing border and migration control—one that the wider European public has yet to recognize. A national expert claimed, for example, "it is the biggest undertaking in the European Union that has ever taken place […] but it will take a little while […] until it also hits the public as what it is" (Interview 18, 2019). Interoperability represents a certain technological momentum (Hughes 1994) that creates a significant change in the ways that state authorities can access and handle the biometric data of individuals travelling to Europe. While interoperability components are currently still being developed by eu-LISA, their pending implementation has regularly been called into question due to the complex, transnational and heterogenous landscape of biometric databases in Europe (Amelung,

Granja, and Machado 2020; Broeders 2007; Leese, Noori, and Scheel 2022; Trauttmansdorff 2017).

This chapter explores how interoperability has been gradually transformed from an initially obscure, technical concept into something collectively known, articulated and, ultimately, accepted—a powerful policy fiction for digitally infrastructuring borders. It perceives interoperability as a policy on the move (Clarke et al. 2015) that has travelled through the hands of different actors and across various policy arenas, gradually shaping how interoperable biometric borders are imagined as a future solution to sociotechnological problems. In this context, I examine policy making as an exemplary and dynamic subject of what, in Chapter 3, was referred to as infrastructural experimentation in the EU border regime.

To do so, I first contextualize interoperability in the landscape of biometric borders and propose a framework for policy(making) in border regimes. While scholars at the intersection of STS and Critical Border and Security Studies have only recently unearthed some distinct rationalities of the interoperability project, they have largely ignored why, and how, interoperability has become a powerful hegemonic policy in the border regime (cf. Bellanova and Glouftsios 2022a; Bigo 2020; Leese 2022). Therefore, I describe interoperability as the "fabrication of a necessary fiction" (Ezrahi 2012) and analyze three solutionist promises at its core: the production of expert authority, the enactment of simplification, and the goal of (technological) certainty. These promises have shaped the narratives, directed expectations and orientations, and constructed policy coalitions among actors in the EU, guiding them towards a widely shared future of how digital borders must be designed, made accessible and operated.

During my years of empirical research on the EU's digital border regime, I started to trace the creation of the interoperability policy, which has quickly turned out to be a dominant theme in my conversations with officials from eu-LISA and the EC, national delegates and technical experts, officials from the Council Secretariat, or staff in the European Parliament (EP). These actors did not all equally participate in the negotiations that brought interoperability into the formalized EU law adopted in 2019.[2] However, they are highly policy-relevant as they have contributed to the multifaceted process through which interoperability finds "expression through sequences of events; [...] creates new social and semantic spaces, new sets of relations, new political subjects and new webs of meaning" (Shore and Wright 2011, 1). These actors have articulated forms of knowledge, policy-related visions, and regulatory environments shaping the politics of database interoperability. Consequently, these aspects have also been a significant feature in the protocols of my field visits and participant observations during conferences and industry roundtables within the border regime. In sum, multiple sources have offered valuable insights into interoperability as an evolving policy in the making—the production of its meaning, its promised futures and its increasing influence as a necessary fiction.

Situating interoperability

Interoperability can be characterized as another stepping stone in the "network of information technology to collect, store, check, compare and exchange all kinds of data and profiles extracted from migrants, travelers and their social and professional context" (Dijstelbloem and Broeders 2015, 2). It has hence also become an growing factor in the expanding technological infrastructures and data practices used to render mobilities into actionable objects of governance (Amelung, Granja, and Machado 2020; Glouftsios and Scheel 2021; Leese, Noori, and Scheel 2022; Pelizza 2020). Databases and their infrastructures have led to the "digitally mediated coordination of controls [that] are conducted at varying sites and temporal registers" (Bellanova and Glouftsios 2022b, 8). Not only do they hardwire transnational cooperation between states, organizations and agencies involved in bordering processes, but they have also emerged as "catalysts for new social relations among disparate sectors, creating areas for collaboration and competition, compliance and conflict" (Andersson 2016, 22). IT systems like Eurodac or the Schengen Information System have expanded their scopes and purposes of control over time, notably including additional data categories and widening their access to authorities (Brouwer 2008; Tsianos and Kuster 2016b). They have caused new, conflicting agendas between national states and their interests, EU agencies and Commission officials as they produce uneven power relations, empower new agencies and disempower others (Bellanova and Glouftsios 2022a; Trauttmansdorff and Felt 2023; Tsianos and Kuster 2016b). Consequently, interoperability is expected to also produce tensions in regard to institutional reordering processes (Pelizza 2016a, 2020). In other words, interoperability represents a process of "datastructuring—re-organising, linking and re-purposing data", which inevitably brings to the fore both the weaknesses and strengths of European infrastructural security (Bellanova and Glouftsios 2022a, 465). Finally, as legal scholars have emphasized, interoperability introduces a plethora of problems concerning privacy protection and fundamental rights (Aden 2020; Brouwer 2020; Curtin and Bastos 2021; Vavoula 2020).

Importantly, scholars have also begun to pay attention to interoperability's technical details and implications for the changing dynamics of securitization and state power. By interconnecting existing systems with future databases, such as the Schengen-wide Entry-Exit System or the European Travel Information and Authorisation System (which were previously discussed also as smart borders), interoperability feeds into the logic of multipurpose use and access to border, migration and visa systems (Brouwer 2020).[3] Both Bigo

(2020) and Leese (2022) discard the view of interoperability's components as "neutral" technological solutions, such as the Common Identity Repository (CIR) or the shared Biometric Matching System (sBMS), and interpret them as political instruments in the datafication of (border) security.

Leese suggests that interoperability introduces a "significant move from the border as a site of identity production to the (digital) border as a space of identity management" (2022, 12). Introduced digital tools must fix the state vision by rendering migrant identity ever-more legible and classifiable. Interoperability's CIR, which creates individual data files of a person registered in at least one of the databases, has accordingly been criticized as disproportionally intrusive and a "deathblow" to data protection and privacy rights (Vavoula 2020). Similarly, Curtin and Bastos predict that interoperability provides "one of the battlegrounds for many contemporary ethical issues that the deployment of technologies raises in the exercise of public power" (2021, 69). Most recently, Bellanova and Glouftsios have delved into the various "operational and epistemic anxieties" (2022a, 460) that underpin interoperability's design and mechanisms.

However, these scholars tend to neglect the processes through which such anxieties are imagined and constructed, carefully framing interoperability as both an acceptable and sustainable future policy solution. This chapter will therefore propose unpacking interoperability through the lens of policy formation, one that necessitates the repeated performances of sociotechnical visions and promises. This approach offers two significant advantages: Firstly, it allows us to better understand how interoperability operates as a collectively imagined and repeatedly articulated policy *fiction* of future border control, effectively shaping the contemporary landscape and politics of digital borders. Secondly, it delineates the contingent and disputed processes through which policies become powerful agents in infrastructuring the regimes of borders and migration control. In sum, this chapter investigates how interoperability gradually became translated from an unfamiliar technical concept into a widely embraced fiction, entailing several key promises of problem diagnosis and resolution.

Conceptualizing policy formation in the border regime

Policies on the move

Policies in border regimes can be understood in terms of what De Genova calls "reaction formations", that is, the mechanisms and tactics of (re)bordering that respond to the "volume and velocity of human mobility" (2017a, 13). This perspective positions policy making as an integral component of the ongoing repair work that border regimes undergo to govern mobility (Sciortino 2004), and which occur in various, non-linear and procedural ways. As Clarke et al. (2015) stress, policies are also made meaningful in the process of their formation; they are both sites and instruments of meaning-making, forming "mutable assemblages of keywords, technologies, things, action and passions [that] create potentialities for action" (Nielsen 2011, 83). Policies emerge as products of the laborious work of assemblage and translation, as Clarke and colleagues claim, rendering "power and policy operative within the dynamics of societal transformation" (2015, 53). This work showcases and performs policies during their formation, actions that thereby travel through the hands of different actors and across different social worlds. For instance, in order to become a seemingly intelligible and coherent program of biometric (re)bordering, interoperability also had to be repeatedly articulated to "real and imagined audiences, attempting to make specific proposals or projects appear as if they are logical, innovative, necessary, obvious" (2015, 31).

This dynamic process of formation signals the crucial role played by collective imagination in policy making. In *The Governance of Problems*, Hoppe argues that policies are usually confronted with problems presented as the "gap between a current situation and a more desirable future one" (2010, 23). Likewise, STS scholars have frequently drawn on Jasanoff and Kim's (2015) call to explore the role of sociotechnical imaginaries of futures as instruments that create and stabilize social and political order. Thus, policy imagination must create a quasi-common social and semantic terrain that fosters certain ways of knowing and seeing and renders pathways for desirable futures as taken-for-granted. Howarth points to the phantasmatic logics and narratives that allow a policy to be produced and sustained, enabling it to "displace antagonisms and demands, thus enabling the smooth reproduction of a practice or regime" (2010, 323). His neo-Gramscian approach emphasizes how power and hegemony operate as essential practices and forms of governance in policy making, particularly by making and breaking projects and coalitions, but also by maintaining certain policy frames and trajectories. Policy formation then becomes a crucial field of inquiry because it "expresses in condensed terms the hegemonic forms of social order" (Feldman 2005, 678). Importantly, policy formation explains how diverse, policy-relevant actors in the border regime—officials, experts, agency representatives, national delegates and industry actors—come to collectively interpret problems, accordingly generating outcomes and consent and pursuing specific sociotechnical trajectories.

Policy (as) solutionism

The field of digitized border control is often said to be permeated by what Morozov (2013) defines as techno-solutionism. As Martins and Jumbert suggest, what is framed as a problem of border and migration management simultaneously becomes "amenable to a technological solution" (2022, 1441)—most notably, in the form of border technologies and the ever-growing expansion of databases. As in so many domains, policy is at the forefront of promoting technological innovations as panaceas to social and political challenges, seemingly realizing progressivist visions of the future (Pfotenhauer and Jasanoff 2017; Pfotenhauer, Juhl, and Aarden 2019). Critical Policy Studies contain ample analysis of rulers, elites or other policy actors engaging in problem structuring that open and close down debates surrounding particular social questions, "serve entrenched interests, or dissuade others from introducing new problems" (Turnbull 2005, 222; see also Colebatch 2014; Fischer et al. 2015; Hoppe 2010). In the literature, techno-solutionism can be seen as a problem-solving strategy (Hoppe 2010, 23–28)—one that works towards consensus, shifting the focus of attention from debating and questioning the meaning of a problem to reaffirming the technological solution. This typically obscures why "something is seen as a problem worth fixing in the first place" (Klimburg-Witjes and Wentland 2021, 1322).

But how, then, is policy making imagined, showcased or performed to create hegemonic effects? And how does this enact and reproduce solutionism? There are two central characteristics to account for in analyses of border control policies. First, solutionist policies frequently conjure and act upon an assumed single reality—one that can be changed and manipulated in singular and linear ways. To capture this assumption, Law and Singleton (2014) propose the notion of "ontological singularity", which frames reality as inhibiting problem-solutions that inevitably fail to account for the multiple realities through which humans (and non-humans) encounter the world. In other words, ontological singularity creates abstract and simplifying epistemic conditions.

Such conditions also permeate the violent and dehumanizing practices of border and migration regimes. EU policy practices tend to confront migration in radically simplifying ways, transmuting mobile individuals, as Feldman suggests, "from three-dimensional human subjects into two-dimensional policy objects […] through textual practices of policy representation, policy making and policy implementation" (Feldman 2011a, 44). Second, solutionism mobilizes specific actors and forms of knowledge that are eligible for articulating policy "draw on technical languages, visionary promises, and other forms of exclusive expertise to assert causal relationships and credibility" (Pfotenhauer et al. 2022, 16). Policies then cut problems "into smaller, discrete pieces that warrant ready-made solutions, which are in turn owned or controlled by specialized organizations or individuals" (Pfotenhauer et al. 2022, 16). Solutionism, in other words, relies on expert authority to stabilize its promises and meanings and secure consensus on otherwise highly complex and contested issues. Exploring how solutionist policies are formatted allows the observation of how expertise is brought into being and legitimized, while other forms of knowledge become excluded. In this context, expertise is never a stable category, but rather organized forms of knowledge that define "who participates, in what ways [...]; who has rights and responsibilities to speak authoritatively about knowledge" (Miller 2017, 912). Solutionism should then be considered as a performative technique that establishes expert authority over certain issues, reframes technological/infrastructural innovations as coherent and necessary, and legitimizes certain social actors as responsible for policy design and implementation. This is a particularly problematic process, mainly because of the "technical mystique [… that] envelop[s] experts with a misleading aura of objective rationality" (Fischer et al. 2015, 7). The authority of experts and their knowledge, in other words, hampers and distracts from alternative framings and problematizations, thereby potentially marginalizing policy dissent and contestation.

In what follows, I read the making of interoperability through the repeated solutionist articulations of migration and border control. In the words of a Commission representative, "from the onset, the term interoperability in technical terms is something completely different [...]. Our interoperability as such has nothing to do with it" (Interview 21, 2019). I explain this discordant statement by showing how three solutionist promises fabricate and stabilize something different: a necessary policy fiction for the reinfrastructuring of EU borders. First, this fiction invokes expert authority to solve what is ambiguously identified as a "crisis" in the governing of the border regime; second, it enacts simplification to solve the complexity and fragmentation of digital borders; third, it promises technological certainty in the ambiguous regime of identification and verification of mobile identities.

Forging expert authority
Bringing it back from the archives

In early documents on border and migration management, the idea of interoperability was sketched out only hypothetically and imprecisely (EC 2003, 2005). In the main policy arena of the EC, interoperability has previously been described as operationally vague and politically risky— especially in its implications for data protection and fundamental rights. In 2010, the EC still warned, "such a system would [...] constitute a gross and illegitimate restriction of individuals' right to privacy and data protection" (EC 2010, 2). However, the so-called migration and refugee crisis in 2015 prompted officials to bring this idea back from the archives (Interviews 21 and 13 with EC officials, 2019).

In 2016, the *Communication on Stronger and Smarter Information Systems for Borders and Security* set a new tone, invoking "European citizens" that would "expect external border controls on persons to be effective, to allow effective management of migration and to contribute to internal security" (EC 2016a, 2). A multifaceted "crisis", produced by migrant movements and terrorist attacks in Europe, was associated with a set of "shortcomings" and "gaps" in the Europe's data architecture, a "fragmented" landscape of digital borders, and uncertainties in the identification of immigrants.[4]

Proclaiming the crisis invoked that "the more prolonged temporalities of democratic debate and deliberative processes" were no longer affordable (Stierl et al. 2016, 11) and it allowed to introduce interoperability as an urgent governmental intervention. It was particularly articulated as a response by experts and "some [of their] deep-thinking around the use of all kinds of data, captured and processed for different purposes, different reasons, by different systems, coming from different authorities" (Interview 21, 2019). Simultaneously, the conservative European People's Party (EPP) pressured the EC on concrete proposals to prove to the electorate that the EU can deliver on these things in a speedy manner; thus, interoperability became "the flagship file" for the upcoming European parliamentary elections (Interview 22 with EP member, 2019).

These moves laid the groundwork for promoting interoperability as a promise to (re-)establish expert authority over border policy making in times of crisis. Moreover, it aimed to delegitimize prominent voices such as those by the European Data Protection Supervisor (EDPS) who had criticized interoperability on the grounds of data protection principles, which were now considered as "mistakes" and "misbeliefs" unfit to meet the urgent challenges to the EU and its Schengen borders.

Making issue-experts

A crucial tool for translating interoperability from an opaque idea into an expert-driven solution was the High-Level Expert Group on Information Systems and Interoperability (HLEG). The group was described by a Commission representative as a "whole big consultation process" and (somewhat paradoxically) was called an "evangelization process" to convince sceptical (national) stakeholders of interconnecting existing and future databases (Interview 21, 2019). The HLEG aimed to settle institutional competition over the border regime, appeasing and enroling national authorities that were less receptive to a burgeoning "policy activism" in Brussels. A carefully selected set of mid-level representatives from 12 member states formed a subgroup on interoperability: "There was a lot of preparation […] and a lot of consultation, but they [the HLEG] knew where they were heading' (Interview 6 with EU official, 2019).

The group formed what Asdal (2015) calls issue-experts, claiming that they possessed "knowledge on the relevant issue" (p. 83) but were guided independently from political interests. Its members spoke as practitioners and pioneers, being knowledgeable of the challenges in the "real world" of border security professionals. They introduced interoperability as an everyday problem that could no longer be contested on principled political grounds.

In a series of documents, most notably the so-called *Final Report*, the group's gatherings were described as a "platform for exchange of experience and knowledge between peers" that served as "a bridge between technical expert level and the policy discussion at senior official level" (HLEG 2017, 6). Despite the notable presence of the EDPS and the EU's Fundamental Rights Agency, who had voiced concerns regarding interoperability's risks for individuals and its disproportionate measures, interoperability was rearticulated as a collective and fairly consensual endeavour, leaving protest against such measures unheard and isolated. Instead, the group's issue-experts described interoperability as a "shared European vision on the ways ahead" (HLEG 2017, 6) with a set of tools that were deemed both acceptable and necessary. These tools did not simply emerge from the group's debates (although they were frequently presented as such) but mirrored what the EC had previously proposed (see, for example, EC 2016a). The HLEG thus launched a certain vision of interoperability using its acquired authority and leveraged its components to smoothly enter subsequent policy documents.[5]

Keeping components together

Mobilizing this expert authority proved crucial to overcoming political resistance and building coalitions on interoperability's path to legislative passage. Political parties in the EP, such as the European Greens, feared a dystopian vision of a "super database" and a dangerous precedent for data protection and fundamental rights.[6] Similarly, the Alliance of Socialists and Democrats (S&D) criticized interoperability for its centralized data pool underlying all IT systems of border and migration control. According to them, the CIR represented a standalone database that would store and link biometric templates across IT systems in the future, overriding fundamental principles of purpose limitation and data minimization. Although they agreed with interoperability's vague political objectives—to officially "improve the effectiveness and efficiency of border checks" and "contribute to the prevention and the combating of illegal immigration" (EU 2019a, Article 2)—the S&D group was opposed to the CIR as altogether disproportionate.

The S&D's political position, however, was gradually undermined. The HLEG's exclusive form of expertise was effective in mobilizing against political opposition. Proponents, such as the EC, the EPP or eu-LISA, insisted repeatedly that the CIR would not constitute a database because it would not collect new data but only link existing information together while maintaining "virtual separation" (Interview 23 with EP member, 2019).[7] Proponents added that interoperability would only function by keeping all its components together. According to the HLEG, the CIR constituted the central pillar of interoperability—it was promoted as a single, convoluted puzzle complete only with all its pieces. The S&D successively lost the battle of arguments, as one EP member explained:

> The argument got quite technical and at some point, if you're not an IT expert, […] you have nothing beneath your feet anymore. […] As I said, there is a line between policy and information technology, and, at some point, […] the Commission were very strong in their argument that this was required in order for the systems work properly. In the end, that was determined to be the right course. (Interview 23, 2019)

Expert authority thus successfully performed the boundary work of what counted as political and necessary technical components of interoperability, determining what had to be legitimate policy knowledge and required policy components: "If you're trying to sell a message, […] to explain your policies to the outside world; you can't vote against interoperability because the Common Identity Repository is there. It's just not something that anybody will understand" (Interview 23, 2019). This transformed interoperability into a single piece of policy built on expert knowledge. It posited interoperability as a consensual means of overcoming opposing political positions, framing it as an informed response to crisis, and as an expert solution.[8]

Enacting simplification

> To break the silos, it's really to break also your way of thinking about it. (Interview 27 with EU official, 2019)

In public presentations at conferences, as well as in conversations with EU officials, interoperability was habitually introduced by avoiding any precise definition—invoking, for instance, that it meant "significantly more than one would think of it" (Interview 17 with member state representative, 2019). Interoperability, I was told, had become the talk of the town among national politicians, delegates and experts, despite being notoriously difficult to define. On the upper echelons of political representation, one official recounted that "all ministers were all of a sudden talking about interoperability, [but] no one had a clue what it was" (Interview 13, 2019). Another EU institution representative complained, "you have the crux of the whole matter now, it is extremely difficult to explain" (Interview 27, 2019). An expert from the EC wondered how he could "always mess up totally in explaining it" (Interview 21, 2019). Another interviewee suggested that it was impossible to comprehend interoperability in all its technological complexity. Its vaguely defined yet blunt political objectives disguised the fact that it would be extremely difficult to explain to "average voters": "I would say, silently or quietly, that not so many people understand fully what we are currently doing" (Interview 9 with EU official, 2019).

Paradigm change: talking to each other

Such complexities present policy-relevant actors with the problem of both explaining and justifying their policies as consensual solutions to their pre-structured problems. In the case of interoperability, EU officials, such as EC or eu-LISA representatives, developed and routinely followed the script of simplification, providing useful metaphorical and committing rhetoric. Accordingly, it became less important whether these officials explained, or even understood, interoperability's full scope or details.

The script captured the public imaginations and performances of interoperability by shifting techno-legal intricacies and complexities aside (for example, those one might find in the regulatory texts). Interoperability was instead attached to a strong desire to overcome a static data architecture inherited from an outdated past. Biometric databases, such as the Eurodac or VIS—initially designed to operate in categorically separated ways and with limited purposes—were now "isolated silos" to be brought down in a "new era". A conference report by eu-LISA argued that we were "enter[ing] an interoperability era", which would bring down the artificial silos of large-scale IT systems (eu-LISA 2019). Similarly, proponents of interoperability singled out and challenged the old-fashioned view that failed to recognize silos as pillars of a fragmented architecture that was keeping data in so-called "cages". Integrating interoperable methods was publicly lauded as overcoming "the siloed view", adopting one's "mindset" and releasing potentialities through a "new way of thinking" (field note, eu-LISA conference, 16 October 2019).

This "new way" instead acknowledged the urgency of having IT systems talking to each other. Communication invoked here a natural, positive value that one should associate with interoperability and its technological components. The property of databases "simply talking" (as opposed to being categorically separated) has here become an almost omnipresent feature in the simplified descriptions of interoperability: "So, interoperability, fundamentally, what you see written on paper, what is introduced, is the ability of systems to speak to each other" (Interview 4 with EU official, 2018). Another EC official claimed that "the concept of interoperability means creating a new environment where systems talk to each other, and then we just need to see what they need to do" (Interview 25, 2019).

Tidying up, creating order

These portrayals mediate seemingly simple virtues that are highly regarded in the management of migration. They must reflect the quasi-natural impulses that policy making seems to require (and avoid reminders of its complicated technical and regulatory implications).

At a conference, a Commission representative presented interoperability to a broader audience of industry actors, policy makers, national delegates and agency representatives by inviting them to "look at the real world" (field note, eu-LISA conference, 16 October 2019). He compared interoperability with the habits and challenges of daily life and order (for example, with misplacing socks or keys), developing an analogy with some basic principles for tidying up a house and keeping things in order (popularized by the bestselling author and consultant Marie Kondo). According to his analogy, databases for migration management were like "the children" of the EU and member states had put their belongings, like socks, all over the place. As he insisted, interoperability was simply devotion to the task of order and realignment, corresponding to a "common sense" of making data available when they are needed. In the same vein, it was repeatedly argued that it was imperative to have "the information where it's needed at the right time' (Interviews 12 and 21 with EU officials, 2019).

The persuasive power of this script lies in its seemingly innocent and consensual simplicity. The solution offered is a trade of complexity for simple order—hence the analogy to Kondo's bestselling motto, "Tidy your space, transform your life". Policy officials feed into an appealing and self-reassuring discourse of migration management facilitation, following an impulse to neatly frame migration as a continuous source of ambiguity and complexity (Feldman 2012). Interlinking biometric databases were then promoted as natural approaches through which "the EU is putting its own house in order", as one high-level national delegate stated (fieldnote, OSCE conference, 10–11 April 2019). These performances reframed the "problem" of migration in terms of "information gaps" in an outdated data architecture at risk of being abused by migrants and their complex patterns of movement (EC 2016a). The EU, as an eu-LISA official once claimed, was then only "lagging behind with filling up the gaps in the information architecture" (Interview 1, 2018).

The promise of simplification sets plain metaphors of future transformation against a defective present state defined by legal and regulatory intricacies, infrastructural compromises and patchy border regulations. Interoperability was naturalized as a sort of common-sense solution, but one that endowed officials with seemingly progressivist mentalities and activities. That is how interoperability promises a "change in mentality" or a "new way of thinking", with officials "catching up", "entering a new era", or overcoming "static mentalities" (Interviews 6 and 27, 2019; field note, eu-LISA conference, 16 October 2019).

Simplification has thus become a metaphorizing strategy, not only perpetuating the fiction of techno-scientific progress but, crucially, also suggesting action against concrete measures and principles that limit the purpose of border databases, protect individual data privacy, or safeguard fundamental rights. The imperative of simplification seems to encourage and normalize (rather than prevent) the extended access of law-enforcement authorities to asylum and visa data and suggests the multi-purpose use of border IT systems as a natural goal for policy making. This fiction implicitly works against the EU's predominant conception of an effective data protection regime, framing the separation of purposes of databases, proportionality, and strictly defined access to sensible personal data as nothing more than artificial and outdated design choices.

The promise of technological certainty

> This [is] essentially about being more certain about the identity of the person that you are investigating. That is [...] the big chunk of interoperability. (Interview 13 with EU official, 2019)

The third core solutionist element in fabricating this necessary fiction relates to what policy officials call interoperability's identity management. Its objective is the swift and accurate construction and standardization of authentic (digital) identity from the ambiguous, and thus problematic, patterns of individual mobility—a process promoted by interoperability's data matching and verification technologies. Interoperability offers a future guarantee—one that would make it "finally possible now to verify identity with almost certainty" (Interview 15 with member state representative, 2019).

Catching and matching identities

This promise should appeal to security authorities and professionals grappling with unknown mobile identities. It promotes not only interoperable, but also significantly expanded, databases for more "comprehensive", "proper" or "correct" identification in the future (Interviews 15 and 18 with member state representatives, 2019).

Scholars have often noted that the biometrization of control at Europe's borders establishes biometric representations as "allegedly infallible proof of [a traveler's] identity" (Leese, Noori, and Scheel 2022, 14), problematizing migrants as deviant subjects by targeting their bodies as sources of true knowledge. The fiction of interoperability offers an affirmation and reinforcement of such assumptions, particularly demonstrable by two central components—the Multiple Identity Detector (MID) and the Common Identity Repository (CIR). Both components are designed to detect "multiple identities" (stored in different databases). For officials, multiple identities are treated as a strategic unknown (McGoey 2012), which could be key indicators of fraud in the digital management of migration. As an EP member explained, "there was no possibility to actually verify that we knew already this person [or] this person is committing identity fraud" (Interview 23, 2019). Officials have, notably, located the problem of multiple identities in the context of asylum-seeking: "somebody could just fraudulently apply for asylum, then ask for a visa, and with a different identity just to try to come to Schengen by different means" (Interview 25 with EU official, 2019). Another EC official argued that "it is, first of all, good to know who is standing before you, in what context, and if that is really a refugee" (Interview 27 with EU official, 2019).

This strategic unknown nurtures an underlying suspicion that reinforces the nexus of criminality and asylum. The applicant's identity is imaged as a source of deceit, mutability and uncertainty, inducing a call for its necessary stabilization through biometric means. Interoperability jumps in to promise a new regime of evidence, appropriately targeting bodies as a source of evidence-based and verified knowledge in the precarious business of identification.[9] Once biometric borders are interoperable, the existence and extent of fraudulent identity are expected to be revealed; authorities are promised new ways of reading, matching and authenticating digitized fragments of identities across both existing and future border databases.

Reproducing uncertainty

Two components of this envisioned regime of evidence deserve further attention. The CIR creates identity files of fingerprint templates, facial images and biographical information retrieved from any one of the databases, thereby standardizing biometric markers for testing and verifying identities. As Leese argues, this single confirmation file would serve as a "verified and cross-validated baseline truth as the basis for knowledge production and government" (2022, 125).

On this basis, the MID automatically creates identity links that indicate whether individual data is present in more than one database. White, green, yellow and red links form part of what officials occasionally call a "traffic light system" and are intended to signal to authorities whether claims of identity can be read as authentic or inauthentic. The ideal result is a red link: the confirmed mismatch of data in different systems (for example, between biometric features and the person's presented biographic data or identity documents at the border). A red link must automatically confirm the authorities' suspicions:

> In case there is an identity difference for the same person where it shouldn't be, we create this famous red link—that's the whole center part of all the shit [sic] we are proposing here. […I]f you have a red link, all the purpose limitations and access control rights are void! We are going to tell everybody this person is known under a different identity in an illegal way. (Interview 21 with EU official, 2019)

A red link delivers the promise of technological certainty—a crucial element in the formation of interoperability. Occasionally, however, officials have revealed the fragility of this promised solution. Firstly, digital identification relies on algorithmic matching and verification, which remains a comparative and translational enterprise prone to variant degrees of uncertainty (Pelizza 2021; Schinkel 2020). Migrant bodies frequently escape biometric practices at the border; the attachment of biometric markers to individual bodies can always be detached. Colour links thus produce knowledges that are not (automatically) actionable. In other words, "deceptability governs the border […]. Deceptive mimicry, deceit, camouflage, must of necessity be possible" (Schinkel 2020, 561).

Moreover, comparing identities to biometric templates is a probabilistic undertaking, relying heavily on the minimization of error rates and inaccuracy that are likely to increase with growing data and template collections. As a report for the Civil Liberty and Justice Committee states, "the more databases there are, the more potential risks [of misidentification] there may be" (LIBE 2018, 41).[10]

But the promise of certainty might also be shaken by the MID's design itself. The MID operates as an inscription device (Latour 1987) that automatically accredits the validity of newly verified knowledge on a migrant's identity, seeking to eradicate uncertainty qua red link to confirmed fraud. However, once all interoperability components are in operation, the MID will first produce a plethora of yellow links to files where "manual verification of different identities has not yet taken place" (EU 2019a, Article 30).

The so-called traffic light system thus requires most cases to be manually cleared to confirm or reject suspicion about travel documents and biometric templates. The MID falls back on a single human decision. If a border guard "sees a yellow link, […] you have to take a decision—you cannot measure" (Interview 6 with EU official, 2019). Another EU official involved in negotiating the final interoperability regulations admitted:

> If the guy [the border guard] is afraid that maybe we will [let] someone pass that should not, he is not sure […], he will always put a red link.

[...] Or it's the other way round—he doesn't want any trouble, he says: "Okay, anyway there are many mistakes in the systems, probably a mistake, the guy seems honest, I trust my gut feeling, I put a green link." (Interview 6 with EU official, 2019)

Such accounts contradict the premise of technologically eradicating uncertainty. Instead, it confirms the multiple contingencies of interoperable border control, which rely on the environments and local infrastructures, data quality, the specific technological devices of bordering and even arbitrary decisions by border guards.

Conclusion

This chapter has carefully traced how the making of interoperability has been woven into dominant imaginations, rationales and promises involved in digitally infrastructuring the EU border regime. I analyzed interoperability as a policy on the move, that is, a process wherein actors, promises, narratives, knowledges and components are assembled and translated into a shared and powerful fiction. This approach demonstrated how arguments for interoperability enacted three core solutionist promises, conjuring both problem constructions and their fixes: expert authority, simplification, and technological certainty. Such promises have operated as convenient means to tailor the border regime's "crisis" and its problems in order to justify interoperability as a consensual policy solution.

The formation of interoperability hence created what we call a necessary policy fiction. Borrowing this term from Ezrahi, it emphasizes the power of imagination to produce "deliberate performance[s] of illusions or fictions" that can create an "obvious deviation from the world normalized for us by common-sense realism" (2012, 40). As such, interoperability between biometric borders operates as a powerful way to "gloss over criticism of the present order" (2012, 40). It becomes necessary and alluring precisely because it deviates from the fundamentally social and political problems of the EU's so-called migration management.

Instead, it unfolds a promissory future of perfectly aligned streams, interconnected points and seamless processing of biometric data. Simultaneously, the concept of interoperability becomes saturated with the rhetoric of paradigm change and innovation, conjuring technological irreversibility and a vague but nonetheless redemptive future in which migration is governed through simplified, unambiguous and authoritative means. As a necessary policy fiction, then, interoperability steers the visions, narratives and epistemic orientations of diverse groups of actors within the border regime, holding officials, agency representatives, industry and national delegates together with solutionist ways of thinking and speaking about migration. At the same time, however, this fiction strategically closes the door on significant alternative principles of purpose limitation and data minimization in IT systems, as well as the protection of fundamental rights and personal privacy; they appear increasingly incompatible with the seemingly natural solutions and promises of interoperability.

The rise of interoperability as a policy fiction illustrates the enduring importance of attending to sociotechnical imagination, which informs not only contemporary policy-making practices but also the ongoing spiraling dynamics of securitization (Bello 2022). As core drivers of legitimizing and naturalizing digital borders, their classificatory infrastructures, as well as their increasingly discriminatory regimes of stratifying human mobility, a critique of these hegemonic forms of imagination in policy making remains as vital as ever.

Justification, Techno-Determinism, and Sanitized Realities: The Perils of Imagining Future Borders

The preceding chapters have explored the eu-LISA Agency as an empirical laboratory, which offered us insights into the various actors, activities and technological projects involved in reshaping Europe's borders. Rather than providing an exhaustive summary of all empirical findings, this concluding chapter aims to succinctly draw some of them together. Its purpose is to emphasize some of the problematic implications and risks associated with these findings, serving as a foundation for further reflection on countering the worrying trends and developments in contemporary digital border management. This includes, for instance, the severe power imbalances and forms of automated suspicion introduced and reinforced by digital technologies at the border (Askew 2023; Borelli, Lindberg, Wyss 2022; Noori 2022). In the following, I suggest engaging with three primary critiques of the digital transformation of the European border regime: justification, techno-determinism, and the perils stemming from imagining future borders.

Problematizing new modes of justification

The construction of shared visions of future digital borders around which this book has revolved is grounded in specific value systems, moral standards, principles of evaluations and grammars of worth. These elements form part of the repertoires of justification that legitimize the claims for new digital borders in Europe and make them socially acceptable. Justifications, as Boltanski and Thévenot (2006) argue in their influential work on orders of worth, are crucial means of legitimization, enabling actors to refer to higher generalizable value principles or internalized ideas of worth. Justificatory claims are thus conceived of as situated practices—that is, actors find themselves "driven to explain their judgement and to support it by drawing from the resources of the present situation" (Boltanski and Thévenot 2000, 216). In other words, these claims are connected to valuations that stem from shared ideas of a greater good or benefit (although these can be competing); actors then "typically do not invent false pretexts to explain their actions, [...] but rather try to act in ways that can withstand the test of justification" (Sharon 2018, 4).

Drawing from the field of Valuation Studies, we can understand how important justifications are for imagining and enacting future digital borders. This approach allows us to uncover the underlying evaluative undercurrents in the digital transformation of the border regime and better scrutinize how technological solutionism has served as a consistent and enduring destination for various actors involved.[1] Jeandesboz (2016a) has argued in a similar direction when claiming that justification must be understood as a vital part in the routine practices within migration management, because it "highlights the ways in which EU border control is not only about adopting the 'right' measure—the efficient, proportionate or acceptable measure—but also involves shifting the boundaries of what is considered justifiable" (p. 222).

To this end, I suggest problematizing one of the more recently emerging repertoires of justification—the *project repertoire of justification*—and scrutinizing its increasingly dominant value framework and principles of worth that underpin many of today's claims for digital borders.[2] Notably, within the EU's border regime, numerous components and principles of this project repertoire have become visible and gained prominence with the creation of eu-LISA, its subsequent growth and power, as well as its very explicit engagement with the security industry.[3] In this justificatory repertoire, success and the "state of greatness" is usually measured against values such as experimentation, adaptability, flexibility or connectivity. Sharon (2018) contends that moments of mobilizing the project-oriented repertoire "will be at work wherever notions like experimentation, innovation, 'thinking outside the box' and 'shaking things up' are promoted as valuable" (p. 7). Information technologies seem to belong to the natural directory of this world, as inherently worthy objects, and they are repeatedly and unambiguously embraced and celebrated. In this context, actors feel compelled to create an environment conducive to their full realization since these technologies are perceived as the harbingers of an innovative future. The discourse and rhetoric of this repertoire prevail in conferences and policy gatherings, where participants showcase their presumably innovative, forward-thinking and anticipatory mindsets. Policy officials and Agency representatives, for example, emphasize this repeatedly by framing the new developments of large-scale IT systems as milestones on what they refer to as "our digital journey". "This is [an] ongoing process; it hasn't finished yet" (Interview 1, 2018).

When mobilizing this repertoire, individuals allude to the unfettered belief (or delusion) in the power of innovation (Vinsel and Russel 2020). Core elements here considered are experimentation, scalability or adaptability. During a conference, a participant included a quote by Henry Ford in his PowerPoint presentation to underscore the necessity of innovation in the border regime simply by disrupting the status quo: "If you always do what you've always done, you'll always get what you've always got" (field note, eu-LISA Conference, 16 October 2019). The emphasis is hereby placed on the latent potentials and synergies offered by digital solutions in the context of border control. These potentials are not necessarily limited to the build-up of specific databases, but instead promoted as a nebulous broader project that facilitates multiple enactments of digital technology. As one official remarked: "The smart border is not only one system, it's many systems. It's different obligations and possibilities. We are not blocking the situation, limiting choice, but open[ing] possibilities to different border control" (field note, eu-LISA Industry Roundtable, 24 April 2019).

In this view, the digital transformation of borders is articulated as a constant, quasi-autonomous evolution, fostering a technological momentum for significant change in both politics and society: "It is simply because technology is evolving!" proclaimed one enthusiastic conference participant at a roundtable (field note, eu-LISA Industry Roundtable, 24 April 2019). In the project world, society must adapt naturally to digital innovation, which is often linked to automation and scalability. Obstacles in this transformation are frequently attributed to unfortunately low levels of public acceptance of non-human labour or automation. These narratives suggest that members of the public, travelers, or even border guards and authorities require a longer learning curve to adjust to the new systems and technologies. For instance, the interoperability initiative has been repeatedly justified as a gateway to increased automatization at borders (mainly due to its Multiple Identity Detector component) but would require so-called change management to accustom border guards and authorities at their work. Likewise, smart borders have been said to be promising first steps to further automatization in the future, possibly steering and implementing artificial intelligence applications or blockchain technologies later on (field note, eu-LISA Conference, 16 October 2019).

A previous chapter (Chapter 4) has emphasized the eu-LISA Agency's events as the most valuable platform for actors to showcase anticipation of the future as a particularly significant epistemic orientation. By drawing on the project repertoire of justification, actors moreover demonstrate "positive thinking" about innovation and express their expectations for future success. This optimism is often encapsulated in slogans, such as "we can and we will succeed", or "we should be able to envision what is possible in [the] future" (field note, eu-LISA Conference, 16 October 2019). More generally, events are considered as best practices for establishing contacts, exchanging ideas with the industry professionals, brainstorming sessions and sharing knowledge. Within these social arenas, "mediation" is invoked as a positive value in its own right (Boltanski and Chiapello 2018, 207). Mediation facilitates the formation of networks through which worth can be realized and it propels other projectivist qualities such as, problem–solution capabilities, foresight, entrepreneurialism and flexibility.

All this corresponds well to the Agency's renewed 2018 mandate, which encourages more independence for carrying out pilot projects, proofs of concept, testing or research and permits the Agency participating in EU Framework Programmes for Research and Innovation. eu-LISA's frequent emphasis on their image as a "centre of excellence" showcases itself as a hub of evolving expertise, networks, new working methods, as well as gradually expanding experimental initiatives. As such a novel site of infrastructuring EU borders, Agency representatives are often viewed as pioneering experts engaged in experimental modes of research and development.

Digitizing borders is legitimized because it becomes framed in terms of a "unique project" and the willingness of those involved to "do the impossible"—as another official told me: "[This] is something, which for many people has been considered […] impossible" (Interview 13 with EU official, 2019). This forms an integral part of *justification*: digitizing borders is a "project on a mission". On a PowerPoint presentation during eu-LISA's annual conference, an Agency representative stated that "It's the act of getting the right information at the right time, to the right person, with the goal of furthering an agency's mission." The quote concluded with the statement, "technology simply enables the mission" (field note, eu-LISA Conference, 16 October 2019). Similarly, eu-LISA's former Director Krum Garkov invited participants in his speeches "to join in this broader project" (field note, eu-LISA Industry Roundtable, 17 October 2019).

In this justificatory repertoire, then, technological innovation is not so much a measure of social progress as it is a *project*; a form of production that moulds the conditions of social reality. As Boltanski and Chiapello argued, project worlds must demonstrate the constant pursuit of "activity" as a paramount condition for creating worth, "what is relevant is to be always pursuing some sort of activity" (Boltanski and Chiapello 2005, 169). The need for constant activity is thus another rhetoric at eu-LISA events: "We don't have the luxury to sit and enjoy what we have achieved so far, we need to continue" (field note, eu-LISA Conference, 16 October 2019). Frequently, building and expanding databases is legitimized based on enhancing innovation, maintaining activity, preventing discontinuity or interruption—regardless of how empty or even tautological the purpose of the activity appears. The emphasis on activity is encapsulated in a semi-official eu-LISA slogan: "We're making it happen". Subjects considered worthy are therefore active, utilizing their presumed creative potential to solve technical challenges. Political and ethical reflection seem alien in this context. They are unwelcome and discouraged because they stand in the way of the worth-creating and self-fulfilling purpose of the mission, the activity, the innovation.[4]

Problematizing justificatory repertoires unveils how making digital borders is always part of what Aradau and McCluskey term *the politics of acceptability* of certain arguments (2021, 7). The creation of new databases for border control and the efforts to interconnect them may seem like natural and convenient responses to cross-border mobility, but this perception stems from the repeated alignment with overarching principles of (e)valuation that render them acceptable and worth striving for. Justifications encapsulate specific values, ideas and solutions that underlie the aspirations and collective visions. Projectivist worlds increasingly shape the ways people and organizations speak, write, act and interact, and therefore create the conditions that enable solutionist ideologies and allow them to thrive in the European border regime. They form part of the politics of acceptability and thus the prerequisites of legitimate dispute.

The politics of acceptability encompass the claims and arguments with which actors not only establish legitimate (border) policy and practice, but also mobilize them to defend themselves against valid criticisms. Problematizing justification may therefore help us also to develop and cultivate an analytical vocabulary that creates our own meaningful evaluations and critiques of the border regime—by gaining a better understanding of the conditions of legitimate dispute. But finding ways to articulate justified or valid criticism might not be enough; we also need to develop strategies to create repertoires that make the creation and continuous expansion of digital borders in Europe less acceptable and normalized.

The myths and fallacies of techno-determinism

Throughout the book, I have delved into the promises, hopes and futures associated with the development and maintenance of databases at eu-LISA. All these elements have portrayed the new databases and digital technologies as indispensable necessities in the transformation. It is therefore imperative also to shed light on the—sometimes more, sometimes less—concealed techno-determinist logics and make explicit how they obscure the normative structures, infrastructural efforts and political decisions that underpin this digital border regime.

To this end, let us revisit the statement from eu-LISA that was cited at the outset of this book. The Agency's former Director asserted that "the virtual world of IT is now part of the equation", and emphasized "the importance of sophisticated, flexible and integrated IT systems and solutions". In the subsequent chapters, I have identified and explored at least two implicit, interrelated points of view embedded within this statement, serving as the focal points of this book's inquiry.

The first stance relates to the inevitability of the digital transformation (see especially Chapter 2). This position suggests that technological change is a non-negotiable, inescapable part of our future and, thus, governments must embrace specific measures, such as the production and ever-expanding accumulation of migrant data. The second position revolves around the promises and benefits of digital technologies and data in the management of borders and migration. This position holds that the expansion of databases would enable states to effectively master the challenges, complexities and uncertainties brought about by our interconnected global world and its diverse forms of mobility.

As the book's findings suggest, both positions were found to be problematic. First, the idea of inevitability attempts to prepare us for the permanent arrival of the so-called virtual world, but is essentially flawed and misleading because it conflates digital change with progress. Moreover, it presents "the virtual" as a black box, rendering visible only its presumed input (that is, data and information) and promised output (that is, greater security, better cooperation). Inevitability both obfuscates and naturalizes the digital, ignoring its contentious histories, the infrastructural inner workings, or the intricate networks required to bring it into existence and hold it in place. The position of inevitability also ignores the multiple performances, varying interests (both political and economic), disparate objectives of different actors, and the laborious infrastructural work that shape our sociotechnical trajectories. Consequently, one main objective of this book's investigation has been to unseal this black box and demystify the "virtual"—paying close attention to the manifold epistemic and material practices at eu-LISA that have been invested in realizing future borders in Europe.

The position of inevitability is, of course, not only limited to the realms of digital border and migration control. More than two decades ago, Cornelius Castoriadis (1991) exposed the inherent fallacy of what he perceived as a widespread and enduring ideology. According to him, this ideology falsely assumed the separation between technological systems and society, implying that societal norms and values would simply follow, or align with, technological values and codes. Inevitability advocates for the deterministic idea of technological change as an "out-of-control history-shaping process" (Dafoe 2015). It suggests that the sheer power of invention and innovation represents itself to be unstoppable or at least irreversible, largely detached from social factors. Thus, while this position may recognize the power of technology to penetrate social structures, rebuild political order, and even shape individual bodies, it also obscures the intricate relationship between the social and the material—and the networks of actors, visions, practices and infrastructures that sustain or transform this relationship.

Previous chapters have examined various empirical situations in which this fallacy was exposed. For example, I have observed the eu-LISA's distinct performances of the sociotechnical imaginary of digital transformation that framed the digitization of migration and border governance as a unidirectional, stable process. Similarly, the fallacy was evident in the portrayals of database interoperability as an irreversible momentum and "necessary policy fiction". This perception of inevitability strategically shields the controversial policy trajectories and technopolitical interventions from criticism. Consequently, the logics and rationalities underpinning large-scale, interconnected IT systems for border and migration governance are rarely challenged in official government policies, reinforcing their status as vital components of sociopolitical order.

The second position that this book opposes revolves around the simplistic promises and principles of solutionism, solutionist thinking and argumentation. The book has argued that digital borders are never ready-made answers or straightforward outcomes of rational scientific reasoning and planning. Instead, it is a fiction—upheld by a set of beliefs and values held by elite actors and officials, which are continuously re-enacted to accredit and legitimize the ongoing investments in the digital border regime and its digital infrastructures. In its most frequently articulated form, digital solutionism shapes the projects and policies related to digital borders by prioritizing the governmental desires for certainty, unambiguity and mastery over the complex and messy realities of the ever-evolving mobilities of people.

This position resembles, again, Castoriadis's (1991) characterization of the "blatant absurdity of the idea of total mastery" (p. 193), which he once identified as the hidden motor of modern techno-capitalist development. Consequently, solutionism of this kind possesses a troubling yet highly seductive eschatological quality; it holds out the promise of future rewards, the materialization of governmental desires, and the fulfillment of border security through technological advancements. Many attempts to validate solutionism assume that, once databases and border technologies are put into operation, they work flawlessly, delivering reliably on the policy goals and objectives. Databases then become seen as finely calibrated machines, expected to meet the security, economic or efficiency demands of governmental authorities. This mistaken belief in their flawless performances also haunts the critical analysis of digital borders (Glouftsios and Scheel 2021). By leaving the predefined problem–solution framework unchallenged, including the biases inherent in professional planning and technological development, critical analyses can involuntarily lend support to the policy claims and justifications of government officials or industry representatives.

Ultimately, solutionist promises also perpetuate the myth of unintended consequences (Jasanoff 2016, 21–26). In this scenario, the recurrent failures of technologies, but also their violent or harmful social effects, are consistently perceived as mere anomalies or deviations resulting from a lack of adequate foresight (typically attributed to policy professionals and technical experts). This serves to reassure us once more of the supposedly enduring, progressive character of digital transformations. The myth of unintended consequences and the promises of solutionism are two sides of the coin: when technology fails as a solution, it is considered to be because its consequences were not sufficiently anticipated, prompting experts and designers to readjust their interventions. Both perspectives are grounded in what experts, professionals and designers of digital border control define as the space between what is and what ought to be. Both perspectives reinforce the existing problem–assumptions, established solution promises, and their normative and justificatory frameworks in the development of digital border infrastructure in Europe.

Sanitized realities

Imagining future borders, as this book has investigated, occasionally fosters a sense of belonging and collectivity among an otherwise dispersed network of actors within the digital border regime. eu-LISA officials thus frequently evoke a shared path or a "common journey". Chapter 4 has outlined the typical conditions and concerted efforts to draw in a diverse range of people—officials, professionals, brokers, delegates—thereby establishing (at least temporarily) a sense of unity and coherence: the repetition of policy events, meticulous conference arrangements, or standardized modes of communication. The imaginary of digital transformation, as explored in Chapter 2, serves as an example of how a particular vision of the future became embedded, and only gradually stabilized, within a broader network of stakeholders. The imaginary blended fact, fiction and emotion as it addressed these actors as a collective political community with a common future. Once this vision became sufficiently collectivized, the future of digitizing border (in)security appeared compelling and totalizing, creating opportunities for action while silencing dissenting voices. In another example analyzed in Chapter 3, eu-LISA positioned itself as a European spokesperson, and its "infrastructural performances" aimed at cultivating ideas of European identity and infrastructural integration. EU officials and other representatives promoted the Agency as an entity capable of forging cohesion from fractionality, order from disorder or chaos. Practices of imagination served to establish connection, and different experiences and daily practices were framed to represent a single European regime. The diversity of human mobility was therefore translated into logistical populations and coherent entities for migration management (see Chapter 4). Metaphorically, collective imagination can therefore indeed "operate as both glue and solvent [...] to preserve continuity across the sharpest ruptures of innovation or, in reverse, to upend firm worlds and make them anew" (Jasanoff 2015a, 29). In summary, such shared modes and conditions of sociotechnical imagination generate a temporary sense of coherence and collectivity, binding together the multiple factions of policy officials, professionals and delegates within the border regime.

Imagining future borders, as demonstrated in previous chapters, creates powerful effects, notably simplification and abstraction, which deserve closer attention. In a broader context, simplification and abstraction have always served as crucial tools for the exercise of modern state power. According to political anthropologist James Scott (1998), state authorities must establish clear demarcations and distinct categories to ensure the legibility of people within a world characterized by multiplicity and hybridity. Similarly, Timothy Mitchell (2002) reminds us of a fundamental tenet of expert governance: "Politics itself [... is] working to simplify the world" (p. 34).[5] However, simplifications are not merely generalizable templates, readily at hand or universally applicable for state officials to impose on populations. In the book's empirical case of eu-LISA, simplifications are brought into existence through the imaginative efforts and capabilities of specific individuals and organizations.

Simplification and abstraction must hereby provide epistemic keys to a world in which borders, mobilities, populations can be known and represented as manageable. We have seen how eu-LISA's recurrent depictions of mobility and border dynamics were accompanied by reassuring expertise and a sense of mastery. As exemplified in Chapter 4, various communities could come together to co-laborate and negotiate knowledge, representations and semantics of border control by crafting an entire epistemology full of acronyms, logistical vocabulary, boundary objects and abstract, calculative reasoning. This epistemological framework for digital borders is not simply a product of technoscientific rigorism. Instead, it reflects the governmental desire to simplify social realities of mobility and border management as well as their inherent inconsistencies. At the same time, officials, bureaucrats and industry representatives employ rhetorical devices and the tractable language of logistics to position themselves as planners, experts and strategists of control.

Simplification also played a pivotal role in assembling the policy of interoperability (see Chapter 5). This policy essentially revolved around the promise of reducing the complexity of what authorities term "identity management" in border control. Simplification, in this example, was integral for envisioning database interoperability as a "necessary policy fiction". It had to convey the sense of mastery and meet the desire to exert control over the intricacies of IT systems, the multifaceted bureaucratic complications, and the overall infrastructural configurations of borders—complexities that can be difficult even for their administrators or operators to fully grasp.

The sense of mastery and control that visions of future borders need to convey is closely tied to creating distance and obscuring the actual realities of bordering on the ground. This distancing provides an opportunity to ignore friction and conflict arising from human mobility, including acts of resistance against border control measures. The same detachment is invoked and reinforced through what I referred to as "a view from beyond" within the imaginary of digital transformation (see Chapter 2)—a specific, professionalized way of seeing migration. I analyzed this view from beyond as something that envisions migration and border control within laboratory-like settings, as the business of managing virtualized data streams (as illustrated in Figure 2.1).

This professional "gaze" intentionally diverges from the realities of bordering and border enforcement as a locally grounded practice and encounter between human beings. Instead, it conceptualizes bordering as an abstract alignment and interconnection of data points—a futuristic, seamless world of virtual control. It invokes the imagery of the laboratory where data serves as an instrument for sifting through and calibrating population flows, determining whether a traveler qualifies as a legitimate object of circulation or a potentially threatening intruder. Through "the view from beyond", human subjects eventually vanish from the picture because the actual violence of border operations and acts of political resistance would contradict the imagination of an all-encompassing and smooth functioning digital border.

In contrast to the imagery of walls and barbed wire fences, widely recognized for their violent aesthetic and inhumane symbolism, future borders are here imagined, portrayed and promoted differently. They aim to invoke what I called sanitized realities or futures.[6] This can be particularly exemplified, as Chapter 4 illustrated, in the projects of border smartification. In their insightful discussion of smart borders in the US, Aizeki and colleagues (2021) point out that smart border security promulgates a so-called "humane alternative" to physical border zones, walls, or fences—and not only because of its innovative promise to counter new threats.[7]

Instead, the visions surrounding new digital borders seem to offer escape from the increasing violence that migrants face on a daily basis in contemporary border regimes. This escape, however, is not rooted in the fact that smart borders would be more humane but because their representations are dehumanized. New digital borders are proposed as potential alternatives because the sanitized versions of reality they propagate render the presence of humans invisible—that is, human elements are erased from the polished representations of control, security, surveillance or circulation. This might provide another layer of meaning behind a hope expressed by an EU official when asked about the future of migration and border security in Europe: "I hope that we can largely eliminate the human factor in border control" (Interview 21, 2019).

Smart or digital borders become, both conceptually and rhetorically, portrayed as distinct from supposedly non-digital territorial boundaries. This separation produces a misleading dichotomy, focusing public attention on the prominent symbols of deterrence—walls, fences, and fortresses—while risking not paying attention to the subtler but equally concerning infrastructures of smart bordering: filtering, categorizing, selecting, detaining and deporting people. As Benjamin (2019) argues elsewhere, there is an imminent danger that "the equivalent of slow death—the subtler and even alluring forms of coded inequity—get a pass" (p. 24). These false dichotomies between smart/digital and hard/geographical boundaries, the virtual and the territorial, should therefore be discarded: they mask the fact that borders are underpinned by similar objectives and visions that drive the extensive extraction and collection of data related to migration. They divert attention from the multiple infrastructural practices that classify individuals into categories of worthy travelers, on the one hand, and unworthy travelers, anomalies or intrusions on the other. In other words, the dichotomy between smart and hard borders tends to obscure the more complex assemblages of actors, technologies, knowledge practices and values through which otherness is produced and processed, ultimately determining the status of mobile individuals within or outside the boundaries of legality. As Heller and Pezzani (2017) observe, the productive dimension and benefits for today's governments of pursuing these forms of constructing otherness is never far from view, including "attracting the populist vote, keeping the surveillance and military industries buoyant, and [...] providing the labor market with a ready supply of deskilled and precaritized laborers" (p. 104).

Envisioning the sanitized realities of digital borders not only has the tendency to make human elements disappear but equally bypass crucial questions concerning responsibility and accountability. Sanitized realities within Europe's digital border regime represent small "islands of order" (Scott 2012, 141) for government authorities, and their proliferation aims to block our view from the messy and complex realities as much as divert us from the disastrous consequences of European borders. Yet, as mobile individuals continue to face persistent violence and injustice, these questions appear more relevant than ever before. Who can be accountable for the errors, wrongdoings, vulnerabilities and suffering at the sites of (digital) border infrastructures? At what (human) expense should these sanitized realities and their spaces of experimentality be brought into being? Such questions should lie at the heart of imagining and making future digital borders. Because, as Hannah Arendt (2017 [1948]) once noted, "[i]n a totally fictitious world, failures need not be recorded, admitted, and remembered" (p. 508).[8] Arendt's observations are instructive in this context, highlighting the totalitarian potential of contemporary imaginations of digital borders—particularly when they replace any deliberations of the social consequences of technoscientific change and innovation. The predominant tendency to construct visions of borders and their digital transformations as dehumanized, abstract and sanitized futures is thus not merely a façade; they prevent us from the essential dialogue we must begin about the social failures, responsibilities and accountabilities for the systemic injustice that persist within border regimes today.

A final note on another politics of responsibility

The politics of migration in Europe is often described as a malfunction in state cooperation or as "lack of courage" among politicians or policy makers. While such assessments are not entirely wrong, they tend to overlook the deliberate construction of sanitized realities and futures. It is important to reflect on how those contribute to what we can call a form of organized irresponsibility (cf. Beck 1995). Beck's well-known concept asserts that while individuals or organizations may be responsible for the harmful risks and consequences of their own actions, conditions are established that prevent specific individuals or organizations from being held accountable. More than just being a failure, sanitized constructs can be considered a strategic method and effect, when they obfuscate the hierarchies, vulnerabilities and arbitrary responses of state authorities dealing with migrations across the various bordering contexts. Within the Schengen border laboratory, state authorities and supranational institutions may indeed be responsible for the infrastructural violence and its harmful consequences; today, however, there are few means available for holding these authorities accountable.

Contemporary border governance in Europe is not only reliant on invoking exceptional scenarios or states of emergency—although this does recur as a method through which states respond to human movement. But we should keep in view the multitude of infrastructural practices of bordering—surveilling, identifying, verifying, categorizing and deporting—that routinely result in extreme situations: they entail intensified mechanisms of selection and sorting, the inclusion of travelers into the smooth circuits of mobility as much as the arbitrary detainment and expulsion of human beings from European territory (Dijstelbloem 2021, 181). These situations are not necessarily exceptional but an extreme form of routine; they produce precarity and violence on a daily basis—circumstances where the rights of migrants and responsibilities of state authorities become blurred, fragmented or even suspended.

Against this backdrop, let us revisit one of eu-LISA's prosaic claims that it operates border databases "24 hours a day, seven days a week [... which] allows the continuous, uninterrupted exchange of data between the national authorities" (eu-LISA 2014, 3) through the prism of organized irresponsibility. The imperative to expand the digital infrastructure of borders and the fervent solutionist belief in the unfettered power of data are closely intertwined with sanitized portrayals in which rights and responsibilities are, at best, sidelined. The claims made by the Agency depict the operations of digital border infrastructures as clean, orderly, routine and almost imperceptible, appearing to bypass the potentially violent and extreme circumstances upon which these operations are founded. This stands in contrast to the numerous "unofficial" evidence of how data is extracted and collected, frequently building upon unequal hierarchies and violent encounters between migrants and authorities. For instance, migrants may find themselves forced to provide fingerprints or facial images against their will; monitoring technology tracks refugees' boats while choosing to ignore and abandon individuals at sea.[9]

In the face of organized irresponsibility, how could the contours of a counterprogramme be outlined? One possible source of inspiration could lie in Akrich's (1992) concept of a geography of responsibility. A geography of responsibility would have to start from revealing—rather than concealing—the ways in which infrastructural arrangements within the EU border regime distribute responsibility, power and agency across institutions, places and technologies. As Oudshoorn elaborated on this concept, the idea of geography can sensitize us "to distributions of responsibilities which grant agency and power to specific actors and places while restricting or silencing the agency of others" (2012, 137). A geography of responsibility, at the very least, would have to unravel again the political and legal accountabilities of national and supranational actors in Europe. It should compel these diverse actors to engage in a genuine dialogue about how they can make their duties and practices transparent, and how they can fulfil their duties to respond to, rather than ignore or conceal, the various injustices and acts of violence occurring at Europe's borders.

The two closely intertwined perspectives proposed in this book, infrastructure and collective imagination, have exposed borders as manifestations of the policing and surveillance efforts that shape our perception of who is imagined to be "genuine" European or non-European, citizen or non-citizen, intruder or tourist, and who is entitled to protection or must face deportation. Therefore, a geography of responsibility must first acknowledge that borders and their infrastructural configurations are markers for how societies seek to realize their desired futures, political objectives and notions of justice and injustice. Border infrastructures inherently have a global dimension, reflecting how societies and their polities address human movement. A geography of responsibility could then offer a political programme that truly challenges the fundamental social categories that structure mobility in today's global world, including the colonial infrastructures that have an intimate legacy in the profound structural inequality persisting within mobilities today.

Ultimately, we cannot simply advocate for abolishing digital technologies or databases. Instead, a counterprogramme would have to aim to unsettle and fundamentally redirect the prevailing imaginaries of the future that underpin the border regime's fixation on "technological solutions". This reflection would most likely extend beyond the important conversations about data protection and personal privacy in light of today's unparalleled collection of traveler data. It would also require consideration of how we can imagine a future that breaks with the prevailing cycles of mobility that determine an individual's inclusion or exclusion largely on the basis of the presumed birthright, which remains the main guarantor of legitimate cross-border movement today. Otherwise, it will be impossible to reflect on how technology can be reimagined to contribute to, rather than obstruct, future mobility justice on this planet (Sheller 2018a).

None of the above represents a straightforward template for creating a better, or even a utopian, future. But it would be overly presumptuous to claim to possess all the answers to the questions posed by this book. Nevertheless, the book aimed to carve out a clearer sense of where to direct our attention and to underscore the pressing need to envision alternative sociotechnical infrastructures that challenge a dystopian status quo and work toward fostering greater mobility justice.

In the future, border infrastructures will continue to be constructed and (digitally) transformed, only to eventually perish again. The simple reason for this lies in the fact that the movements of people will never neatly conform to the sanitized digital realities that governmental experts or officials wish for their future borders. On the contrary, as Sheller highlights, mobilities are concrete and diverse, "uneven, differential, and unequal, and come together through these combined lived experiences that are both physical and meaningful" (Sheller 2018b, 20). To prevent further violence and suffering, an initial step can only be an acceptance of the irreducible multiplicity of mobility realities and futures (rather than fighting or sanitizing them). People will continue to shape these realities by persisting in being mobile and claiming their right to cross borders—whether they seek refuge, escape persecution, or search for a better life.

Coda

Recently, eu–LISA and industry representatives have been actively advocating for Artificial Intelligence (AI) and big data in the realm of border control and surveillance. Despite being notoriously vague terms, much of their appeal stems from the novel machine-learning techniques they employ to automatize routine tasks—including deep learning, translation, evaluating and sorting data, and the automated interpretation and analysis of potential risks. However, the ways in which machine learning, big data and their associated promises are performed are firmly rooted in the broader sociotechnical imaginary of the digital transformation of borders and its underpinning narratives of an inevitable and unidirectional path toward technological change.

For example, the event report from eu–LISA's industry roundtable "Artificial Intelligence and Large-Scale IT Systems: Opportunities and Challenges" claims that "[i]n order to understand the importance of AI as a disruptive technology, it needs to be considered in the broader context of digital transformation" (eu–LISA 2022c, 6). In a report titled *Artificial Intelligence in the Operational Management of Large-Scale IT Systems*, the Agency states:

> [I]mplementation of AI is not a question of "if", but "when" and "to what extent". The EES and ETIAS both foresee a certain level of artificial intelligence or automation and will therefore have an immediate effect on individuals. Considering that the precision of AI systems based on machine learning algorithms depends to a significant extent on data sets used for training, and the quality of data sets used for the training of biometric recognition systems to be used in the EES will to a significant extent determine the quality of the AI systems. (eu–LISA 2020, 32)

Meanwhile, algorithms are already in active use, or being tested or under consideration for implementation in border control. According to a report by the nonprofit organization Statewatch, the EU has allocated €341 million for 51 research projects aimed at exploring AI for border and migration control purposes (Statewatch 2022). Automated technologies are already applied in biometric identification, including fingerprint search and comparison systems; AI applications are employed in risk assessments, monitoring and analysis; projects funded by the EU are experimenting with emotion detection at borders (Dumbrava 2021).

In May 2023, the European Parliament voted on the AI Act, a prospective binding legislation intended to regulate AI in the EU. The proposed Act includes a provision to prohibit AI technologies categorized as harmful, such as emotion recognition or predictive policing. Notably, the AI Act acknowledges:

> AI systems used in migration, asylum and border control management affect people who are often in particularly vulnerable position and who are dependent on the outcome of the actions of the competent public authorities. The accuracy, non-discriminatory nature and transparency of the AI systems used in those contexts are therefore particularly important […]. (EC 2021b, 28)

While this is undoubtedly an important statement, it does not comprehensively address the problematic consequences of digitally filing, categorizing and sorting migrants in large-scale databases, a matter certainly not fully covered by the AI Act. Nonetheless, the regulation of AI has already evolved in a contentious domain influenced by the politics of classification, which involves evaluating and ranking AI technology as "harmful", "high" or "low risk".

Border control in Europe is therefore expected to continue leveraging various forms of algorithmic power (Beer 2009), impacting how data is interpreted, what decisions are made, and what actions are undertaken. Consequently, there will be an increasing need for rigorous empirical investigations that can delve into the manifold contexts in which AI and big data techniques are enacted through sociotechnical practice.

The infrastructural character of digital border surveillance only hints at the numerous ways in which AI can reconfigure notions of sovereignty, territory and mobility: being deployed at automated gates in airports, biometric registration centres at hotspots, or in drone monitoring and pushback operations along the EU's maritime borders. In these instances, algorithms do not operate in a vacuum; they work based on preconceived notions and assumptions, which carry the risk of objectifying or perpetuating existing inequalities and patterns of discrimination.

Furthermore, these new technological artefacts invite a plethora of actors—ranging from researchers, engineers and private companies to official experts and policy makers—to engage in the design, development and implementation of machine-learning techniques, consequently shaping the infrastructural configurations of border control. This necessitates research into the complex compositions of AI, the individuals or entities involved in AI, and the functions that AI fulfils. AI and big data raise significant questions about whether, and to what extent, their mechanistic design introduces autonomous decision-making at borders. As Amoore (2021) explores in her concept of the "deep border", machine learning redefines the border "as world-making, or as a means of reordering what the border is, what it could be, and how it imagines and bounds political community" (p. 7).

Parts of this book were written and discussed amid the unfolding global pandemic. COVID-19 has either caused, or rather exposed, multiple social, political, economic and infrastructural crises. It has fundamentally reshaped border infrastructures around the globe. It has, moreover, given rise to new narratives of inclusion and exclusion and redrawn boundaries between communities, territories and nation-states.

One of the earliest responses taken by European countries was the attempt to contain the highly contagious virus and its variants. These measures included travel restrictions and other forms of containing human movement, often resulting in dramatic and entirely unforeseen consequences. At the same time, the introduction of bans, mobility restrictions and border closures often served as symbolic gestures in the pandemic theatre, rather than genuinely effective strategies for safeguarding public health and medical safety. For example, European states made drastic attempts to close borders, which, at best, only slowed the spread of COVID-19 rather than prevent it. When the Omicron variant emerged towards the end of 2021, the US promptly closed its borders and banned entry for non-citizens from South Africa, where laboratories initially detected the variant (US citizens traveling from South Africa were still permitted to enter). European authorities followed suit, implementing travel bans or border closures for African countries, even though the variant had likely already spread beyond South Africa and had reached their own countries. Such border control measures by Global North countries were thus perceived as racially biased scapegoating rather than being founded on scientific rationale.[1] These performative political actions, sometimes contradicting scientific reasoning, left a bitter aftertaste, particularly when considering the significant disparities in global vaccine distribution.

Furthermore, the COVID-19 pandemic offered a convenient pretext for authorities to exert greater policing methods against migrants and refugees, thereby increasing the risk of their exclusion, expulsion or deportation. As reported by the nongovernmental organisation Picum, varying levels of vaccine access for undocumented individuals across Europe were observed, with some countries offering good access while others had inconsistent or no access at all.[2]

For migrants, public spaces have gradually evolved into areas where they could potentially face identity and police checks, often linked to COVID-19 certification controls. Checking personal identification has become normalized, carried out by both state or non-state entities, and it continues to hold potentially severe consequences for undocumented migrants. Throughout the pandemic, migrants and refugees, in general, were not treated as subjects whose safety or health were potentially at risk; instead, the pandemic exacerbated their categorization *as* risky subjects. In many respects, as Tazzioli (2020a) emphasized, COVID-19 did not lead to enhanced protection for migrants; rather, it led to them being "spatially confined and hampered from getting access to asylum in the name of safety". Finally, regardless of how strict European countries were in enforcing travel bans and general lockdowns in the name of safety, they did not halt the deportations, thereby putting lives in jeopardy.

COVID-19 has also been utilized as a pretext to advance the digitization of the existing European border regime. No opportunity has been missed to underscore how the pandemic condition has made our lives increasingly digital across all facets. For instance, eu-LISA pointed out "that this unparalleled crisis must be embraced as an opportunity to implement long-awaited changes" (eu-LISA 2021, 4).

During its virtual conference in November 2020, the Agency's opening speech highlighted how the ongoing trend of digital transformation would be accelerated due to the global health crisis (field note, eu-LISA Conference, 26 November 2020). Similarly, in the industry roundtable "Contactless Travel in Post-COVID Times", eu-LISA explained that "the COVID-19 crisis has provided an additional impetus for the digital transformation of the EU Security Ecosystem, opening new opportunities for the entire community" (eu-LISA 2021, 4).

It is evident that the global pandemic has established a highly visible, discursive connection between health, mobility and security. Transnational health infrastructures are either being newly established or overhauled. Personal health data has now become an indispensable component of security measures in Europe. In other words, the realm of digital health has become an integral element of border infrastructures and their operations. Health infrastructures and the collection of health data have expanded the scope of intervention for a vast network of actors, practices and technologies. This domain will be a significant area of focus in the future, where new discourses on (in)security and risk will emerge, controversies will unfold, and technopolitical orders will be constructed.

Overview of Existing and Future Large-Scale IT Systems Under eu-LISA's Management

SIS II	
Description	In operation since 2001, the Schengen Information System (SIS) is the oldest centralized transnational database in Europe. Its current version dates from April 2013 and is known as SIS II. The system officially supports intergovernmental cooperation on law enforcement and external border management. It shares data among those state authorities that participate in the so-called Schengen Agreement Application Convention—currently consisting of 31 European countries, including 22 Schengen member states, the four associated countries Iceland, Liechtenstein, Norway and Switzerland, and countries that cooperate with Schengen members in law enforcement (such as Bulgaria, Romania and the UK). The central system can be accessed by law enforcement, border control, visa and customs authorities as well as vehicle registration authorities. EU agencies such as Europol and Eurojust have limited access to data (in accordance with their legal mandates).

SIS's origins lie in the creation of the Schengen space in 1985, when it was envisioned as a compensatory measure for the dissolution of borders between members of the newly founded Schengen community. After 2004, during the process of EU enlargement, SIS had to be made newly operational for countries planning to join Schengen. The EU's expansion also provoked a debate about significantly expanding the system's purpose and technical capacities. A so-called second generation of the system was envisioned to implement the "latest technological developments and added functions such as new categories of alerts, a facility to link alerts and the capacity to store documents associated with an alert" (European Court of Auditors 2014, 1). SIS was thus subsequently transformed from a simple hit/no-hit system to a broader search and intelligence tool, introducing new biometric data as sole identifiers, new possibilities for creating links between stored entries and categories, and new access possibilities to national authorities and intergovernmental organizations such as Europol (see Brouwer 2008). SIS II ultimately planned to go online at the end of 2006, which would enable new EU countries to operate as full Schengen members. However, the realization of this project failed. The onset of operations was postponed by more than six years and ended up with a budget eight times higher than originally estimated (Parkin 2011).

Operational details	SIS II is an alert system that contains data categories for both persons and objects. It provides authorities with information, for example, on people involved in crime or denied entry into the Schengen space, missing persons, or on the kind of action to be taken by authorities in case of so-called misused identities. SIS II also contains data on stolen or lost objects (for example, vehicles, firearms, documents, credit cards and banknotes). In November 2018, the EU adopted a proposal for reinforcing the system and preparing its interoperability with other systems. Moreover, it decided to expand its capacity to collect additional biometric data, including fingerprints, palm prints, facial images of so-called suspects and DNA records of missing persons. Additionally, the role of SIS II in the EU countries' strategies of deporting migrants has been strengthened, for instance, by including a new alert category on return decisions. In March 2023, the renewed version of the system went "live". According to eu-LISA's annual statistics, SIS II was accessed and searched over 12 billion times in 2022. It stored more than 86 million alerts in its central system, of which more than one million alerts corresponded to persons.[1]

VIS

Description	The Visa Information System (VIS) became operational in 2011. It connects immigration authorities at external border crossing points of Schengen states and consular posts in countries outside the EU. The VIS is a tool to implement the EU's common visa policy by assisting authorities in the management of applications for short-stay visas. Today, the system is one of the largest (biometric) databases in the world, registering both granted and refused visa applications, copies of travel documents and applicants' biometric data. Its main purpose is to verify the traveler at the external Schengen border, establish their biometric identity, and check whether it corresponds to the issued visa. Therefore, authorities enrol fingerprints at the border and match them with the system's stored templates. The VIS thereby aims to prevent the so-called practice of visa shopping, that is, when individuals repeatedly seek to obtain visa permission following the rejection of a previous application. Rejections are digitally stored in the VIS instead of being stamped into the passport (which can potentially be reissued). Furthermore, the VIS seeks to forestall the strategy of using a visa by a so-called lookalike, that is, an individual using someone else's passport with a valid Schengen visa (see Scheel 2017).
Operational details	The system is designed as a central database, which registers visa permissions and refusals of individuals over 12 years of age. However, EU member states plan to also include data of children over six years of age and information on long-stay visa holders. The VIS stores categories of biographical data, within which are included names, place and date of birth, travel details (that is, the purpose of stay), application status, type of visa or visa sponsors, facial images, and a full set of 10 fingerprints. According to eu-LISA, the VIS communication network processes fingerprints for identity verification between a border crosser and their visa application within 0.87 seconds.

eu-LISA's report on the technical functioning of the VIS claims that, at the end of 2021, the system had 73 million visa application and 56 million storedfingerprint sets; while in pre-COVID times almost 43 million operations in VIS were carried out at borders, this fell to 7.5 million in 2021.

Eurodac

Description	Eurodac is the abbreviation for the European Dactyloscopy database. As a large-scale fingerprint database, it primarily targets asylum seekers. The legislation for its implementation was first introduced in 2002. Eurodac has been operational since 2003 and seeks to determine the responsible country for assessing an asylum application lodged within an EU member state (or Schengen Associated country) using the technique of fingerprint comparisons. The principle of this responsibility is enshrined in the Dublin Regulation (currently Dublin III, Regulation [EU] No. 604/2013), which aims to prevent the uncontrolled movement of asylum seekers within (and across) EU member state territories. Eurodac thus stores an asylum seekers' fingerprints to help detect, for instance, multiple asylum applications in different EU member states—a practice derogatively termed asylum shopping. Authorities usually store a set of fingerprints taken during an application and, depending on the individual's purpose and category, search it against existing templates in Eurodac. The transmission of data between member states should ensure that multiple application claims are attributable to the country where the individual first arrived or applied for asylum. Currently, member states intend to significantly expand Eurodac to ensure its interoperability with other systems, store additional facial images, and include biometric data of children aged six years or older. The expanded Eurodac system should thus become a cornerstone in the interoperability project currently developed by eu-LISA. Moreover, member states have demanded to reinforce the system in the future by including data of third countries to facilitate deportations.
Operational details	Eurodac stores various categories of fingerprint sets, overall more than 5.8 million in 2021. Category 1 includes sets of applications of asylum seekers aged 14 or older that are stored for 10 years. Category 2 relates to third-country nationals (or stateless persons) that have "irregularly" crossed the border and are not turned back (which will be stored for 18 months). Category 3 relates to third-country nationals aged 14 or older who are "illegally" found on the territory of a member state. However, this data is only transmitted for a search. Categories 4 and 5 are sets of fingerprints used for searches by law-enforcement authorities to prevent, detect or investigate terrorist offences or criminal offences. In 2021, 855,478 fingerprints were transmitted to Eurodac, of which around 510,500 sets of fingerprints belong to asylum applications, more than 132,000 to individuals in Category 2, and roughly 212,000 checks are related to Category 3.

EES	
Description	The Entry/Exit System (EES) will become an information system for the registration of travelers from third-country nationals each time they cross the external border of the EU and regardless of their traveler status (that is, short-stay visa holders or visa-exempt travelers). A joint system to register entries has been a long-standing vision of the European Commission, which ultimately promoted and introduced it as part of the Smart Borders Package proposal. eu-LISA has officially been tasked to develop this system, which was expected to enter into operation in the first half of 2022 (however, the process has been significantly delayed).
	The EES is expected to become one of the world's biggest biometric databases, recording both entries and exits as well as refusals of entry (for visits up to 90 days). It will replace the current practice of visa authorities to manually stamp passports with an electronic registration of biometric information, thereby creating more reliable data on border crossers. From the beginning, the EES was meant to become interoperable with the VIS because it also targets so-called over-stayers, that is, travelers who have legally traveled to Schengen with a short-term visa (for example, as tourists) but remain after their visa expiry. The EES thus officially aims to prevent "irregular immigration" by biometrically identifying persons who are no longer eligible for staying and automatically alerting national authorities once this stay is exceeded.
Operational details	The EES will register a person's name, their biographical information and the type of travel document, and capture and store five fingerprints and a facial image. A central system must operate as a computerized database, which stores biometric and alphanumerical data. National interfaces in each EU member state serve as a channel between the central systems of both the EES and the VIS to enable data comparison. The design also includes a data repository for statistical reports—which will likely inform future visa policies of EU member states (that is, restricting visa policy based on the system's new statistical information). Furthermore, carriers are currently required to install so-called web services that enable them to verify third-country nationals and their short-stay visa status when using carrier services.
ETIAS	
Description	The European Travel Information and Authorisation System (ETIAS) will be a new border management information system that introduces an online authorization process for all visa-exempt third-country nationals before they embark on their journey to a Schengen country. This pre-travel authorization system must verify whether a traveler meets the entry requirements of a Schengen country. It obliges travelers to complete an online application, with identity information mostly related to passport data or another travel document, residence information, contact details and credit card information. The system will therefore resemble similar pre-clearance systems of other countries, such as the US ESTA system, Canada's eTA system or Australia's ETA system. Information provided by ETIAS should be automatically

checked against the other EU IT systems (SIS, VIS, Eurodac, EES and ECRIS-TCN) and Interpol databases. ETIAS aims to complement—or rather compensate—the EU's various visa liberalization policies. As a preemptive dataveillance mechanism, it targets third-country nationals who should usually be exempt from visa requirements.

A significant part of the system is constituted by the creation of a watchlist that will identify connections between data in application files and individuals on the watchlist to filter out "risk subjects"—whether in terms of migration, security or public health risks. Watchlist data can be entered by Europol or national authorities, although the conditions or obligations for entering and screening data are still unclarified. The ETIAS regulation (EU 2018b) mandates that the foreseen watchlist contains persons "suspected or having committed or having taken part in a terrorist offence or other serious criminal offence or regarding whom there are factual indications [...] to believe that they will commit a terrorist offence or other serious criminal offences" (Article 28). An ETIAS Screening Board composed of representatives from so-called ETIAS National Units and Europol, will serve as an advisory body to define and evaluate so-called risk indicators on a rolling basis.

Operational details	ETIAS will have the capacity to store personal data, travel documents, information on the intended stay, information related to criminal records, presence in conflict zones, country bans, or previous return decisions. The online application will cost €7 for applicants between 18 and 70 years old, providing a valid travel authorization for three years. Applicants may appeal if the authorization is refused. Carriers such as airlines, boat and bus companies are required to enrol into the ETIAS control system and verify travel authorizations prior to boarding. At any border crossing point, border guards will decide on the approval or refusal of entry based on a valid ETIAS authorization and a successful biometric registration for the EES. While eu-LISA develops and operates ETIAS, Frontex will be responsible for its central unit. The central unit includes the various application files and establishes screening rules in consultation with the ETIAS Screening Board.

ECRIS-TCN

Description	The European Criminal Record Information System on Third-Country Nationals (ECRIS-TCN) will allow authorities to store and process information on convicted non-EU citizens. ECRIS-TCN builds on ECRIS, an existing decentralized electronic system for the exchange of information on convicted EU citizens. Since 2012, ECRIS has enabled member states to notify each other about citizens' convictions or criminal proceedings. The European Commission proposed a comparable centralized system for third-country nationals in 2017, reaching an agreement with the Council and the Parliament in 2019. ECRIS-TCN was part of the "European Agenda on Security", which promoted increased information exchange among EU member states to safeguard security in Europe. ECRIS-TCN is intended to contribute to more efficient exchange within border management by fighting cross-border crime. It will allow authorities to not only identify the criminal records of a third-country national or a stateless person, but also to file requests for retrieving information on convictions. Its official objective is to provide

judges and prosecutors with access to the criminal records and histories of non-EU citizens. ECRIS-TCN plans furthermore to include data on dual nationals.

Operational details	ECRIS-TCN should technically operate like a hit/no hit search system. In accordance with interoperability, it stores and exchanges biographic data, fingerprints and facial images. Regulation (EU) 2019/816 defines various situations in which ETIAS can also be accessed by Eurojust (the EU agency for Criminal Justice Cooperation), Europol, or the so-called European Public Prosecutor's Office of the European Union (EPPO) (see EU 2019c).

Interoperability

Description	Interoperability is a large-scale IT project currently being developed by the eu-LISA Agency. Its legal specificities are enshrined in two legal regulations: (EU) 2019/817 on borders and visa, and (EU) 2019/818 on police and judicial cooperation, asylum and migration (EU 2019a, 2019b). Although the content of these regulatory texts is almost identical, they differ on judicial grounds because some countries are associated with Schengen but do not engage in judicial cooperation (for example, Switzerland or Iceland). Interoperability should allow the exchange of data across the six major databases in border, migration and visa management. Furthermore, it seeks to provide faster and facilitated access to the databases to authorized national authorities (that is, police and migration officials, visa authorities or border guards). Interoperability is repeatedly described as an EU response to a series of terrorist attacks in member states that occurred in 2016 and the migrant movements of 2015. Politicians and policy makers have linked these events to the existence of unconnected EU databases, insufficient data sharing on third-country nationals, identity fraud, and the existence of aliases in databases. Among the official objectives were the improvement of "effectiveness and efficiency of border checks at external borders", "the prevention and the combating of illegal immigration", and "a high level of security" (EU 2019a, Article 2). Furthermore, the interoperability regulations include legal provisions that facilitate national authorities to access and query Europol's data pool and Interpol's Stolen and Lost Travel Document database. The policy famously followed the recommendations developed by the so-called High-level Expert Group on Information Systems and Interoperability, a group established by the EC in 2016.
Technological components	The interoperability policy includes four main technological components. First, it has designed the European Search Portal (ESP), an interface for national authorities that enables harmonized and simultaneous query across all six systems (SIS II, VIS, Eurodac, EES, ETIAS and ECRIS-TCN). Second, it will introduce the shared Biometric Matching Service (sBMS), which underlies all IT systems as a data engine, thereby enabling authorities to query and cross-match biometric information. The sBMS entails a central infrastructure that replaces the respective communication infrastructures of other systems (SIS, VIS, Eurodac, EES and ECRIS-TCN) and enables searches with biometric data. Third, the Common Identity Repository (CIR) creates and stores individual data files for every person registered in at least one of the existing or future systems (due to previously established data formats, SIS II must be externally connected to the CIR). The CIR

represents a centralized data pool of a limited set of data extracted from one of the systems. It thus operates like a "book index" (Interview 10 with EU official, 2019) and represents interoperability's backbone. With its distinct storage capacity, the CIR on its own could represent a fully-fledged database. However, individual files are stored there only for the period in which the corresponding data is stored in the original system. The controversial conditions of access to CIR have been debated and are now outlined in Articles 20–22 of the interoperability regulations. For example, police authorities can access the repository once there "are reasonable grounds to believe that [its] consultation […] will contribute to the prevention, detection or investigation of terrorist offences or other serious criminal offences" (EU 2019a, Article 22). Lastly, the Multiple Identity Detector (MID) should create and store confirmation files. It is designed as an instrument for the automatic matching of queried identities against other systems—for example, whether a screened fingerprint in one system can be linked to multiple names in other systems. The MID must accordingly establish and contain different links, which can indicate any potential (mis)match of identity data in different systems. It must determine whether and how biometric information corresponds (correctly or incorrectly) to biographic identity (stored in the CIR) and confirms whether different identities of the same person exist in EU systems. National authorities are then tasked to further evaluate and act upon MID links.

List of Conducted Interviews and Sites of Participant Observation

Conducted Interviews

Interview 1 with eu–LISA official, 21/09/2018
Interview 2 with member state representative, 03/10/2018
Interview 3 with EU official, 18/10/2018
Interview 4 with EU official, 30/11/2018
Interview 5 with private consultant, 08/01/2019
Interview 6 with EU official, 04/03/2019
Interview 7 with member state representative, 11/03/2019
Interview 8 with member state representative, 15/03/2019
Interview 9 with EU official, 19/03/2019
Interview 10 with EU official, 26/04/2019
Interview 11 with EU official, 29/04/2019
Interview 12 with EU official, 29/04/2019
Interview 13 with EU official, 29/04/2019
Interview 14 with two EU officials, 30/04/2019
Interview 15 with member state representative, 27/05/2019
Interview 16 with EU official, 14/06/2019
Interview 17 with member state representative, 01/07/2019
Interview 18 with member state representative, 11/07/2019
Interview 19 with EU official, 18/03/2019
Interview 20 with member state representative, 24/03/2019
Interview 21 with EU official, 08/08/2019
Interview 22 with member of the European Parliament, 18/09/2019
Interview 23 with member of the European Parliament, 11/10/2019
Interview 24 with member state representative, 16/10/2019
Interview 25 with EU official, 21/10/2019
Interview 26 with member state representative, 31/10/2019
Interview 27 with EU official, 28/11/2019
Interview 28 with EU official, 29/11/2019

Sites of Participant Observation

OSCE conference "ID@Borders and Future of Travel", 10–11/04/2019, Vienna, Austria.

eu-LISA industry roundtable "Making EU Land and Sea Border Crossings Seamless and Secure—Operational Solutions", 24/04/2019, Bucharest, Romania.

eu-LISA annual conference "The New Information Architecture as a Driver for Efficiency and Effectiveness in Internal Security", 16/10/2019, Tallinn, Estonia.

eu-LISA industry roundtable "Towards Practical Implementation of the New JHA Information Architecture", 17/10/2019, Tallinn, Estonia.

Visionbox "Smart Borders explained: Air, Land and Sea—Travel Ecosystem", 30/09/2020, online.

eu-LISA industry roundtable "Data Quality and Interoperability: Addressing the Capability Gaps through Standardisation", 03–05/11/2020, online.

eu-LISA annual conference "Building Digital Resilience for the EU Justice and Home Affairs", 26/11/2020, online.

eu-LISA industry roundtable "Contactless Travel in Post-Covid Times: Enhancing the EU Security Ecosystems", 01–02/06/2021, online.

Notes

Chapter 1

[1] The relatively innocuous abbreviation "LISA" has been chosen in contrast to another infamous acronym associated with a European Union Agency, "FRONTEX". This latter acronym, with its rather martial connotations stemming from the French phrase for external borders, "frontières extérieures", and its practice of naming operations after Greek gods like Poseidon and Triton, has undoubtedly contributed to the Agency's notoriety and negative public image.

[2] The terms "Europe" and "European" can be understood in various geographical, regional, political, or cultural ways. Whenever I refer to "Europe" in this book, it will reference the political constitution of Schengen Europe and the borders of the EU as I seek to understand how these formations shape mobility and migration on the continent. I also use "European border regime" when referring to the actors, infrastructures, and practices involved in the bordering of Europe. Border regimes, as conceptualized by numerous scholars in critical migration and border studies, have emphasized the multiple (and often conflicting) interests, actors, institutions, practices, legal regulations, discourses, migratory movements, and material technologies that construct and shape borders. A regime thus denotes the always partial and fragmented field that involves numerous human and nonhuman elements. For an extended discussion about this notion, see, for example, Casas-Cortes et al. 2015; Eule, Loher, and Wyss 2018; Papadopoulos, Stephenson, and Tsianos 2008; Tsianos and Karakayali 2010.

[3] The statement is made by the former Executive Director Krum Garkov, who led eu-LISA for almost eight years. On 16 March 2023, the Agency's second Executive Director Agnès Diallo took office.

[4] For reviews on the development of the field of border studies, see, for example, *A Companion to Border Studies* (Wilson and Donnan 2016) or Chris Rumford's insightful article, "Theorizing Borders" (2006a).

[5] The idea of borderlands, for instance, points to the phenomena of whole countries or regions becoming zones of transition and no longer having territorial fixity (Balibar 2009, 2010; Rumford 2006b; Squire 2011). Even more widely cited is the concept of borderscapes, which is mobilized as an epistemic viewpoint for exploring the performances, practices, and discourses of borders—and their distinct spatial, temporal, and political dimensions—that uncover the hidden geographies and distributions of categories of belonging (see here for example Brambilla 2015; Dell'Agnese and Szary 2015; Rajaram and Grundy-Warr 2007).

[6] For an extended discussion on the biopolitical turn at the intersection of critical border studies and STS, see Trauttmansdorff (2022).

[7] In a widely recited passage, Foucault traces biopolitics as a form of governance back to the development of towns in the eighteenth century when the problem of regulating and

surveilling populations was first encountered. The objective of governance changed from being concerned with territorial domination to the challenge of managing the influx and circulation of populations: governance became a matter of "organizing circulation, eliminating its dangerous elements, making a division between good and bad circulation, and maximizing the good circulation by diminishing the bad" (2009, 18).

[8]   For an overview of these systems, see the Appendix. A system that is less relevant in the border regime and will not be addressed in this book it the so-called e-Codex system. eu-LISA has also begun operating this "e-Justice Communication via Online Data Exchange", which is the EU's flagship project to exchange judiciary data among member states.

[9]   There is no space here to dwell on the different meanings and implications of these very similar notions, or even on broader concepts such as digitization, although the latter has been done in more recent contributions by Glouftsios and Scheel (2021) and Witteborn (2022). For this book, I make pragmatic use of terms such as "digital borders" when referring to the large-scale border security databases in the EU.

[10]   Previous accounts on borders and migration which have emphasized this point in different ways include Bellanova and Glouftsios (2022a), Dijstelbloem (2017, 2021), Feldman (2012), Leese (2018), Pollozek and Passoth (2019), Tazzioli and Walters (2016), or Walters (2011).

[11]   Foucault elsewhere defines the apparatus as a dispositif consisting of "strategies of relations of forces supporting, and supported by types of knowledge" (Foucault in Rabinow 2003, 53). Bussolini (2010) points to this concept's anticipatory and logistical orientation in referring to its etymology: "Apparatus, or adparatus, from apparo in Latin, refers to a preparation or making ready for something: a furnishing, providing, or equipping. It has the sense of laying in sufficient supplies, provisions or instruments, of establishing a plan to deal with a situation by ensuring the proper supplies" (p. 96). Slota and Bowker's (2017) definition of infrastructure is also highly reminiscent of what Foucault's apparatus or *dispositif* aimed to unravel—"infrastructure," they argue, "is not so much a single thing as a bundle of heterogeneous things (standards, technological objects, administrative procedures […])—which involves both organizational work as well as technology" (p. 531).

[12]   Although now becoming highlighted by STS-influenced scholars on border and migration infrastructures, this aspect is still too often neglected (see Bellanova and Glouftsios 2022a; Dijstelbloem 2021; Glouftsios 2021; Graham and Thrift 2007; Sontowski 2018).

[13]   As Foucault (2009) notes, one of the core features of apparatuses is "that one works on the future" and a permanent preoccupation with anticipating and regulating an "indefinite series of events" (p. 20). The very idea, then, of defining security as a problem of managing populations is partly grounded in (re-)imagining the operations, strategies, and techniques that bring it into being as a new form of governmentality. Security, in Foucault's words, is the "ensemble formed by the institutions, procedures, analyses and reflections, the calculations and tactics that allow the exercise of this very specific albeit complex form of power, which has as its target population, political economy as its major form of knowledge, and apparatuses of security as its essential technical instrument" (Foucault 2009, 108). Scholars have often analyzed this central concern with the future in the so-called "war on terror" through the prism of risk (Amoore 2011; Aradau and van Munster 2013; Hall and Mendel 2012; Opitz and Tellmann 2015b).

[14]   A vast literature in STS has explored how technological and scientific innovation pursue and shape collective visions and ideals of larger social groups. They crystalize in collectively imagined futures that guide individuals and societies in organizing life and order and articulate "society's shared understanding of good and evil" (Jasanoff 2015a, 4). Similar things can be said of making material infrastructures (Aarden 2017; Anand, Appel, and

Gupta 2018; Fujimura 2003; Hetherington 2016; Larkin 2013). Ribes and Finholt (2009), for example, speak of "the long now" of material infrastructures that testify to the social desires and futures inscribed into their design or by continuing maintenance work to keep them alive. Imagination shapes infrastructuring processes such as the creation and design of large-scale technological systems, the construction of standards and interfaces, or the practices of classification through which societies envision the governing of subjects (Bowker and Star 1999; Scott 1998).

[15] By numbers provided only by the International Organization of Migration's Missing Migrants Project, there have been over 29,200 missing in the Mediterranean Sea since 2014; see https://missingmigrants.iom.int/region/mediterranean.

[16] Scholars like Taylor, Appadurai, and Anderson have acknowledged this in different ways by framing imagination as an "organized field of social practice". As Appadurai (2010) claimed, "no longer mere fantasy [...], no longer simple escape [...], no longer elite pastime [...], no longer mere contemplation", but a central component for the making of new worlds and global orders (p. 31). Likewise, Taylor (2004) anchors the imaginary as an emerging, underpinning *fait social* of collective social life in Western modernity. It does not merely mark out a set of ideas or beliefs, but rather "is what enables, through making sense of, the practices of a society" (p. 2). For Taylor, the imaginary of modernity becomes a socially accepted form of moral and social order, generating a natural sense of legitimacy for institutions such as the modern market economy, the public sphere, or the self-governing of people.

[17] Examples of this strand of work that seeks to capture the perpetual interplay between technology, politics, and society are plenty. They include concepts such as "technological imagination" to study how artistic or political movements such as the Italian futurists were created (Berghaus 2009), or "techno-scientific imaginaries" (Marcus 1995) to grapple with how social knowledges and the materiality of technoscience are mutually entangled. Prasad's concept of "technocultural imaginaries" (Prasad 2014) points to manifold narratives, desires, and material worlds that interweave the realities and (national) myths in techno-scientific developments. As a space of knowledge-making, laboratory activities, and technical expertise, techno-science is inevitably engrained in local cultures and hierarchical networks of power and administration. Similarly, the anthropologist Marcus (1995) described the "technoscientific imaginaries" to elaborate on "various kinds of scientific practice in their fully embedded social and cultural contexts" (p. 4).

[18] Initially, the modern nation-state has been perceived as a primary unit of analysis to trace the emergence of imaginaries (Jasanoff and Kim 2009, 2013). Nations were hereby not conceived as analytical black-boxes or containers, but rather as dynamic formations that needed to be continually (re)imagined and performed along with the projected visions of progress. STS has produced robust literature on national imaginaries, which are particularly germane to the study of large-scale technological innovation operating "as sites of contemporary state-making and societal reconfiguration" (Pfotenhauer and Jasanoff 2017, 788). But sociotechnical imaginaries are also reservoirs of power that are mobilizable by a myriad of collectives on different scales. They can solidify on a global level (Miller 2015), manifest on regional scales, or be translated from supranational into national contexts (Baur 2023; Mager 2017); they can also be carried and promoted by smaller "vanguard" groups (Hilgartner 2015)—for instance, by commercial and industrial collectives (Sadowski and Bendor 2019), professional experts (Ruppert 2018), and global elites (Schiølin 2020).

[19] The conception of imaginaries thereby differs from ideologies in so far that they do not necessarily represent entrenched, explicit systems of ideas and ideals. Nor do they

represent the distorted interests of the people or simply articulate false consciousness. The imaginary forms a potentially powerful, productive quality because it is (often emotionally) embedded into social practice and (tacitly) encoded into scientific production, material infrastructure, and technological innovation.

[20] As reported by the nonprofit organization Statewatch in 2022, eu-LISA was given roughly €1.5 billion between 2014 and 2020 to spend on private contracts and fund the construction of these new systems (Jones, Valdivia, and Kilpatrick 2022). At the 2022 conference organized by eu-LISA, the Commissioner for Home Affairs, Ylva Johansson described the Agency's growth as a transformation from a "start-up agency at the edge of Europe to the digital heart of the Schengen area in a mere 10 years" (see its report https://eulisaconference.eu/report-2022/#OpeningRemarks). See also Chapter 3, for a brief analysis of the usage of this metaphoric language.

[21] I should mention that I was not granted access to the highly protected site in Sankt Johann im Pongau, Austria, where eu-LISA runs a business continuity site for its IT systems.

[22] Participant lists usually revealed the wide range of actors and institutions that take part in these events, such as EC officials, parliamentary representatives, delegates of foreign and interior ministries, diplomats, representatives of agencies such as the EDPS or FRA, officials from eu-LISA, Frontex, and EUAA (formerly EASO), industry actors, brokers, consultants and IT companies, and researchers.

[23] All quotes from interviews in this book are either in the original English or translated into English by the author.

Chapter 2

[1] Acknowledgement: this chapter is a modified version of a research article written and published together with Ulrike Felt, in *Science, Technology, and Human Values* 48 (3), available online: https://journals.sagepub.com/doi/full/10.1177/01622439211057523.

[2] See also Chapter 5 and Appendices for a description of how the use of databases has significantly expanded, that is, by gradually extending access opportunities to law-enforcement authorities.

[3] While Tallinn (Estonia) became the city of eu-LISA's headquarters, French authorities insisted that Strasbourg remained the operational data centre. It had previously hosted both the central systems of SIS II and the Visa Information System. The EC in turn ensured that many of its staff were transferred to the agency, while the member states took the opportunity to recommend their own national bureaucrats to the agency (see also Chapter 4).

[4] This quarterly was published by the International Border Management and Technologies Association, which describes itself as a "not for profit international nongovernmental organization" bringing together experts, practitioners, policy makers, and technology providers (see http://www.ibmata.org/about/).

[5] The eu-LISA pilot study report ultimately claimed that a large-scale biometric system (such as the EES) and its comprehensive enrolment at the Schengen external borders were, in principle, "feasible (in terms of accuracy, effectiveness and impact)" (eu-LISA 2015b, 12).

Second Interlude

[1] "Neue Macht für die obskurste Behörde der EU" by Jannis Brühl, available at https://www.sueddeutsche.de/digital/fluechtlinge-eurodac-eu-datenbanken-migration-ueberwachung-kriminalitaet-1.4219070, accessed 4 April 2023.

[2] The video can be found online at https://www.youtube.com/watch?v=Nz3kVrlwcnc, accessed 5 April 2023.

3 My own translation, quoted from Jannis Brühl's article "Neue Macht für die obskurste Behörde der EU", available at https://www.sueddeutsche.de/digital/fluechtlinge-euro dac-eu-datenbanken-migration-ueberwachung-kriminalitaet-1.4219070.

Chapter 3

1 On this perspective, see, for example, Korn et al. (2019) who argue that infrastructuring offers a "shift of perspective from a structuralist or system theory-led approach that attempts to characterize systems as entities to a practice theory-inspired view on phenomena as results of systematically linked and synchronised practices" (p. 17).

2 The video is available on eu-LISA's YouTube channel. See https://www.youtube.com/watch?v=F50ecVl8Chw, Min. 00:13–00:24, accessed 5 April 2023.

3 This presents an opportunity for smaller states to participate and act alongside more powerful states, such as Germany and France, and alongside big industry players too who manufacture the devices and systems of digital bordering.

4 See https://estonianworld.com/technology/eus-it-agency-sets-up-in-estonia/, last accessed 5 April 2023. As reported by the online magazine *Estonian World*, the state had promoted its candidacy for the agency seat long before any draft EU regulation for eu-LISA was presented in 2011. Another magazine called *The Baltic Course* quoted a former Minister of the Interior on the "symbolic significance" of building the Agency's headquarters in Tallinn: "This reinforces the image of Estonia as [an] IT capable state [...]. It is no less important that the strategic planning team will be located here who will handle the IT systems development work" (*The Baltic Course*, 11 December 2014). See http://www.baltic-course.com/eng/real_estate/?doc=100028&ins_print&output=d, last accessed 5 April 2023.

5 Mariam Fraser (2009) discusses this principle in her reflection on Whitehead's concept of the event (and in conversation with Latour, Stengers, and Deleuze). She notes that "the singularity of an entity is derived from a multiplicity of diverse elements that are inextricably conjoined [...] by way of prehensive relations grasped in the unity of an event" (p. 66).

6 To shed light on both the materiality and movability of borders, Dijstelbloem (2021) deploys the notion of "infrastructural compromise", stressing that they emerge from all kinds of sociotechnical mediations in the context of border security. He likewise holds that compromises concern the "transformation of conflicting requirements and opposing views into a workable composition by adding new elements, foregrounding certain aspects, and backgrounding others" (p. 32).

7 Accordingly, the first official to lead eu-LISA's operational centre was a member of the French police.

8 This "magic mountain", as one interviewee called it, had housed a (previously secret) war room called "Einsatzzentrale Basisraum", designed in the 1970s after the experiences of the Prague Spring when Soviet troops occupied the Czechoslovak Socialist Republic. Feeling threatened by a potential Soviet attack from the east, Austria's political leaders decided to set up an emergency government room in the event that Vienna, the capital, was overrun by Soviet troops.

9 Usually, only individual components or applications need to be switched to the Austrian site and operated remotely from Strasbourg. It is not clear how often these scenarios take place. According to one of my interlocutors, they occur frequently and, at times, for longer periods (Interview 7, 2019).

10 As scholars have argued, clearing data in the bordering process not only involves complex chains of actions that can incrementally improve data quality but also means sorting out different approaches to what data quality should actually mean (Pelizza 2016b; Pollozek 2020).

11 Translated from the interviewee's German use of this expression: "Wer schlechte Daten in das System eingibt, muss mit ihnen rechnen".

12 This is also one of the reasons why a significant amount of repair work must be outsourced to external contractors: "You know, if you need to fix a bug, then already we would ask the contractor to do it. If it's more coordination, you know, some issue which is not a technical problem, [...] there can be many questions that a help desk needs to reply [to] from member states, too. So, the bulk of the work is for us, but if there are some technical, real[ly] technical details, then we again involve the industry. But these are the same contracts. So it's not only for building the system but also for maintaining it and fixing it" (Interview 27 with an Agency official, 2019).

13 Recently, Eileen Murphy Maguire (2023) has convincingly argued that such *service management* of IT systems has contributed to establishing the legitimacy and authority of the eu-LISA Agency in the EU.

14 See also this radio interview with an agency representative from 10 October 2020, entitled "Eu-LISA: Strasbourg, le cœur numérique de l'espace Schengen." Available at https://rcf. fr/actualite/le-grand-invite-alsace?episode=51744, last accessed 5 April 2023. Likewise, eu-LISA's ten-year Anniversary Conference on 13 October 2022, was titled "10 years as the Digital Heart of Schengen".

15 A range of contributions has studied the infrastructural making of Europe (Badenoch and Fickers 2010b; Kaiser and Schot 2014; Misa and Schot 2005; Schipper and Schot 2011). At the same time, contrary to Scott's hegemonic role of the state, these works have made clear that this process has been shaped by a multiplicity of both state and non-state actors and that "several co-existing Europe-oriented forms of governance overlapped, competed, or sometimes reinforced each other" (Schipper and Schot 2011, 252).

Chapter 4

1 For more information on the role of private actors working with eu-LISA, see the exceptional report on the Agency's network of lobbying and industrial groups by Lemberg-Pedersen, Hansen, and Halpern (2020).

2 A wide range of contributions has been made to the smart border literature. See, for example, Amoore, Marmura, and Salter (2008); Bigo (2011); Côté-Boucher (2008); Leese (2016); Sparke (2006); and Vukov and Sheller (2013), among others. On Europe specifically, Tsianos and Kuster (2016) describe the smart border as an "instrument that enables the deterritorialization of the external European border and potentially extending it to the whole Schengen area" (p. 236). Jeandesboz (2016b) argues that smart borders enhance the mass dataveillance of mobility while promoting the reconcilement between intensified securitization (mobility control) and the increasing imperatives of the global economy (mobility facilitation) (see also Leese 2016). In similar terms, Bigo (2011) contends that smart borders officially foster speed of movement, mobilized as an important economic resource, while at the same time reinforcing control and the banishment of those classified as risky subjects. Finally, Sontowski (2018) identifies this dilemma as one of the reasons smart borders reproblematize "cross-border movements and their control on the level of [... their] various temporalities" (p. 2734).

3 See the Appendix for additional details about these systems.

4 On this point, see, for instance, Scheel (2017) who notes that most illegalized migrants in the EU arrive by legal means on a Schengen visa and subsequently become "illegal" upon its expiration.

5 Both the EES and ETIAS implementations were planned to be completed in 2023, but, at the time of writing, are already expected to be delayed.

[6] According to Torpey (1998, 1999), embracement encompasses the various means used by modern states to expropriate the "legitimate means of movement", most notably by the invention of the passport. Expropriation (used in reference to Marx and Weber) describes the historical practice of modern states gradually appropriating the right to move from individuals and private entities, particularly across international boundaries.

[7] In addition, there is usually a speaker from the US, Canada or Australia at eu-LISA roundtables. They serve as an important gateway to the market for transatlantic stakeholders. Generally, there is a long list of examples of conferences and policy meetings at which eu-LISA itself is listed as a speaker and/or participant. This includes, for example, the "Border Security 2021" summit, a conference in the framework of an EU-funded project on facial recognition called the "European Security Summit". The agency's participation in these events is usually listed in digital newsletters under the rubric "Happenings", available at https://eulisa.europa.eu/SiteAssets/Bits-and-Bytes/002.aspx, accessed 5 April 2023.

[8] For example, at an online conference during the COVID-19 pandemic, eu-LISA hired BBC World moderator Joe Lynam for welcome remarks and moderation. This may seem like an attempt to break with routine by employing the services of a professional event moderator, but, in fact, it reinforces this formality, giving a strong impression that the content of the speeches and discourse is less important than its form.

[9] To further illustrate this point, we can refer to an online interview with eu-LISA's former Executive Director, conducted by eu-LISA and published on its website, entitled "A Leader of a Successful Organization Knows that Progress Never Stops". Here, Garkov emphasizes the importance of managerial skills and discusses his management background. Available at https://www.eulisa.europa.eu/Newsroom/News/Pages/Leader-Successful-Organisation-Progress-Never-Stops.aspx, accessed 4 April 2023. Likewise, eu-LISA's new Director Agnès Diallo was introduced as someone with managerial capacities and ties to the industry and consultancies. Diallo served, for instance, as Vice-President of IN Groupe, a well-known French company specialized in document security and had worked for the consultancy McKinsey & Company. See also https://www.eulisa.eur opa.eu/Newsroom/PressRelease/Pages/Agn%C3%A8s-Diallo-takes-office-as-Execut ive-Director-of-eu-LISA.aspx, accessed 5 April 2023.

[10] The business card competition also reminds one of Feldman's observations (2014) at a policy meeting, at which a teddy bear was presented to the host of the upcoming conference meeting. For Feldman, these acts must invoke "Olympic team spirit" (p. 49), but also essentially conceal the general lack thereof.

[11] The first statement was originally written by the sociologist Daniel Bell. The second was taken from Marc Benioff, US investor and owner of the cloud computing company Salesforce.

[12] On the privatization processes in border regimes, see for example Baird (2018); Lemberg-Pedersen (2013, 2018); Binder (2020); Lemberg-Pedersen, Hansen, and Halpern (2020).

[13] In this instance, the term "European" is used as a casual way to describe the borders of the Schengen space, which are repeatedly used metaphorically to invoke the greater political project of a united Europe. See also earlier, in endnote 2 of Chapter 1.

[14] A widespread assumption at all roundtables and conferences—notably before the outbreak of the pandemic—was that global flows of mobility will inevitably increase. Unsurprisingly, the tourism sector was predicted to become one of the fastest-growing sectors of state economies. Seen as a highly profitable but relatively "unproblematic" category of mobility, it would thereafter demand speedier and simplified border checks. Compare this to the argument of an Agency representative who claimed: "[Y]ou cannot [...] separate it [anymore ...]. You always will have to look to the needs of border management and

security. There [are] always going to be different business needs for each one [...] because one without the other, it doesn't exist anymore" (Interview 12, 2019).

15 Similarly, Torpey (1998) uses the term "sheriff's deputies" to describe private entities' participation in controlling movement.

16 These enrolment processes are not simple. The overall initiative of smart borders depends, to a certain degree, on the private actors that are part of this infrastructural experimentation. One eu-LISA official argued that the "implementation [of smart borders] is not only in the hands of the agency but requires [a] joint effort, [...] the integration of all those stakeholders" (field note, Visionbox online event, 30 September 2020). Another representative even admitted that "to be honest, I don't know how it's going to work [...]. I have some doubts that any train—you know—manager [conductor] is able to check a third-country national. I mean, I hope it will work, but it will be definitely very hard in the beginning" (Interview 28 with EU official, 2019).

17 In her article on nuclear language, which is my main inspiration for the reflections here, Cohn raises an important point about how abstractions and sexual imagery can fashion a language of nuclear power that disguises the messy, uncontrollable and destructive reality of nuclear weapons.

18 For a discussion on the increasing logistification of migration and border regimes, see, for example, Moritz Altenried and colleagues (2017, 2018), who see the emergence of this rationality as a new attempt at governing migration to resolve a central contradiction between states' economic need for (migrant) labour and the politico-cultural logic of shielding nation-states from foreigners. Accordingly, theories and practices of managing migration would be increasingly plagued by a "delivery rationality" and the fantasy of a "just-in-time" and "to-the-point" migration that promotes the integration of labour mobility into national capitalist economies (2018, 299).

19 On the notion of platformization as an attractive way to signal state-of-the-art thinking in infrastructural and economic terms and as an increasingly dominant model in media and data environments, see Helmond (2015) and Srnicek (2017).

20 In addition to its connotations in biology, the notion of ecosystems has previously been applied to corporate strategies. See, for example, James F. Moore's (1998) early article on the rise of a "new corporate form": ecosystems are defined as "communities of customers, suppliers, lead producers, and other stakeholders interacting with one another to produce goods and services and coevolving capabilities" (p. 168).

21 For the meeting, eu-LISA also drafted a report by the joint advisory group on the EES that depicted various scenarios at these different locations and how borders were to be crossed there (eu-LISA 2019d).

22 The practice of "timeboxing" in the implementation of new, large-scale IT systems is a widely recognized, problematic practice in the EU that has led to wholly unrealistic timelines for these implementation plans.

Chapter 5

1 Acknowledgement: This chapter is derived in part from an article in *Critical Policy Studies*, 15 November 2022, copyright Taylor & Francis, available online: https://www.tandfonl ine.com/doi/full/10.1080/19460171.2022.2147851

2 The EU ultimately adopted two legal regulations on interoperability in May 2019.

3 Interoperability consists of four main components. The shared Biometric Matching Service (sBMS) underlies all central IT systems in the EU as a joint "engine" that queries and cross-matches data based on biometric templates, such as fingerprints and facial images. The Common Identity Repository (CIR) creates individual files (of extracted data) for every person that is registered in at least one of the databases. The Multiple

Identity Detector (MID) seeks to automatically check queried identities against other databases (for example, whether a screened fingerprint can be linked to multiple names). The European Search Portal is envisioned as a search engine/interface for harmonizing national accesses. For a detailed description of the components, see the Appendices.

4   Subsequent documents up until 2015 show only a few notable references to interoperability, or in relation to a future Entry-Exit Program. The trajectory was set out in *Stronger and Smarter Information Systems* (EC 2016a) as well as in another Communication called *Enhancing security in a world of mobility: improved information exchange in the fight against terrorism and stronger external borders* (EC 2016b).

5   The 2019 regulations referred to the HLEG as a prime case for which "it was necessary and technically feasible to work towards practical solutions for interoperability" (EU 2019a, 3).

6   The parliamentarian Cornelia Ernst of the Left in the European Parliament stated, "There evolves a huge, super database with data of third-country nationals [...]. Welcome in the brave new world!" (See https://www.europarl.europa.eu/doceo/document/CRE-8-2019-03-27-ITM-024_EN.html?redirect; accessed 12 April 2023; own translation).

7   This reasoning was a sort of "legal trick," as one interviewee admitted, ironically remarking, "to me, it's a database [...] but that's something you are not supposed to talk about—okay [*laughing*]?' (Interview 6 with EU official, 2019).

8   The votes of the S&D Group provided the EPP with a majority to pass its "flagship file" as official EU law in May 2019.

9   Matching and verifying can be seen as a series of testing procedures around which a "true" identity must be constructed; identification basically becomes a test based on the "comparison of one body with a multitude of bodies" (Schinkel 2020, 560).

10   A related problem is data quality, another widely acknowledged source of uncertainty. The report highlights that the issue of "insufficient data and poor data quality" is well-known and will remain so because "interoperability in itself does not lead to improvement in the completeness, accuracy and reliability of data" (LIBE 2018, 51).

Chapter 6

1   Scholars of valuation have insisted that the study of justification contributes to a better understanding of contemporary transformations, such as digitization, quantification or neoliberalization (Lamont 2012; Mau 2019; Stark 2009).

2   The definition of "repertoires of justification" stems from the vast literature of Valuation Studies, which usually highlight legitimate orders or justificatory regimes. To describe this "project and innovation repertoire", I draw particularly on Boltanski and Chiapello's *The New Spirit of Capitalism* (2018 [1999]), in which they thoughtfully trace the various projectivist narratives, ideologies and values. A comprehensive valuography (Dussauge, Helgesson, and Lee 2015) of the digital border regime cannot be offered here, but would certainly have to explore the multiple sets of justifications, values and normative assumptions in the ongoing expansion of border databases. It would thus include several different repertoires of justification, such as a security repertoire, an economic or market repertoire, an industrial repertoire. Such valuography would also have to elaborate on the implicit tensions, inconsistencies and contradictions when repertoires contradict each other.

3   Accordingly, these are also the actors who mobilize this repertoire of justification most visibly and frequently. It remains less frequently used by actors such as national delegates or operators who are concerned with adapting their practices to new legislation or who must manage IT systems on the ground.

4   This is reminiscent of Gregory Feldman's useful remarks (2015, 53–84) about the relationship between "activity" and "connectivity" in neoliberal societies and the process of the atomization of the individual that this results in.

5   There are numerous examples in the social sciences that explore simplification and abstraction in a variety of contexts but especially concerning the relationship between science, technology and modernity. For instance, Latour (1986) describes the flattening of the modern world, enabled by the creation of immutable mobiles—that is, simplified technoscientific representations that make it possible to disseminate knowledge and draw actors together at a distance. The works of Bowker and Star (1999), Hacking (1990) or Porter (2020 [1995]) discuss how people's realities, looks, personal attributes or behaviours are translated into the tractable language of numbers and comparable categories and, in turn, allow modern institutions to pursue their business of ordering. Compare this also to Busch's (2011, 116–117) observation of how standards are intimately connected to power and that simplification is used often as a less pejorative term than standardization. In an early account, Star (1983) states that technoscientific work entails simplification: "Scientific work involves the representation of chaos in an orderly fashion" (p. 205).

6   See Chapter 4 for a comprehensive discussion about sanitization, referring to Carol Cohn's work.

7   In this report by the Immigrant Defense Project's Surveillance, Tech & Immigration Policing Project and the Transnational Institute, Aizeki et al. (2021) observe how the rhetoric of smart borders has been broadly embraced by both the Democratic party and moderate Republicans—as if smart borders represent a humane response to border insecurity and an alternative to former US President Donald Trump's hardline stance on immigration and his obsession with "The Wall" along the US–Mexico border. In short, "there is a belief that a 'smart' border—the expansive use of surveillance and monitoring technologies including cameras, drones, biometrics, and motion sensors—offers a humane alternative […]" (p. 4).

8   Arendt (2017 [1948]) makes this observation about totalitarian ideology that must constantly free itself from individual reason, factuality and experience in an attempt to establish and verify its fiction against the odds of reality and its own inconsistencies. Accordingly, she claims, "Factuality itself depends for its continued existence upon the existence of the nontotalitarian world" (p. 508). In this sense, individuals are expected to fully conform to totalitarian rule, which seeks to eliminate human spontaneity and individual responsibility. For Arendt, the concentration and extermination camps were the ultimate consequences of the totalitarian quest for complete domination, where its beliefs and ideology had to be enforced with the requisite terror. While I do not want to assess the general validity of Arendt's claims with regard to the National Socialists' murderous programme of annihilation, we should also note her use of the metaphor of the laboratory to describe "the ghastly experiment of eliminating, under scientifically controlled conditions, spontaneity itself as an expression of human behavior […]" (pp. 578–579).

9   See, for example, the report "Death by Rescue" published by the Forensic Architecture project. Available at https://forensic-architecture.org/investigation/death-by-rescue-the-lethal-effects-of-non-assistance-at-sea, accessed 7 March 2023.

Chapter 7

1   See, for example, https://blog.ucsusa.org/derrick-jackson/omicron-in-blackface-racist-us-travel-ban-scapegoats-africa/, accessed 5 April 2022.

2   See Picum's report on their website, https://picum.org/covid-19-undocumented-migrants-europe/, accessed 5 April 2022.

Appendices

1   Statistical data that are used for this overview are accessible on eu-LISA's official website. See www.eu-LISA.europa.eu.

References

Aarden, Erik. 2017. "Projecting and Producing 'Usefulness' of Biomedical Research Infrastructures; or Why the Singapore Tissue Network Closed." *Science and Public Policy* 44 (6): 753–762. doi:10.1093/scipol/scx010.

Adams, Vincanne, Michelle Murphy, and Adele E. Clarke. 2009. "Anticipation: Technoscience, Life, Affect, Temporality." *Subjectivity* 28 (1): 246–265. doi:10.1057/sub.2009.18.

Aden, Hartmut. 2020. "Interoperability Between EU Policing and Migration Databases: Risks for Privacy." *European Public Law* 26 (1): 93–108.

Adey, Peter. 2012. "Borders, Identification and Surveillance. New Regimes of Border Control." In *Routledge Handbook of Surveillance Studies*, edited by Kevin D. Haggerty and David Lyon, 193–200. London: Routledge.

Aizeki, By Mizue, Geoffrey Boyce, Todd Miller, Joseph Nevins, and Miriam Ticktin. 2021. *Smart Borders or a Humane World?*. https://www.tni.org/files/publication-downloads/smart_borders_humane_world_2021.pdf.

Akrich, Madeleine. 1992. "The De-Scription of Technical Objects." In *Shaping Technology/Building Society. Studies in Sociotechnical Change*, edited by W.E. Bijker and John Law, 205–224. Cambridge: MIT Press.

Allen, William L., and Bastian A. Vollmer. 2018. "Clean Skins: Making the e-Border Security Assemblage." *Environment and Planning D: Society and Space* 36 (1): 23–39. doi:10.1177/0263775817722565.

Altenried, Moritz. 2019. "On the Last Mile: Logistical Urbanism and the Transformation of Labour." *Work Organisation, Labour and Globalisation* 13 (1): 114–129. doi:10.13169/workorgalaboglob.13.1.0114.

Altenried, Moritz, Manuela Bojadžijev, Leif Höfler, Sandro Mezzadra, and Mira Wallis, eds. 2017. *Logistische Grenzlandschaften. Das Regime Mobiler Arbeit Nach Dem Sommer Der Migration*. Münster: Unrast.

Altenried, Moritz, Manuela Bojadžijev, Leif Höfler, Sandro Mezzadra, and Mira Wallis, eds. 2018. "Logistical Borderscapes: Politics and Mediation of Mobile Labor in Germany after the 'Summer of Migration.'" *South Atlantic Quarterly* 117 (2): 291–312. doi:10.1215/00382876-4374845.

Amelung, Nina, Cristiano Gianolla, Olga Solovova, and Joana Sousa Ribeiro. 2020. "Technologies, Infrastructures and Migrations: Material Citizenship Politics." *Citizenship Studies* 24 (5): 1–20. doi:10.1080/13621025.2020.1784636.

Amelung, Nina, Rafaela Granja, and Helena Machado. 2020. *Modes of Bio-Bordering: The Hidden (Dis)Integration of Europe*. Gateway East, Singapore: Palgrave Macmillan UK.

Amoore, Louise. 2006. "Biometric Borders: Governing Mobilities in the War on Terror." *Political Geography* 25 (3): 336–351. doi:10.1016/j.polgeo.2006.02.001.

Amoore, Louise. 2011. "Data Derivatives: On the Emergence of a Security Risk Calculus for Our Times." *Theory, Culture & Society* 28 (6): 24–43. doi:10.1177/0263276411417430.

Amoore, Louise. 2021. "The Deep Border." *Political Geography*, November. doi:10.1016/j.polgeo.2021.102547.

Amoore, Louise, Stephen Marmura, and Mark B. Salter. 2008. "Editorial: Smart Borders and Mobilities: Spaces, Zones, Enclosures." *Surveillance and Society* 5 (2): 96–101. doi:10.24908/ss.v5i2.3429.

Anand, Nikhil, Hannah Appel, and Akhil Gupta, eds. 2018. *The Promise of Infrastructure*. Durham, NC/London: Duke University Press.

Anderson, Benedict. 1991. *Imagined Communities: Reflections on the Origin and Spread of Nationalism*. Revised ed. London/New York: Verso.

Andersson, Ruben. 2016. "Hardwiring the Frontier? The Politics of Security Technology in Europe's 'Fight against Illegal Migration.'" *Security Dialogue* 47 (1): 22–39. doi:10.1177/0967010615606044.

Appadurai, Arjun. 2010. *Modernity at Large: Cultural Dimensions of Globalization*. Minneapolis, MN: University of Minnesota Press.

Appadurai, Arjun. 2013. *The Future as Cultural Fact: Essays on the Global Condition*. 1. publ. London: Verso.

Aradau, Claudia, and Rens van Munster. 2013. *Politics of Catastrophe: Genealogies of the Unknown*. London: Routledge.

Aradau, Claudia, and Martina Tazzioli. 2020. "Biopolitics Multiple: Migration, Extraction, Subtraction." *Millennium: Journal of International Studies* 48 (2): 198–220. doi:10.1177/0305829819889139.

Aradau, Claudia, and Emma McCluskey. 2022. "Making digital surveillance unacceptable? Security, democracy, and the political sociology of disputes." *International Political Sociology* 16 (1): 1–19. doi:10.1093/ips/olab024.

Arendt, Hannah. 2017. *The Origins of Totalitarianism*. Milton Keynes: Penguin Books.

Asdal, Kristin. 2015. "What Is the Issue? The Transformative Capacity of Documents." *Distinktion* 16 (1): 74–90. doi:10.1080/1600910X.2015.1022194.

Askew, Joshua. 2023. " 'Mass Surveillance, Automated Suspicion, Extreme Power': How Tech Is Shaping EU Borders." *Euronews.Next*, 6 April. https://www.euronews.com/next/2023/04/06/mass-surveillance-automated-suspicion-extreme-power-how-tech-is-shaping-the-eus-borders.

Baar, Huub van. 2017. "Evictability and the Biopolitical Bordering of Europe." *Antipode* 49 (1): 212–230. doi:10.1111/anti.12260.

Badenoch, Alexander. 2010. "Myths of the European Network: Constructions of Cohesion in Infrastructure Maps." In *Materializing Europe. Transnational Infrastructures and the Project of Europe*, edited by Alexander Badenoch and Andreas Fickers, 47–77. Hampshire: Palgrave Macmillan.

Badenoch, Alexander, and Andreas Fickers. 2010a. "Introduction. Europe Materializing? Toward a Transnational History of European Infrastructures." In *Materializing Europe. Transnational Infrastructures and the Project of Europe*, edited by Alexander Badenoch and Andreas Fickers, 1–26. Hampshire: Palgrave Macmillan.

Badenoch, Alexander, and Andreas Fickers, eds. 2010b. *Materializing Europe. Transnational Infrastructures and the Project of Europe*. Hampshire: Palgrave Macmillan. doi:10.1017/CBO9781107415324.004.

Baird, Theodore. 2018. "Interest Groups and Strategic Constructivism: Business Actors and Border Security Policies in the European Union." *Journal of Ethnic and Migration Studies* 44 (1): 118–136. doi:10.1080/1369183X.2017.1316185.

Balibar, Étienne. 2002. *Politics and the Other Scene*. London/New York: Verso. doi:10.1177/030981680608800115.

Balibar, Etienne. 2009. "Europe as Borderland." *Environment and Planning D: Society and Space* 27 (2): 190–215. doi:10.1068/d13008.

Balibar, Etienne. 2010. "At the Borders of Citizenship: A Democracy in Translation?" *European Journal of Social Theory* 13 (3): 315–322. doi:10.1177/1368431010371751.

Barry, Andrew. 2001. *Political Machines: Governing a Technological Society*. Oxford: The Athlone Press. doi:10.5040/9781474213110.

Barry, Andrew. 2006. "Technological Zones." *Journal of Asian and African Studies* 41 (3): 239–253. doi:10.1016/j.bbapap.2005.10.001.

Bauman, Richard, and Charles L. Briggs. 1990. "Poetics And Performance As Critical Perspectives On Language And Social Life." *Annual Review of Anthropology* 19 (1): 59–88. doi:10.1146/annurev.anthro.19.1.59.

Baur, Andreas. 2023. "European Dreams of the Cloud: Imagining Innovation and Political Control." *Geopolitics*: 1–25. doi:10.1080/14650045.2022.2151902.

Bayer, Florian, and Ulrike Felt. 2019. "Embracing the 'Atomic Future' in Post–World War II Austria." *Technology and Culture* 60 (1): 165–191. doi:10.1353/tech.2019.0005.

Beck, Ulrich. 1995. *Ecological Politics in an Age of Risk*. Cambridge, UK: Polity Press.

Beer, David. 2009. "Power through the Algorithm? Participatory Web Cultures and the Technological Unconscious." *New Media and Society* 11 (6): 985–1002. doi:10.1177/1461444809336551.

Bellanova, Rocco, and Georgios Glouftsios. 2022a. "Controlling the Schengen Information System (SIS II): The Infrastructural Politics of Fragility and Maintenance." *Geopolitics* 27 (1): 160–184. doi:10.1080/14650045.2020.1830765.

Bellanova, Rocco, and Georgios Glouftsios. 2022b. "Formatting European Security Integration through Database Interoperability." *European Security* 31 (3): 454–474. doi:10.1080/09662839.2022.2101886.

Bello, Valeria. 2022. "The Spiralling of the Securitisation of Migration in the EU: From the Management of a 'Crisis' to a Governance of Human Mobility?" *Journal of Ethnic and Migration Studies* 48 (6). Taylor & Francis: 1327–1344. doi:10.1080/1369183X.2020.1851464.

Benjamin, Ruha. 2019. *Race after Technology: Abolitionist Tools for the New Jim Code*. Cambridge: Polity.

Benjamin, Walter. 2002. *The Arcades Project*. Cambridge, MA/London: The Belknap Press of Harvard University Press.

Berezin, Mabel. 1997. *Making the Fascist Self. The Political Culture of Interwar Italy*. Ithaca: Cornell University Press.

Berghaus, Günter, ed. 2009. *Futurism and the Technological Imagination*. Amsterdam/New York: Rodopi.

Bigo, Didier. 2011. "Freedom and Speed in Enlarged Borderzones." In *The Contested Politics of Mobility. Borderzones and Irregularity*, edited by Vicki Squire, 31–50. London/New York: Routledge, Taylor & Francis Group.

Bigo, Didier. 2014. "The (in)Securitization Practices of the Three Universes of EU Border Control: Military/Navy – Border Guards/Police – Database Analysts." *Security Dialogue* 45 (3): 209–225. doi:10.1177/0967010614530459.

Bigo, Didier. 2020. "Interoperability: A Political Technology for the Datafication of the Field of EU Internal Security?" In *The Routledge Handbook of Critical European Studies*, edited by Didier Bigo, Thomas Diez, Evangelos Fanoulis, Ben Rosamond, and Yannis A. Stivachtis, 400–417. Abingdon/New York: Routledge. doi:10.4324/9780429491306-26.

Bigo, Didier, and Elspeth Guild. 2005. "Policing at a Distance: Schengen Visa Policies." In *Controlling Frontiers: Free Movement Into and Within Europe*, edited by Didier Bigo and Elspeth Guild, 233–263. Abingdon/New York: Routledge. doi:10.4324/9781315259321-8.

Binder, Clemens. 2020. "Developing Future Borders. The Politics of Security Research and Emerging Technologies in Border Security." In *Emerging Security Technologies and EU Governance. Actors, Practices and Processes*, edited by Antonio Calcara, Raluca Csernatoni, and Chantal Lavallée, 148–163. London: Routledge.

Bojadžijev, Manuela. 2019. "Die Logistik Der Migration." In *Konfliktfeld Fluchtmigration*, edited by Reinhard Johler and Jan Lange, 31–48. Bielefeld: transcript-Verlag. doi:10.14361/9783839447666-003.

Boltanski, Luc, and Eve Chiapello. 2005. "The New Spirit of Capitalism." *International Journal of Politics, Culture and Society* 18 (3–4): 161–188. doi:10.1007/s10767-006-9006-9.

Boltanski, Luc, and Eve Chiapello. 2006. *On Justification. Economies of Worth.* Princeton, NJ: Princeton University Press.

Boltanski, Luc, and Eve Chiapello. 2018. *The New Spirit of Capitalism.* London/New York: Verso.

Boltanski, Luc, and Laurent Thévenot. 2000. "The Reality of Moral Expectations: A Sociology of Situated Judgement." *Philosophical Explorations* 3 (3): 208–231. doi:10.1080/13869790008523332.

Borrelli, Lisa Marie, Annika Lindberg, and Anna Wyss. 2022. "States of Suspicion: How Institutionalised Disbelief Shapes Migration Control Regimes." *Geopolitics* 27 (4): 1025–1041. doi:10.1080/14650045.2021.2005862.

Bosma, Esmé, Marieke De Goede, and Polly Pallister-Wilkins. 2020. "Introduction. Navigating Secrecy in Security Research." In *Secrecy and Methods*, edited by Marieke De Goede, Esmé Bosma, and Polly Pallister-Wilkins, 1–27. Abington/New York: Routledge.

Bourne, Mike, Heather Johnson, and Debbie Lisle. 2015. "Laboratizing the Border: The Production, Translation and Anticipation of Security Technologies." *Security Dialogue* 46 (4): 307–325. doi:10.1177/0967010615578399.

Bowker, Geoffrey C., and Susan Leigh Star. 1999. *Sorting Things out: Classification and Its Consequences. Sorting Things Out.* Cambridge, MA: The MIT Press.

Brambilla, Chiara. 2015. "Exploring the Critical Potential of the Borderscapes Concept." *Geopolitics* 20 (1): 14–34. doi:10.1080/14650045.2014.884561.

Broeders, Dennis. 2007. "The New Digital Borders of Europe: EU Databases and the Surveillance of Irregular Migrants." *International Sociology* 22 (1): 71–92. doi:10.1177/0268580907070126.

Broeders, Dennis, and James Hampshire. 2013. "Dreaming of Seamless Borders: ICTs and the Pre-Emptive Governance of Mobility in Europe." *Journal of Ethnic and Migration Studies* 39 (8): 1201–1218. doi:10.1080/1369183X.2013.787512.

Brouwer, Evelien. 2008. *Digital Borders and Real Rights: Effective Remedies for Third-Country Nationals in the Schengen Information System.* Leiden/Boston, MA: Martinus Nijhoff Publishers.

Brouwer, Evelien. 2020. "Large-Scale Databases and Interoperability in Migration and Border Policies: The Non-Discriminatory Approach of Data Protection." *European Public Law* 26 (1): 71–92.

Busch, Lawrence. 2011. *Standards. Recipes for Reality*. Cambridge, MA/ London: The MIT Press.

Bussolini, Jeffrey. 2010. "What Is a Dispositive?" *Foucault Studies*, no. 10: 85–107.

Callon, Michel, Pierre Lascoumes, and Yannick Barthe. 2009. *Acting in an Uncertain World. An Essay on Technical Democracy*. Cambridge, MA/London: The MIT Press.

Carse, Ashley. 2016. "Keyword: Infrastructure: How a Humble French Engineering Term Shaped the Modern World." In *Infrastructures and Social Complexity: A Companion*, edited by Penny Harvey, Casper Bruun Jensen, and Atsuro Morito, 27–39. London: Routledge. doi:10.4324/ 9781315622880.

Casas-Cortes, Maribel, Sebastian Cobarrubias, Nicholas De Genova, Glenda Garelli, Giorgio Grappi, Charles Heller, Sabine Hess, et al. 2015. "New Keywords: Migration and Borders." *Cultural Studies* 29 (1): 55–87. doi:10.1080/09502386.2014.891630.

Castoriadis, Cornelius. 1990. *Gesellschaft Als Imaginäre Institution. Entwurf einer Politischen Philosophie*. Frankfurt am Main: Suhrkamp.

Castoriadis, Cornelius. 1991. *Philosophy, Politics, Autonomy*. Edited by David Ames Curtis. New York, Oxford: Oxford University Press.

Chouliaraki, Lilie, and Myria Georgiou. 2022. *The Digital Border. Migration, Technology, Power*. New York: NYU Press.

Clarke, John, David Bainton, Noémi Lendvai, and Paul Stubbs. 2015. *Making Policy Move. Towards a Politics of Translation and Assemblage*. Bristol: Policy Press.

Cohn, Carol. 1987a. "Nuclear Language and How We Learned to Pat the Bomb." *Bulletin of the Atomic Scientists*, June.

Cohn, Carol. 1987b. "Sex and Death in the Rational World of Defense Intellectuals." *Signs* 12 (4): 687–718.

Colebatch, H.K. 2014. "Interpretation in the Analysis of Policy." *Australian Journal of Public Administration* 73 (3): 349–356. doi:10.1111/ 1467-8500.12088.

Cooperate Europe Observatory. 2021. *Lobbying Fortress Europe. The Making of a Border-Industrial Complex*. https://corporateeurope.org/en/lobbying-fortress-europe#.

Côté-Boucher, Karine. 2008. "The Diffuse Border: Intelligence-Sharing, Control and Confinement along Canada's Smart Border." *Surveillance and Society* 5 (2): 142–165. doi:10.24908/ss.v5i2.3432.

Cowen, Deborah. 2014. *The Deadly Life of Logistics. Mapping Violence in Global Trade*. Minneapolis/London: University of Minnesota Press.

Curtin, Deirdre, and Filipe Bastos. 2021. "Interoperable Information Sharing and the Five Novel Frontiers of EU Governance: A Special Issue." *European Public Law* 411 (1): 59–70.

Czarniawska, Barbara. 2004. *Narratives in Social Science Research.* London/ Thousand Oaks, CA: Sage Publications.

D'Alessio, Federico Alistair. 2021. "Case Study: Salvini and the Sea-Watch 3." *Academia Letters,* June 1–9. doi:10.20935/al3438.

Dafoe, Allan. 2015. "On Technological Determinism: A Typology, Scope Conditions, and a Mechanism." *Science Technology and Human Values* 40 (6): 1047–1076. doi:10.1177/0162243915579283.

Delamont, Sara. 2007. "Ethnography and Participant Observation." In *Qualitative Research in Practice,* edited by Clive Seale, Giampietro Gobo, Jaber F. Gubrium, and David Silverman, 205–217. London/Thousand Oaks, CA: Sage.

Dell'Agnese, Elena, and Anne Laure Amilhat Szary. 2015. "Borderscapes: From Border Landscapes to Border Aesthetics." *Geopolitics* 20 (1): 4–13. doi:10.1080/14650045.2015.1014284.

Dijstelbloem, Huub. 2017. "Migration Tracking Is a Mess." *Nature* 543: 32–34.

Dijstelbloem, Huub. 2021. *Borders as Infrastructure: The Technopolitics of Border Control.* Cambridge, MA: The MIT Press.

Dijstelbloem, Huub, and A. Meijer, eds. 2011. *Migration and the New Technological Borders of Europe.* London: Palgrave Macmillan UK.

Dijstelbloem, Huub, and Dennis Broeders. 2015. "Border Surveillance, Mobility Management and the Shaping of Non-Publics in Europe." *European Journal of Social Theory* 18 (1): 21–38. doi:10.1177/1368431014534353.

Dijstelbloem, Huub, Rogier van Reekum, and Willem Schinkel. 2017. "Surveillance at Sea: The Transactional Politics of Border Control in the Aegean." *Security Dialogue* 48 (3): 224–240. doi:10.1177/ 0967010617695714.

Dumbrava, Costica. 2021. "Artificial Intelligence at EU Borders. Overview of Applications and Key Issues." *EPRS European Parliamentary Research Service.* doi:10.2861/91831.

Dussauge, Isabelle, Claes-Frederik Helgesson, and Francis Lee. 2015. "Valuography. Studying the Making of Values." In *Value Practices in the Life Sciences and Medicine,* edited by Isabelle Dussauge, Claes-Frederik Helgesson, and Francis Lee, 267–285. Oxford: Oxford University Press.

Easterling, Keller. 2014. *Extrastatecraft: The Power of Infrastructure Space.* London: Verso.

EC (European Commission). 2003. "Development of the Schengen Information System II and possible synergies with a future Visa Information System (VIS)." Brussels, 11.12.2003, COM(2003) 771 final. Accessed 5 April 2022. https://eur-lex.europa.eu/legal-content/EN/TXT/?uri= celex%3A52003DC0771.

EC (European Commission). 2005. "Communication on improved effectiveness, enhanced interoperability and synergies among European databases in the area of Justice and Home Affairs." Brussels, 24.11.2005, COM(205) 597 final. Accessed 5 April 2022. https://eur-lex.europa.eu/legal-content/EN/TXT/?uri=CELEX:52005DC0597.

EC (European Commission). 2008. "Preparing the next steps in border management in the European Union." Brussels, 13.2.2008, COM(2008) 69 final. Accessed 5 April 2022. https://www.eumonitor.eu/9353000/1/j9vvik7m1c3gyxp/vikqhmbrb7zk.

EC (European Commission). 2010. "Overview of information management in the area of freedom, security and justice." Brussels, 20.7.2010, COM(2010) 385 final. Accessed 5 April 2022. https://eur-lex.europa.eu/legal-content/EN/ALL/?uri=CELEX%3A52010DC0385.

EC (European Commission). 2016a. "Stronger and Smarter Information Systems for Borders and Security." Brussels, 6.4.2016, COM(2016) 205 final. Accessed 5 April 2022. https://eur-lex.europa.eu/legal-content/EN/TXT/?uri=COM%3A2016%3A205%3AFIN.

EC (European Commission). 2016b. "Enhancing security in a world of mobility: improved information exchange in the fight against terrorism and stronger external borders." Brussels, 14.9.2016, COM(2016) 602 final. Accessed 5 April 2022. https://eur-lex.europa.eu/legal-content/EN/TXT/?uri=COM:2016:0602:FIN.

EC (European Commission). 2021a. "A strategy towards a fully functioning and resilient Schengen area." Brussels, 2.6.2021, COM(2021) 277 final. Accessed 5 April 2022. https://eur-lex.europa.eu/legal-content/EN/TXT/?uri=CELEX:52021DC0277.

EC (European Commission). 2021b. "Proposal for a Regulation of the European Parliament and the of the Council laying down harmonized rules on artificial intelligence (AI Act) and amending certain Union legislative acts." Brussels, 21.4.2021, COM(2021). Accessed 19 May 2023. https://eur-lex.europa.eu/legal-content/EN/TXT/?uri=celex%3A52021PC0206.

Edwards, Paul N. 2003. "Infrastructure and Modernity: Force, Time, and Social Organization in the History of Sociotechnical Systems." In *Modernity and Technology*, edited by Thomas J. Misa, Philip Brey, and Andrew Feenberg, 185–225. Cambridge, MA: MIT Press.

Engels, Franziska, Alexander Wentland, and Sebastian Pfotenhauer. 2019. "Testing Future Societies? Developing a Framework for Test Beds and Living Labs as Instruments of Innovation Governance." *Research Policy* 48: 1–9. doi:10.1016/j.respol.2019.103826.

Estonian World. 2013. "EU's IT Agency Sets up in Estonia". *Technology*. 23 April 2013. Accessed 12 January 2024. https://estonianworld.com/technology/eus-it-agency-sets-up-in-estonia/.

EU (European Union). 2011. "Regulation (EU) 1077/2011 of the European Parliament and of the Council of 25 October 2011 establishing a European Agency for the operational management of large-scale systems." *Official Journal of the European Union*, L286. Accessed 5 April 2022. https://op.eur opa.eu/en/publication-detail/-/publication/59871ed4-6ddc-48d2-b294-e945bbb9c88f.

EU (European Union). 2017. "Regulation (EU) 2017/2226 of the European Parliament and of the Council of 30 November 2017 establishing an Entry/Exit System (EES) to register entry and exit data and refusals of entry data of third-country nationals crossing the external borders of the Member States [...]." *Official Journal of the European Union*, L327. Accessed 5 April 2022. https://eur-lex.europa.eu/legal-content/EN/TXT/?uri=celex%3A32017R2226.

EU (European Union). 2018a. "Regulation (EU) 2018/1726 of the European Parliament and of the Council of 14 November 2018 on the European Union Agency for the Operational Management of Large-Scale IT Systems in the Area of Freedom, Security and Justice (eu-LISA), and amending Regulation (EC) No 1987/2006 and Council Decision 2007/533/JHA and repealing Regulation (EU) No 1077/2011." *Official Journal of the European Union*, L295. Accessed 5 April 2022. https://eur-lex.eur opa.eu/legal-content/EN/TXT/?uri=celex%3A32018R1726.

EU (European Union). 2018b. "Regulation (EU) 2018/1240 of the European Parliament and of the Council of 12 September 2018 establishing a European Travel Information and Authorisation System (ETIAS) [...]." *Official Journal of the European Union*, L236. Accessed 5 April 2022. https://eur-lex.europa.eu/legal-content/EN/TXT/?uri=celex%3A32018R1240.

EU (European Union). 2019a. "Regulation (EU) 2019/817 of the European Parliament and of the Council of 20 May 2019 on establishing a Framework for interoperability between EU information systems in the field of borders and visa [...]." *Official Journal of the European Union*, L135. Accessed 5 April 2022. https://eur-lex.europa.eu/legal-content/EN/TXT/PDF/?uri=CELEX:32019R0817&from=EN.

EU (European Union). 2019b. "Regulation (EU) 2019/818 of the European Parliament and of the Council of 20 May 2019 on establishing a framework for interoperability between EU information systems in the field of police and judicial cooperation, asylum and migration [...]". *Official Journal of the European Union*, L135. Accessed 5 April 2022. https://eur-lex.europa.eu/legal-content/en/ALL/?uri=CELEX:32019R0818.

EU (European Union). 2019c. "Regulation (EU) 2019/816 of the European Parliament and of the Council of 17 April 2019 establishing a centralised system for the identification of Member States holding conviction information on third-country nationals and stateless persons (ECRIS-TCN) […]" *Official Journal of the European Union*, L135. Accessed 22 January 2023. https://eur-lex.europa.eu/legal-content/EN/TXT/?uri= CELEX%3A32019R0816.

Eule, Tobias G., David Loher, and Anna Wyss. 2018. "Contested Control at the Margins of the State." *Journal of Ethnic and Migration Studies* 44 (16): 2717–2729. doi:10.1080/1369183X.2017.1401511.

eu-LISA. 2014. *eu-LISA in action: IT in the service of a more open and security Europe.* Luxembourg: Publications Office of the European Union. Accessed 5 April 2022. https://op.europa.eu/en/publication-detail/-/publication/ 4ece8474-636d-4739-8e13-9027aea48a44/language-en.

eu-LISA. 2015a. *Annual Work Programme.* Accessed 5 April 2022. https://www.eulisa.europa.eu/Publications/Corporate/eu-LISA_Work Programme 2015.pdf.

eu-LISA. 2015b. *Testing the Borders of the Future. Smart Borders Pilot: The Results in Brief.* Accessed 5 April 2022. https://www.eulisa.europa.eu/ Publications/Reports/Smart%20Borders%20-%20The%20results%20 in%20brief.pdf.

eu-LISA. 2017a. *The eu-LISA Strategy 2018–2020. 2017-149.* Accessed 5 April 2022. https://www.eulisa.europa.eu/Publications/Corporate/eu-LISA%20Strategy%202018-2022.pdf.

eu-LISA. 2017b. *Conference Report. eu-LISA Annual Conference. Going Digital for a Safe and Secure Europe.* Accessed 5 April 2022. https://www.eulisa. europa.eu/Publications/Reports/eu-LISA%20Conference%202017%20Fi nal%20Report%20Web%20Version.pdf.

eu-LISA. 2019a. *Annual Conference 2018–Highlights, part 2.* 17 October 2018. Session 4, Future Outlook, 3:57. Accessed 5 April 2022. https:// www.youtube.com/watch?v=WJNJnK46iYE.

eu-LISA. 2019b. *Elaboration of a Future Architecture for Interoperable IT Systems at eu-LISA. Summary of the Feasibility Study.* Accessed 5 April 2022. https:// op.europa.eu/en/publication-detail/-/publication/590503e5-cf8d-11e9-b4bf-01aa75ed71a1.

eu-LISA. 2019c. *EU Borders – Getting Smarter Through Technology.* Report. eu-LISA and Frontex joint conference. Accessed 5 April 2022. https:// www.eulisa.europa.eu/Publications/Reports/eu-LISA%20Joint%20Con ference%20Report%202018.pdf.

eu-LISA. 2019d. *Entry/Exit System (EES). Working Group on ICT Solutions for External Borders (sea/land) Report.* Accessed 5 April 2022. https://www. eulisa.europa.eu/Publications/Reports/WG%20on%20ICT%20Soluti ons%20for%20External%20Borders%20-%20Report.pdf.

eu-LISA. 2019f. *The New Information Architecture as a Driver for Efficiency and Effectiveness in Internal Security. Annual Conference Report.* Accessed 5 April 2022. https://www.eulisa.europa.eu/Publications/Reports/eu-LISA%20 Annual%20Conference%20Report%202019.pdf.

eu-LISA. 2020. *Artificial Intelligence in the Operational Management of Large-scale IT Systems. Perspectives for eu-LISA. Research and Technology Monitoring Report, July 2020.* Accessed 8 May 2023. https://www.eulisa.europa.eu/ Publications/Reports/AI%20in%20the%20OM%20of%20Large-scale%20 IT%20Systems.pdf.

eu-LISA. 2021. *Contactless Travel in Post-COVID Times: Enhancing the EU Security Ecosystem. eu-LISA Virtual Industry Roundtable, 1–2 June 2021.* Accessed 5 April 2022. https://op.europa.eu/en/publication-detail/-/publ ication/9b46c922-00e9-11ec-8f47-01aa75ed71a1/language-en.

eu-LISA. 2022a. *eu-LISA. About Us. Organisation. Management Board.* Accessed 5 April 2022. https://www.eulisa.europa.eu/About-Us/Organ isation/Eu-Lisa-Management-Board.

eu-LISA. 2022b. *eu-LISA. Activities. Research And Development.* Accessed 5 April 2022. https://www.eulisa.europa.eu/Activities/Research-And-Deve lopment.

eu-LISA. 2022c. *Industry Roundtable November 2021 - Report. Artificial Intelligence and Large-Scale IT Systems: Opportunities and Challenges.* Accessed 5 April 2022. https://www.eulisaroundtable.eu/eulisa_content/uploads/ 2022/01/IR-Nov21-Event-report_compressed.pdf.

European Court of Auditors. 2014. *Special Report Lessons from the European Commission's development of the second generation Schengen Information System (SIS II).* Luxembourg: Publications Office of the European Union. Accessed 5 April 2022. https://op.europa.eu/en/publication-detail/-/publication/ b9cc7886-4d89-4559-be8c-c8329acc37a5.

Ezrahi, Yaron. 2012. *Imagined Democracy. Necessary Political Fictions.* Cambridge: Cambridge University Press.

Feldman, Gregory. 2005. "Culture, State, and Security in Europe: The Case of Citizenship and Integration Policy in Estonia." *American Ethnologist* 32 (4): 676–694. doi:10.1525/ae.2005.32.4.676.

Feldman, Gregory. 2011a. "Illuminating the Apparatus: Steps toward a Nonlocal Ethnography of Global Governance." In *Policy Worlds: Anthropology and the Analysis of Contemporary Power*, edited by Davide Pero, Susan Wright, and Cris Shore, 32–49. New York: Berghahn Books.

Feldman, Gregory. 2011b. "If Ethnography Is More than Participant-Observation, Then Relations Are More than Connections: The Case for Nonlocal Ethnography in a World of Apparatuses." *Anthropological Theory* 11 (4): 375–395. doi:10.1177/1463499611429904.

Feldman, Gregory. 2012. *The Migration Apparatus: Security, Labor, and Policymaking in the European Union.* Stanford, CA: Stanford University Press.

Feldman, Gregory. 2014. "Location, Isolation and Disempowerment: The Swift Proliferation of Security Discourse among Policy Professional." In *The Anthropology of Security. Perspectives from the Frontline of Policing, Counter-Terrorism and Border Control*, edited by Mark Maguire, Catarina Frois, and Nils Zurawski, 46–58. London: Pluto Press.

Feldman, Gregory. 2019. *The Gray Zone. Sovereignty, Human Smuggling, and Undercover Police Investigation in Europe.* Stanford, CA: Stanford University Press.

Felt, Ulrike. 2015. "Keeping Technologies Out: Sociotechnical Imaginaries and the Formation of Austria's Technopolitical Identity." In *Dreamscapes of Modernity: Sociotechnical Imaginaries and the Fabrication of Power*, edited by Sheila Jasanoff and Sang-Hyun Kim, 103–125. Chicago/London: The University of Chicago Press.

Felt, Ulrike. 2017. "Living a Real-World Experiment: Post-Fukushima Imaginaries and Spatial Practices of 'Containing the Nuclear.'" In *New Perspectives on Technology in Society: Experimentation Beyond the Laboratory*, edited by Ibo van de Poel, Lotte Asveld, and Donna C. Mehos, 149–178. London: Routledge.

Fischer, Frank, Douglas Torgerson, Anna Durnová, and Michael Orsini. 2015. "Introduction to Critical Policy Studies." In *Handbook of Critical Policy Studies*, edited by Frank Fischer, Douglas Torgerson, Anna Durnová, and Michael Orsini, 1–24. Cheltenham: Edward Elgar Publishing Limited. doi:10.4337/9781783472352.00005.

Fleck, Ludwik. 1981. *Genesis and Development of a Scientific Fact*. Chicago/London: The University of Chicago Press.

Follis, Karolina S. 2017. "Vision and Transterritory: The Borders of Europe." *Science Technology and Human Values* 42 (6): 1003–1030. doi:10.1177/0162243917715106.

Foucault, Michel. 2009. *Security, Territory, Population. Lectures at the Collège de France, 1977–78.* Edited by Michel Senellart. Hampshire: Palgrave Macmillan.

FRA (European Union Agency for Fundamental Rights). 2018. *Under Watchful Eyes, EU IT Systems and Fundamental Rights.* Luxembourg: Publications Office of the European Union. Accessed 5 April 2022. https://fra.europa.eu/en/publication/2018/under-watchful-eyes-biometrics-eu-it-systems-and-fundamental-rights.

Fraser, Mariam. 2009. "Facts, Ethics and Event." In *Deleuzian Intersections: Science, Technology, Anthropology*, edited by Caspar Brunn Jensen and Kjetil Rödje, 57–82. New York/Oxford: Berghahn Books.

Fujimura, Joan. 2003. "Future Imaginaries: Genome Scientists as Socio-Cultural Entrepreneurs." In *Genetic Nature/Culture: Anthropology and Science Beyond the Two-Culture Divide*, edited by Alan H. Goodman, Deborah Heath, and M. Susan Lindee, 176–199. California: University of California Press.

Garkov, Krum. 2020. "Feature: The Digital Challenge at the Borders." In *Border Management Today*, 27–30. International Border Management and Technologies Association Ltd. Accessed 1 April 2022. https://www.ibmata.org/wp-content/uploads/2020/06/Border-Management-Today-Mag-May2020-FINALd.pdf.

Garud, Raghu. 2008. "Conferences as Venues for the Configuration of Emerging Organizational Fields: The Case of Cochlear Implants." *Journal of Management Studies* 45 (6): 1061–1088. doi:10.1111/j.1467-6486.2008.00783.x.

Genova, Nicholas De. 2017a. "Introduction. The Borders of 'Europe' and the European Question." In *The Borders of "Europe". Autonomy of Migration. Tactics of Bordering*, edited by Nicholas De Genova, 1–36. Durham, NC/London: Duke University Press.

Genova, Nicholas De, ed. 2017b. *The Borders of "Europe." Autonomy of Migration, Tactics of Bordering.* Durham, NC/London: Duke University Press.

Glouftsios, Georgios. 2019. "Designing Digital Borders." In *Technology and Agency in International Relations*, edited by Marijn Hoijtink and Matthias Leese, 164–187. London: Routledge. doi:10.4324/9780429463143-8.

Glouftsios, Georgios. 2021. "Governing Border Security Infrastructures: Maintaining Large-Scale Information Systems." *Security Dialogue* 52 (5): 452–470. doi:10.1177/0967010620957230.

Glouftsios, Georgios, and Stephan Scheel. 2021. "An Inquiry into the Digitisation of Border and Migration Management: Performativity, Contestation and Heterogeneous Engineering." *Third World Quarterly* 42 (1): 123–140. doi:10.1080/01436597.2020.1807929.

Graham, Stephen, and Nigel Thrift. 2007. "Out of Order: Understanding Repair and Maintenance." *Theory, Culture & Society* 24 (3): 1–25. doi:10.1177/0263276407075954.

Guggenheim, Michael. 2012. "Laboratizing and De-Laboratizing the World: Changing Sociological Concepts for Places of Knowledge Production." *History of the Human Sciences* 25 (1): 99–118. doi:10.1177/0952695111422978.

Guiraudon, Virginie, and Gallya Lahav. 2000. "The Case of Migration Control." *Comparative Political Studies* 33 (2): 163–195. doi:10.1177/0010414000033002001.

Hacking, Ian. 1990. *The Taming of Chance. The Taming of Chance.* Cambridge: Cambridge University Press. doi:10.1017/cbo9780511819766.

Hall, Alexandra, and Jonathan Mendel. 2012. "Threatprints, Threads and Triggers: Imaginaries of Risk in the 'War on Terror.'" *Journal of Cultural Economy* 5 (1): 9–27. doi:10.1080/17530350.2012.640551.

Harney, Stefano, and Fred Moten. 2013. *The Undercommons: Fugitive Planning & Black Study. The Undercommons: Fugitive Planning and Black Study.* Wivenhoe/New York/Port Watson: Minor Compositions. http://www.minorcompositions.info/wp-content/uploads/2013/04/undercommons-web.pdf.

Heller, Charles, and Lorenzo Pezzani. 2017. "Liquid Traces. Investigating the Deaths of Migrants at the EU's Maritime Frontier." In *The Borders of "Europe". Autonomy of Migration. Tactics of Bordering*, edited by Nicholas De Genova, 95–119. Durham, NC/London: Duke University Press.

Helmond, Anne. 2015. "The Platformization of the Web: Making Web Data Platform Ready." *Social Media + Society* 1 (2): 1–11. doi:10.1177/2056305115603080.

Hess, Sabine, and Bernd Kasparek. 2017. "Under Control? Or Border (as) Conflict: Reflections on the European Border Regime." *Social Inclusion* 5 (3): 58–68. doi:10.17645/si.v5i3.1004.

Hetherington, Kregg. 2016. "Surveying the Future Perfect: Anthropology, Development and the Promise of Infrastructure." In *Infrastructures and Social Complexity: A Companion*, edited by Penny Harvey, Casper Bruun Jensen, and Atsuro Morito, 40–50. London: Routledge. doi:10.4324/9781315622880.

Hilgartner, Stephen. 2000. *Science on Stage: Expert Advice as Public Drama*. Stanford, CA: Stanford University Press.

Hilgartner, Stephen. 2015. "Capturing the Imaginary. Vanguards, Visions and the Synthetic Biology Revolution." In *Science and Democracy. Making Knowledge and Making Power in the Biosciences and Beyond*, edited by Stephen Hilgartner, Clarke A. Miller, and Rob Hagendijk, 33–55. New York/London: Routledge, Taylor & Francis Group.

Hilgartner, Stephen, Clarke A. Miller, and Rob Hagendijk. 2015. "Introduction." In *Science and Democracy: Making Knowledge and Making Power in the Biosciences and Beyond*, edited by Stephen Hilgartner, Clarke A. Miller, and Rob Hagendijk, 1–14. New York: Routledge.

HLEG (High-level Expert Group on Information systems and Interoperability). 2017. *Final Report*. Accessed 5 April 2022. https://ec.europa.eu/transpare ncy/expert-groups-register/screen/expert-groups/consult?do=groupDet ail.groupDetail&groupID=3435.

Hobsbawm, Eric, and Terrence Ranger, eds. 1983. *The Invention of Tradition*. Cambridge: Cambridge University Press.

Hoppe, Robertus. 2010. *The Governance of Problems: Puzzling, Powering and Participation*. Bristol: The Polity Press.

Horst, Maja, and Mike Michael. 2011. "On the Shoulders of Idiots: Re-Thinking Science Communication as 'Event.'" *Science as Culture* 20 (3): 283–306. doi:10.1080/09505431.2010.524199.

Howarth, David. 2010. "Power, Discourse, and Policy: Articulating a Hegemony Approach to Critical Policy Studies." *Critical Policy Studies* 3 (3–4): 309–335. doi:10.1080/19460171003619725.

Hughes, Thomas P. 1994. "Technological Momentum." In *Does Technology Drive History. The Dilemma of Technological Determinism*, edited by Merritt Roe Smith and Leo Marx, 101–114. Cambridge, MA/London: The MIT Press.

Jasanoff, Sheila. 2005. *Designs on Nature: Science and Democracy in Europe and the United States*. Princeton, NJ: Princeton University Press. doi:10.1515/9781400837311.

Jasanoff, Sheila. 2015a. "Future Imperfect: Science, Technology and the Imaginations of Modernity." In *Dreamscapes of Modernity: Sociotechnical Imaginaries and the Fabrication of Power*, edited by Sheila Jasanoff and Sang-Hyun Kim, 1–49. Chicago/London: The University of Chicago Press.

Jasanoff, Sheila. 2015b. "Imagined and Invented Worlds." In *Dreamscapes of Modernity: Sociotechnical Imaginaries and the Fabrication of Power*, edited by Sheila Jasanoff and Sang-Hyun Kim, 321–341. Chicago/London: The University of Chicago Press.

Jasanoff, Sheila. 2016. *The Ethics of Invention. Technology and the Human Future.* New York/London: W.W. Norton & Company.

Jasanoff, Sheila. 2017. "Virtual, Visible, and Actionable: Data Assemblages and the Sightlines of Justice." *Big Data & Society* 4 (2): 1–15. doi:10.1177/2053951717724477.

Jasanoff, Sheila, and Sang-Hyun Kim. 2009. "Containing the Atom: Sociotechnical Imaginaries and Nuclear Power in the United States and South Korea." *Minerva* 47 (2): 119–146. doi:10.1007/s11024-009-9124-4.

Jasanoff, Sheila, and Sang-Hyun Kim. 2013. "Sociotechnical Imaginaries and National Energy Policies." *Science as Culture* 22 (2): 189–196. doi:10.1080/09505431.2013.786990.

Jasanoff, Sheila, and Sang-Hyun Kim, eds. 2015. *Dreamscapes of Modernity: Sociotechnical Imaginaries and the Fabrication of Power.* Chicago/London: The University of Chicago Press.

Jeandesboz, Julien. 2016a. "Justifying Control: EU Border Security and the Shifting Boundaries of Political Arrangement." In *EU Borders and Shifting Internal Security: Technology, Externalization and Accountability*, edited by Raphael Bossong and Helena Carrapico, 221–238. Springer International Publishing. doi:10.1007/978-3-319-17560-7.

Jeandesboz, Julien. 2016b. "Smartening Border Security in the European Union: An Associational Inquiry." *Security Dialogue* 47 (4): 292–309. doi:10.1177/0967010616650226.

Jensen, Casper Bruun, and Atsuro Morita. 2015. "Infrastructures as Ontological Experiments." *Engaging Science, Technology, and Society* 1: 81–87. doi:10.17351/ests2015.21.

Jensen, Ole B., and Tim Richardson. 2004. *Making European Space: Mobility, Power and Territorial Identity.* London/New York: Routledge, Taylor & Francis Group.

Jones, Chris. 2017. "Market Forces. The Development of the EU Security-Industrial Complex." *Transnational Institut and Statewatch.* https://www.tni.org/files/publication-downloads/marketforces-report-tni-statewatch.pdf.

Jones, Chris, Ana Valdivia, and Jane Kilpatrick. 2022. "Funds for Fortress Europe: Spending by Frontex and Eu-LISA." *Statewatch.* https://www.statewatch.org/analyses/2022/funds-for-fortress-europe-spending-by-frontex-and-eu-lisa/.

Kaiser, Wolfram, and Johan Schot. 2014. *Writing the Rules for Europe. Experts, Cartels, and International Organizations.* Hampshire: Palgrave Macmillan.

Klimburg-Witjes, Nina, and Paul Trauttmansdorff, eds. 2023. *Technopolitics and the Making of Europe. Infrastructures of In/Security.* London: Routledge, Taylor & Francis Group.

Klimburg-Witjes, Nina, and Alexander Wentland. 2021. "Hacking Humans? Social Engineering and the Construction of the 'Deficient User' in Cybersecurity Discourses." *Science Technology and Human Values* 46 (6): 1316–1339. doi:10.1177/0162243921992844.

Klimburg-Witjes, Nina, Matthias Leese, and Paul Trauttmansdorff. 2022. "Expanding Boundaries: Unmaking and Remaking Secrecy in Field Research." *Political Anthropological Research on International Social Sciences* 3 (2): 168–197. doi:10.1163/25903276-bja10039.

Knorr Cetina, Karin. 1999. *Epistemic Cultures: How the Sciences Make Knowledge.* Cambridge, MA/London: Cambridge University Press. doi:10.2307/2653984.

Knorr Cetina, Karin. 2009. "The Synthetic Situation: Interactionism for a Global World." *Symbolic Interaction* 32 (1): 61–87. doi:10.1525/si.2009.32.1.61.62.

König, Magdalena. 2016. "The Borders, They Are a-Changin'! The Emergence of Socio-Digital Borders in the EU." *Internet Policy Review. Journal on Internet Regulation* 5 (1): 1–14. doi:10.14763/2016.1.403.

Korn, Matthias, Wolfgang Reißmann, Tobias Röhl, and David Sittler. 2019. *Infrastructuring Publics.* Edited by Matthias Korn, Wolfgang Reißmann, Tobias Röhl, and David Sittler. *Infrastructuring Publics.* Wiesbaden: Springer Fachmedien Wiesbaden. doi:10.1007/978-3-658-20725-0.

Laak, Dirk van. 2001. "Infra-Strukturgeschichte." *Geschichte Und Gesellschaft: Zeitschrift Für Historische Sozialwissenschaft* 27: 367–393.

Lamont, Michèle. 2012. "Toward a Comparative Sociology of Valuation and Evaluation." *Annual Review of Sociology* 38: 201–221. doi:10.1146/annurev-soc-070308-120022.

Larkin, Brian. 2013. "The Politics and Poetics of Infrastructure." *Annual Review of Anthropology* 42: 327–343. doi:10.1146/annurev-anthro-092412-155522.

Latour, Bruno. 1986. "Visualisation and Cognition: Drawing Things Together." In *Knowledge and Society Studies in the Sociology of Culture Past and Present*, edited by Henrika Kuklick, 1–40. Greenwich: Jai Press.

Latour, Bruno. 1987. *Science in Action. How to Follow Scientists and Engineers through Society.* Cambridge, MA: Harvard University Press.

Latour, Bruno. 1993. *The Pasteurization of France.* Cambridge, MA and London: Harvard University Press.

Law, John. 1991. "Introduction: Monsters, Machines and Sociotechnical Relations." In *A Sociology of Monsters. Essays on Power, Technology and Domination*, edited by John Law, 1–25. London/New York: Routledge.

Law, John. 2002. *Aircraft Stories: Decentering the Object in Technoscience.* Durham, NC: Duke University Press.

Law, John. 2004. *After Method: Mess in Social Science Research.* London/New York: Routledge, Taylor & Francis Group.

Law, John. 2015. "What's Wrong with a One-World World?" *Distinktion* 16 (1). Taylor & Francis: 126–139. doi:10.1080/1600910X.2015.1020066.

Law, John, and Vicky Singleton. 2014. "ANT, Multiplicity and Policy." *Critical Policy Studies* 8 (4): 379–396. doi:10.1080/19460171.2014.957056.

Leese, Matthias. 2016. "Exploring the Security/Facilitation Nexus: Foucault at the 'Smart' Border." *Global Society* 30 (3): 412–429. doi:10.1080/13600826.2016.1173016.

Leese, Matthias. 2018. "Standardizing Security: The Business Case Politics of Borders." *Mobilities* 13 (2): 261–275. doi:10.1080/17450101.2017.1403777.

Leese, Matthias. 2022. "Fixing State Vision: Interoperability, Biometrics, and Identity Management in the EU." *Geopolitics* 27 (1): 113–133. doi:10.1080/14650045.2020.1830764.

Leese, Matthias, Simon Noori, and Stephan Scheel. 2022. "Data Matters: The Politics and Practices of Digital Border and Migration Management." *Geopolitics* 27 (1): 5–25. doi:10.1080/14650045.2021.1940538.

Lemberg-Pedersen, Martin. 2013. "Private Security Companies and the European Borderscapes." In *The Neoliberalized State and the Growth of the Migration Industry*, edited by Thomas Gammeltoft-Hansen and Ninna Nyberg Sørensen, 152–173. Abington, Oxon: Routledge.

Lemberg-Pedersen, Martin. 2018. "Security, Industry and Migration in European Border Control." In *The Routledge Handbook of the Politics of Migration in Europe*, edited by Agnieszka Weinar, Saskia Bonjour, and Lyubov Zhyznomirska, 239–250. London: Routledge. doi:10.4324/9781315512853-23.

Lemberg-Pedersen, Martin, Johannes Rübner Hansen, and Oliver Joel Halpern. 2020. *The Political Economy of Entry Governance.* Copenhagen: Aalborg University. chrome-extension://efaidnbmnnnib pcajpcglclefindmkaj/https://vbn.aau.dk/files/321478293/AdMiGov_ POLITICAL_ECONOMY_OF_ENTRY_GOVERNANCE_for_publi c_dissemination.pdf.

LIBE (Civil Liberties, Justice and Home Affairs). 2018. *Interoperability of Justice and Home Affairs Information Systems.* Study for the LIBE committee. Accessed 5 April 2022. https://www.europarl.europa.eu/RegData/etudes/ STUD/2018/604947/IPOL_STU(2018)604947_EN.pdf.

Lin, Weiqiang, Johan Lindquist, Biao Xiang, and Brenda S.A. Yeoh. 2017. "Migration Infrastructures and the Production of Migrant Mobilities." *Mobilities* 12 (2): 167–174. doi:10.1080/17450101.2017.1292770.

Longo, Matthew. 2017. *The Politics of Borders.* Cambridge: Cambridge University Press. doi:10.1017/9781316761663.

M'charek, Amade, Katharina Schramm, and David Skinner. 2014. "Topologies of Race: Doing Territory, Population and Identity in Europe." *Science Technology and Human Values* 39 (4): 468–487. doi:10.1177/0162243913509493.

Mager, Astrid. 2017. "Search Engine Imaginary: Visions and Values in the Co-Production of Search Technology and Europe." *Social Studies of Science* 47 (2): 240–262. doi:10.1177/0306312716671433.

Maguire, Eileen Murphy. 2023. "Security-as-Service in the Management of European Border Data Infrastructures." *JCMS: Journal of Common Market Studies*: 1–16. doi:10.1111/jcms.13543.

Marcus, George E., ed. 1995. *Technoscientific Imaginaries. Conversations, Profiles, And Memoirs*. Chicago/London: The University of Chicago Press.

Martins, Bruno Oliveira, and Maria Gabrielsen Jumbert. 2022. "EU Border Technologies and the Co-Production of Security 'Problems' and 'Solutions.'" *Journal of Ethnic and Migration Studies* 48 (6): 1430–1447. doi:10.1080/1369183X.2020.1851470.

Mau, Steffen. 2019. *The Metric Society. The Quantification of the Social World*. Cambridge, MA: Polity Press.

Mau, Steffen. 2021. *Sortiermaschinen. Die Neuerfindung Der Grenze Im 21. Jahrhundert*. München: C.H. Beck.

McGoey, Linsey. 2012. "Strategic Unknowns: Towards a Sociology of Ignorance." *Economy and Society* 41 (1): 1–16. doi:10.1080/03085147.2011.637330.

McLeod, Carmen, and Brigitte Nerlich. 2017. "Synthetic Biology, Metaphors and Responsibility." *Life Sciences, Society and Policy* 13 (13): 1–13. doi:10.1186/s40504-017-0061-y.

Mezzadra, Sandro. 2011. "The Gaze of Autonomy: Capitalism, Migration and Social Struggles." In *The Contested Politics of Mobility. Borderzones and Irregularity*, edited by Vicki Squire, 121–142. London/New York: Routledge, Taylor & Francis Group.

Mezzadra, Sandro. 2017. "Digital Mobility, Logistics, and the Politics of Migration." *Spheres – Journal for Digital Cultures*, no. 4: 1–4. http://spheres-journal.org/digital-mobility-logistics-and-the-politics-of-migration/.

Mezzadra, Sandro. 2019. *Sealing Borders? Rethinking Border Studies in Hard Times*. Working Paper Series B/Orders in Motion. doi:10.11584/B-ORDERS.3.Lizenz.

Mezzadra, Sandro, and Brett Neilson. 2013. *Border as Method, or, the Multiplication of Labor*. Durham, NC: Duke University Press.

Miller, Clarke A. 2015. "Globalizing Security: Science and the Transformation of Contemporary Political Imagination." In *Dreamscapes of Modernity: Sociotechnical Imaginaries and the Fabrication of Power*, edited by Sheila Jasanoff and Sang-Hyun Kim, 277–299. Chicago/London: The University of Chicago Press.

Miller, Clarke A. 2017. "Engaging with Societal Challenges." In *The Handbook of Science and Technology Studies*, edited by Ulrike Felt, Rayvon Fouché, Clark A. Miller, and Laurel Smith-Doerr, 909–913. Cambridge, MA/London: The MIT Press.

Misa, Thomas J., and Johan Schot. 2005. "Introduction. Inventing Europe: Technology and the Hidden Integration of Europe." *History and Technology* 21 (1): 1–19. doi:10.1080/07341510500037487.

Mitchell, Timothy. 2002. *The Rule of Experts. Egypt, Techno-Politics, Modernity.* Berkeley/Los Angeles/London: University of California Press.

Moore, James F. 1998. "The Rise of a New Corporate Form." *The Washington Quarterly* 21 (1): 167–181. doi:10.1080/01636609809550301.

Moraña, Mabel, ed. 2021. *Liquid Borders. Migration as Resistance.* London: Routledge.

Morozov, Evgeny. 2013. *To Save Everything, Click Here. Technology, Solutionism and the Urge to Fix Problems That Don't Exist.* London: Allen Lane.

Muller, Benjamin J. 2011. "Risking It All at the Biometric Border: Mobility, Limits, and the Persistence of Securitisation." *Geopolitics* 16 (1): 91–106. doi:10.1080/14650045.2010.493775.

Munster, Rens van. 2009. *Securitizing Immigration: The Politics of Risk in the EU. Palgrave Studies in International Relations Series.* Hampshire: Palgrave Macmillan.

Murphy, Eileen, and Mark Maguire. 2015. "Speed, Time and Security: Anthropological Perspectives on Automated Border Control." *Etnofoor* 27 (2): 157–177.

Nielsen, Gritt B. 2011. "Peopling Policy: On Conflicting Subjectivities of Fee-Paying Students." In *Policy Worlds: Anthropology and the Analysis of Contemporary Power,* edited by Cris Shore, Susan Wright, and Davide Pero, 68–85. New York: Berghahn Books.

Niewöhner, Jörg. 2015. "Epigenetics: Localizing Biology through Co-Laboration." *New Genetics and Society* 34 (2): 219–242. doi:10.1080/14636778.2015.1036154.

Noori, Simon. 2022. "Suspicious Infrastructures: Automating Border Control and the Multiplication of Mistrust through Biometric E-Gates." *Geopolitics* 27 (4): 1117–1139. doi:10.1080/14650045.2021.1952183.

Nowotny, Helga. 1994. *Time. The Modern and Postmodern Experience.* Cambridge: Polity Press.

Ohmae, Kenichi. 1990. *Managing in a Borderless World. Power and Strategy in the Global Market Place.* London: HarperCollins.

Olwig, Karen Fog, Kristina Grünenberg, Perle Møhl, and Anja Simonsen, eds. 2019. *The Biometric Border World. Technologies, Bodies and Identities on the Move.* London: Routledge. doi:10.4324/9780367808464.

Opitz, Sven, and Ute Tellmann. 2015a. "Europe as Infrastructure: Networking the Operative Community." *South Atlantic Quarterly* 114 (1): 171–190. doi:10.1215/00382876-2831356.

Opitz, Sven, and Ute Tellmann. 2015b. "Future Emergencies: Temporal Politics in Law and Economy." *Theory, Culture & Society* 32 (2): 107–129. doi:10.1177/0263276414560416.

Oudshoorn, Nelly. 2012. "How Places Matter: Telecare Technologies and the Changing Spatial Dimensions of Healthcare." *Social Studies of Science* 42 (1): 121–142. doi:10.1177/0306312711431817.

Paasi, Anssi. 1998. "Boundaries as Social Processes: Territoriality in the World of Flows." *Geopolitics* 3 (1): 69–88. doi:10.1080/14650049808407608.

Paasi, Anssi. 2018. "Borderless Worlds and beyond: Challenging the State-Centric Cartographies." In *Borderless Worlds for Whom? Ethics, Moralities and Mobilities*, edited by Anssi Paasi, Eava-Kaisa Prokkola, Jarkko Saarinen, and Kaj Zimmerbauer, 21–36. London: Routledge.

Papadopoulos, Dimitris, Niamh Stephenson, and Vassilis Tsianos. 2008. *Escape Routes. Control and Subversion in the Twenty-First Century*. London/Ann Arbor, MI: Pluto Press.

Parkin, Joanna. 2011. "The Difficult Road to the Schengen Information System II: The Legacy of 'laboratories' and the Cost for Fundamental Rights and the Rule of Law." *CEPS Working Paper*. Liberty and Security in Europe. http://www.ceps.eu.

Pelizza, Annalisa. 2016a. "Developing the Vectorial Glance: Infrastructural Inversion for the New Agenda on Government Information Systems." *Science Technology and Human Values* 41 (2): 298–321. doi:10.1177/0162243915597478.

Pelizza, Annalisa. 2016b. "Disciplining Change, Displacing Frictions Two Structural Dimensions of Digital Circulation Across Land Registry Database Integration." *TECNOSCIENZA Italian Journal of Science and Technology Studies* 7 (2): 35–60.

Pelizza, Annalisa. 2020. "Processing Alterity, Enacting Europe: Migrant Registration and Identification as Co-Construction of Individuals and Polities." *Science Technology and Human Values* 45 (2): 262–288. doi:10.1177/0162243919827927.

Pelizza, Annalisa. 2021. "Identification as Translation: The Art of Choosing the Right Spokespersons at the Securitized Border." *Social Studies of Science* 51 (4): 487–511. doi:10.1177/0306312720983932.

Pezzani, Lorenzo, and Charles Heller. 2019. "AIS Politics: The Contested Use of Vessel Tracking at the EU's Maritime Frontier." *Science, Technology, & Human Values* 44 (5): 881–899. doi:10.1177/0162243919852672.

Pfotenhauer, Sebastian, and Sheila Jasanoff. 2017. "Panacea or Diagnosis? Imaginaries of Innovation and the 'MIT Model' in Three Political Cultures." *Social Studies of Science* 47 (6): 783–810. doi:10.1177/0306312717706110.

Pfotenhauer, Sebastian, Joakim Juhl, and Erik Aarden. 2019. "Challenging the 'Deficit Model' of Innovation: Framing Policy Issues under the Innovation Imperative." *Research Policy* 48 (4): 895–904. doi:10.1016/j.respol.2018.10.015.

Pfotenhauer, Sebastian, Brice Laurent, Kyriaki Papageorgiou, and Jack Stilgoe. 2022. "The Politics of Scaling." *Social Studies of Science* 52 (1): 3–34. doi:10.1177/03063127211048945.

Pickersgill, Martyn. 2011. "Connecting Neuroscience and Law: Anticipatory Discourse and the Role of Sociotechnical Imaginaries." *New Genetics and Society* 30 (1): 27–40. doi:10.1080/14636778.2011.552298.

Ploeg, Irma van der. 2000. "The Illegal Body: 'Eurodac' and the Politics of Biometric Identification." *Ethics and Information Technology* 1: 295–302. http://www.springerlink.com/index/l5j762825022021t.pdf.

Poel, Ibo Van De, Donna C Mehos, and Lotte Asveld. 2017. "Introduction." In *New Perspectives on Technology in Society. Experimentation Beyond the Laboratory*, edited by Ibo Van De Poel, Donna C Mehos, and Lotte Asveld, 1–15. London: Routledge.

Pollozek, Silvan. 2020. "Turbulences of Speeding up Data Circulation. Frontex and Its Crooked Temporalities of 'Real-Time' Border Control." *Mobilities* 15 (5): 677–693. doi:10.1080/17450101.2020.1801304.

Pollozek, Silvan, and Jan Hendrik Passoth. 2019. "Infrastructuring European Migration and Border Control: The Logistics of Registration and Identification at Moria Hotspot." *Environment and Planning D: Society and Space* 37 (4): 606–624. doi:10.1177/0263775819835819.

Porter, Theodore M. 2020. *Trust in Numbers: The Pursuit of Objectivity in Science and Public Life*. Princeton, NJ: Princeton University Press.

Pötzsch, Holger. 2015. "The Emergence of IBorder: Bordering Bodies, Networks, and Machines." *Environment and Planning D: Society and Space* 33 (1): 101–118. doi:10.1068/d14050p.

Prasad, Amit. 2014. *Imperial Technoscience. Transnational Histories of MRI in the United States, Britain, and India. Imperial Technoscience. Transnational Histories*. Cambridge, MA: The MIT Press. doi:10.4324/9781315106052-1.

Rabinow, Paul. 2003. *Anthropos Today. Reflection on Modern Equipment*. Princeton, NJ: Princeton University Press. doi:10.1515/9781400825905.44.

Rajaram, Prem Kumar, and Carl Grundy-Warr, eds. 2007. *Borderscapes. Hidden Geographies and Politics at Territory's Edge*. Minneapolis/London: University of Minnesota Press.

Rao, H. (2001). "The Power of Public Competition: Promoting Cognitive Legitimacy Through Certification Contests." In The Entrepreneurship Dynamic, edited by Claudia Bird Schoonhoven and Elaine Romanelli, 262–285. Palo Alto, CA: Stanford University Press.

Reekum, Rogier van. 2019. "Patrols, Records and Pictures: Demonstrations of Europe in the Midst of Migration's Crisis." *Environment and Planning D: Society and Space* 37 (4): 625–643. doi:10.1177/0263775818792269.

Renan, Ernest. 1990. "What Is a Nation?" In *Nation and Narration*, edited by Homi K. Bhabha, 8–22. New York: Routledge. doi:10.4324/9780203823064.

Ribes, David, and Thomas A. Finholt. 2009. "The Long Now of Technology Infrastructure: Articulating Tensions in Development." *Journal of the Association for Information Systems* 10 (5): 375–398.

Riles, Annelise. 2000. *The Network Inside Out*. Ann Arbor: The University of Michigan Press.

Rose, Nikolas. 1999. *Powers of Freedom. Reframing Political Thought.* Cambridge: Cambridge University Press.

Rumford, Chris. 2006a. "Introduction: Theorizing Borders." *European Journal of Social Theory* 9 (2): 155–169. doi:10.1177/1368431006063330.

Rumford, Chris. 2006b. "Rethinking European Spaces: Territory, Borders, Governance." *Comparative European Politics* 4 (2–3): 127–140. doi:10.1057/palgrave.cep.6110089.

Ruppert, Evelyn. 2018. "Sociotechnical Imaginaries of Different Data Futures: An Experiment in Citizen Data." *Van Doorn Leerstoel, Erasmus Universiteit Rotterdam, Juni 2018.* https://www.eur.nl/sites/corporate/files/2018-06/3e van doornlezing evelyn ruppert.pdf.

Rygiel, Kim. 2011. "Governing Borderzones of Mobility through E-Borders: The Politics of Embodied Mobility." In *The Contested Politics of Mobility. Borderzones and Irregularity*, edited by Vicki Squire, 143–168. London/New York: Routledge, Taylor & Francis Group.

Sabel, Charles F., and Jonathan Zeitlin. 2010. *Experimentalist Governance in the European Union. Towards a New Architecture*. Oxford: Oxford University Press.

Sadowski, Jathan, and Roy Bendor. 2019. "Selling Smartness: Corporate Narratives and the Smart City as a Sociotechnical Imaginary." *Science, Technology, & Human Values* 44 (3): 540–563. doi:10.1177/0162243918806061.

Salter, Mark B. 2006a. "At the Threshold of Security: A Theory of International Borders." In *Global Surveillance and Policing: Borders, Security, Identity*, edited by Elia Zureik and Mark B. Salter, 36–50. Portland, OR: Willan Publishing.

Salter, Mark B. 2006b. "The Global Visa Regime and the Political Technologies of the International Self: Borders, Bodies, Biopolitics." *Alternatives: Global, Local, Political* 31 (2): 167–189.

Salter, Mark B. 2013. "To Make Move and Let Stop: Mobility and the Assemblage of Circulation." *Mobilities* 8 (1): 7–19. doi:10.1080/17450101.2012.747779.

Scheel, Stephan. 2013. "Autonomy of Migration Despite Its Securitisation? Facing the Terms and Conditions of Biometric Rebordering." *Millennium: Journal of International Studies* 41 (3): 575–600. doi:10.1177/0305829813484186.

Scheel, Stephan. 2017. "'The Secret Is to Look Good on Paper': Appropriating Mobility within and against a Machine of Illegalization." In *The Borders of "Europe". Autonomy of Migration. Tactics of Bordering*, edited by Nicholas De Genova, 37–63. Durham, NC/London: Duke University Press.

Scheel, Stephan. 2020. "Biopolitical Bordering: Enacting Populations as Intelligible Objects of Government." *European Journal of Social Theory* 23 (4): 571–590. doi:10.1177/1368431019900096.

Scheel, Stephan, Evelyn Ruppert, and Funda Ustek-Spilda. 2019. "Enacting Migration through Data Practices." *Environment and Planning D: Society and Space* 37 (4): 579–588. doi:10.1177/0263775819865791.

Schinkel, Willem. 2015. "The Image of Crisis: Walter Benjamin and the Interpretation of 'Crisis' in Modernity." *Thesis Eleven* 127 (1): 36–51. doi:10.1177/0725513615575529.

Schinkel, Willem. 2020. "State Work and the Testing Concours of Citizenship." *The British Journal of Sociology* 71 (3): 556–571. doi:10.1111/1468-4446.12743.

Schiølin, Kasper. 2020. "Revolutionary Dreams: Future Essentialism and the Sociotechnical Imaginary of the Fourth Industrial Revolution in Denmark." *Social Studies of Science* 50 (4): 542–566. doi:10.1177/0306312719867768.

Schipper, Frank, and Johan Schot. 2011. "Infrastructural Europeanism, or the Project of Building Europe on Infrastructures: An Introduction." *History and Technology* 27 (3): 245–264. doi:10.1080/07341512.2011.604166.

Schulze Wessel, Julia. 2015. "On Border Subjects: Rethinking the Figure of the Refugee and the Undocumented Migrant." *Constellations* 23 (1): 46–57.

Schwertl, Maria. 2018. "Die Entmenschlichung Der Grenze. Zur Bedeutung von Technisierung Im EUropäischen Migrations- Und Grenzregime." *Movements. Journal Für Kritische Migrations- Und Grenzregimeforschung* 4 (2): 77–101.

Sciortino, Giuseppe. 2004. "Between Phantoms and Necessary Evils. Some Critical Points in the Study of Irregular Migrations to Western Europe." *IMIS-Beiträge* 24: 17–44. http://www.imis.uni-osnabrueck.de/pdffiles/imis24.pdf.

Scott, James C. 1998. *Seeing like a State: How Certain Schemes to Improve the Human Condition Have Failed.* New Haven, CT: Yale University Press.

Scott, James C. 2012. *Two Cheers for Anarchism.* Princeton, NJ: Princeton University Press.

Sennett, Richard. 1996. *Fleisch Und Stein. Der Körper Und Die Stadt in Der Westlichen Zivilisation.* Berlin: Berlin Verlag.

Shapin, Steven. 2008. *The Scientific Life. A Moral History of a Late Modern Vocation.* Chicago/London: The University of Chicago Press.

Sharon, Tamar. 2018. "When Digital Health Meets Digital Capitalism, How Many Common Goods Are at Stake?" *Big Data and Society* 5 (2): 1–12. doi:10.1177/2053951718819032.

Sheller, Mimi. 2018a. *Mobility Justice: The Politics of Movement in an Age of Extremes.* London/Brooklyn, NY: Verso.

Sheller, Mimi. 2018b. "Theorising Mobility Justice." *Tempo Social* 30 (2): 17–34. doi:10.11606/0103-2070.ts.2018.142763.

Shore, Cris, and Susan Wright. 2011. "Conceptualising Policy: Technologies of Governance and the Politics of Visibility." In *Policy Worlds: Anthropology and the Analysis of Contemporary Power*, edited by Cris Shore, Susan Wright, and Davide Pero, 1–25. New York: Berghahn Books. doi:10.1093/acprof:oso/9780195325102.003.0008.

Silverman, David. 2006. *Interpreting Qualitative Data. Methods for Analyzing Talk, Text and Interaction*. Los Angeles/London/New Delhi/Singapore/Washington DC: Sage.

Simmel, Georg. 2009. *Sociology. Inquiries into the Construction of Social Forms. Volume 1*. Leiden/Boston: Brill.

Slota, Stephen C., and Geoffrey C. Bowker. 2017. "How Infrastructures Matter." In *The Handbook of Science and Technology Studies*, edited by Ulrike Felt, Rayvon Fouché, Clarke A. Miller, and Laurel Smith-Doerr, 529–554. Cambridge, MA/London: The MIT Press.

Smith, Cameron. 2019. "'Authoritarian Neoliberalism' and the Australian Border-Industrial Complex." *Competition and Change* 23 (2): 192–217. doi:10.1177/1024529418807074.

Sohn, Christophe. 2016. "Navigating Borders' Multiplicity: The Critical Potential of Assemblage." *Area* 48 (2): 183–189. doi:10.1111/area.12248.

Sontowski, Simon. 2018. "Speed, Timing and Duration: Contested Temporalities, Techno-Political Controversies and the Emergence of the EU's Smart Border." *Journal of Ethnic and Migration Studies* 44 (16): 2730–2746. doi:10.1080/1369183X.2017.1401512.

Sparke, Matthew B. 2006. "A Neoliberal Nexus: Economy, Security and the Biopolitics of Citizenship on the Border." *Political Geography* 25 (2): 151–180. doi:10.1016/j.polgeo.2005.10.002.

Squire, Vicki, ed. 2011. *The Contested Politics of Mobility. Borderzones and Irregularity*. London/New York: Routledge, Taylor & Francis Group.

Srnicek, Nick. 2017. *Platform Capitalism*. Cambridge, UK/Malden, US: Polity.

Star, Susan Leigh. 1983. "Simplification in Scientific Work. An Example from Neuroscience Research." *Social Studies of Science* 13: 205–228.

Star, Susan Leigh. 1999. "The Ethnography of Infrastructure." *American Behavioral Scientist*, no. 3: 377–391. doi:10.1177/00027649921955326.

Star, Susan Leigh. 2010. "This Is Not a Boundary Object: Reflections on the Origin of a Concept." *Science Technology and Human Values* 35 (5): 601–617. doi:10.1177/0162243910377624.

Star, Susan Leigh, and James R. Griesemer. 1989. "Institutional Ecology, 'Translations' and Boundary Objects: Amateurs and Professionals in Berkeley's Museum of Vertebrate Zoology, 1907–39." *Social Studies of Science* 19 (3): 387–420. doi:10.1177/030631289019003001.

Star, Susan Leigh, and Karen Ruhleder. 1996. "Steps Toward an Ecology of Infrastructure: Design and Access for Large Information Spaces." *Information Systems Research* 7 (1): 111–134. doi:10.1287/isre.7.1.111.

Stark, David. 2009. *The Sense of Dissonance. Accounts of Worth in Economic Life.* Princeton, NJ: Princeton University Press.

Statewatch. 2022. "EU has spent over €340 million on border AI technology that new law fails to regulate." *News.* Accessed 18 May 2023. https://www.statewatch.org/news/2022/may/eu-has-spent-over-340-million-on-border-ai-technology-that-new-law-fails-to-regulate/.

Stierl, Maurice, Huub Van Baar, Irene Peano, Yolande Jansen, Elena Fontanari, Martina Tazzioli, Lisa Riedner, et al. 2016. "Europe / Crisis: New Keywords of 'the Crisis' in and of 'Europe.'" *New Keywords Collective.* http://nearfuturesonline.org/europecrisis-new-keywords-of-crisis-in-and-of-europe-part-2/.

Strauss, Claudia. 2006. "The Imaginary." *Anthropological Theory* 6 (3): 322–344. doi:10.1177/1463499606066891.

Szary, Anne-Laure Amilhat, and Frederic Giraut, eds. 2015. *Borderities and the Politics of Contemporary Mobile Borders.* Hampshire: Palgrave Macmillan.

Taylor, Charles. 2004. *Modern Social Imaginaries.* Durham, NC/London: Duke University Press.

Tazzioli, Martina. 2020a. "Confine to Protect: Greek Hotspots and the Hygienic-Sanitary Borders of Covid-19." *Border Criminologies Blog.*

Tazzioli, Martina. 2020b. *The Making of Migration. The Biopolitics of Mobility at Europe's Borders.* London/Thousand Oaks, CA: SAGE Publications Ltd.

Tazzioli, Martina, and William Walters. 2016. "The Sight of Migration: Governmentality, Visibility and Europe's Contested Borders." *Global Society* 30 (3): 445–464. doi:10.1080/13600826.2016.1173018.

The Baltic Course. 2014. "Estonia builds headquarters for EU IT agency for 8.4 mln euros". *Real Estate.* 11 December 2014. Accessed 15 January 2024. https://www.baltic-course.com/eng/real_estate/?doc=100028&ins_print&output=d.

Torpey, John. 1998. "Coming and Going: On the State Monopolization of the Legitimate 'Means of Movement.'" *Sociological Theory* 16 (3): 239–259. doi:10.1111/0735-2751.00055.

Torpey, John. 1999. *The Invention of the Passport. Surveillance, Citizens and the State.* Cambridge: Cambridge University Press.

Trauttmansdorff, Paul. 2017. "The Politics of Digital Borders." In *Border Politics. Defining Spaces of Governance and Forms of Transgressions*, edited by Cengiz Günay and Nina Witjes, 107–126. Cham: Springer International Publishing. doi:10.1007/978-3-319-46855-6_7.

Trauttmansdorff, Paul. 2022. "Borders, Migration, and Technology in the Age of Security: Intervening with STS." *TECNOSCIENZA Italian Journal of Science and Technology Studies* 13 (2): 133–154. www.tecnoscienza.net.

Trauttmansdorff, Paul, and Ulrike Felt. 2023. "Between Infrastructural Experimentation and Collective Imagination: The Digital Transformation of the EU Border Regime." *Science, Technology, & Human Values* 48 (3): 625–662. doi:10.1177/01622439211057523.

Tsianos, Vassilis, and Serhat Karakayali. 2010. "Transnational Migration and the Emergence of the European Border Regime: An Ethnographic Analysis." *European Journal of Social Theory* 13 (3): 373–387. doi:10.1177/1368431010371761.

Tsianos, Vassilis, and Brigitta Kuster. 2016. "Eurodac in Times of Bigness: The Power of Big Data within the Emerging European IT Agency." *Journal of Borderlands Studies* 31 (2): 235–249. doi:10.1080/08865655.2016.1174606.

Turnbull, Nick. 2005. "Policy in Question: From Problem Solving to Problematology." DPhil. Thesis: University of New South Wales. doi:10.26190/unsworks/22386.

Vaughan-Williams, Nick. 2008. "Borderwork beyond inside/Outside? Frontex, the Citizen-Detective and the War on Terror." *Space and Polity* 12 (1): 63–79. doi:10.1080/13562570801969457.

Vavoula, Niovi. 2020. "Interoperability of EU Information Systems: The Deathblow to the Rights to Privacy and Personal Data Protection of Third-Country Nationals?" *European Public Law* 26 (1): 131–156.

Vinsel, Lee, and Andrew L. Russel. 2020. *The Innovation Delusion. How Our Obsession with the New Has Disrupted the Work That Matters Most.* New York: Currency.

Visvanathan, Shiv. 1997. *A Carnival for Science. Essays on Science, Technology and Development.* Delhi/New York: Oxford University Press. doi:10.1177/030437548701200102.

Vukov, Tamara, and Mimi Sheller. 2013. "Border Work: Surveillant Assemblages, Virtual Fences, and Tactical Counter-Media." *Social Semiotics* 23 (2): 225–241. doi:10.1080/10350330.2013.777592.

Walters, William. 2002. "Mapping Schengenland: Denaturalizing the Border." *Environment and Planning D: Society and Space* 20 (5): 561–580. doi:10.1068/d274t.

Walters, William. 2006a. "Border/Control." *European Journal of Social Theory* 9 (2): 187–203.

Walters, William. 2006b. "Rethinking Borders Beyond the State." *Comparative European Politics* 4 (2–3): 141–159. doi:10.1057/palgrave.cep.6110076.

Walters, William. 2009. "Europe's Borders." In *The Sage Handbook of European Studies*, edited by Chris Rumford, 485–506. Los Angeles/London/New Delhi/Singapore/Washington DC: SAGE Publications, Ltd.

Walters, William. 2010. "Foucault and Frontiers: Notes on the Birth of the Humanitarian Border." In *Governmentality: Current Issues and Future Challenges*, edited by Ulrich Bröckling, Susanne Krasmann, and Thomas Lenke, 138–164. New York: Routledge. doi:10.4324/9780203846476.

Walters, William. 2011. "Rezoning the Global. Technological Zones, Technological Work and the (Un-)Making of Biometric Borders." In *The Contested Politics of Mobility. Borderzones and Irregularity*, edited by Vicki Squire, 51–73. London/New York: Routledge, Taylor & Francis Group.

Wastl-Walter, Doris, ed. 2011. *The Ashgate Research Companion to Border Studies*. Farnham: Ashgate.

Wienroth, Matthias. 2018. "Governing Anticipatory Technology Practices. Forensic DNA Phenotyping and the Forensic Genetics Community in Europe." *New Genetics and Society* 37 (2): 137–152. doi:10.1080/14636778.2018.1469975.

Wilson, Thomas M., and Hastings Donnan, eds. 2016. *A Companion to Border Studies*. Malden/Oxford: Wiley Blackwell.

Witteborn, Saskia. 2022. "Digitalization, Digitization and Datafication: The 'Three D' Transformation of Forced Migration Management." *Communication, Culture and Critique* 15 (2): 157–175. doi:10.1093/ccc/tcac007.

Zaiotti, Ruben. 2011. *Cultures of Border Control. Schengen and the Evolution of European Frontiers*. Chicago: University of Chicago Press.

Zolberg, Aristide R. 2003. "The Archaeology of 'Remote Control.'" In *Migration Control in the North-Atlantic World. The Evolution of State Practices in Europe and the United States from the French Revolution to the Inter-War Period*, edited by Andreas Fahrmeir, Olivier Faron, and Patrick Weil, 195–222. New York: Berghahn Books.

Zolberg, Aristide R. 2006. "Managing a World on the Move." *Population and Development Review* 32: 222–253.

Zureik, Elia, and Mark B. Salter, eds. 2006. *Global Surveillance and Policing. Borders, Security, Identity*. Portland, OR: Willan Publishing. doi:10.1108/17479894200600018.

Index

References to figures appear in *italics*. References to endnotes show the page number and the note number (142n3).

A

abstraction 88–9, 93, 95, 121, 147n17, 149n5
acceptability, politics of 117
acronyms 24, 88–9, 121, 140n1
Adams, Vincanne 78, 79
Adey, Peter 75
Agency *see* eu-LISA Agency
AI (artificial intelligence) 127–9
Aizeki, By Mizue 122, 149n7
Akrich, Madeleine 125
Alliance of Socialists and Democrats (S&D) 104–5, 148n8
Amoore, Louise 7, 129
Anderson, Benedict 11, 142n16
anticipation 32, 36–7, 78–81, *81*, 89, 94, 114, 115, 141n13
Appadurai, Arjun 142n16
Aradau, Claudia 117
Arendt, Hannah 123–4, 149n8
artificial intelligence (AI) 127–9
Artificial Intelligence in the Operational Management of Large-Scale IT Systems 127
Asdal, Kristin 103
Ashgate Research Companion to Border Studies 4
asylum seekers 6, 23, 26, 48, 109, 128, 130, 133
Australia 74, 134
Austria 15, 17, 57, 58, 60, 143n21, 144n8–9

B

backstaging 53, 57, 58, *59*, 60–1, 63, 65–6
backup centre (eu-LISA) *see* eu-LISA Agency; Pongau region (Austria)
Balibar, Étienne 4
Barry, Andrew 61, 83
Barthe, Yannick 29
Bastos, Filipe 99
Beck, Ulrich 124
Belarus 23
Belgium 15, 17, 51

Bellanova, Rocco 99
Bendor, Roy 75
Benjamin, Ruha 123
Benjamin, Walter 35, 54
Berlin Wall 3, 4
Bigo, Didier 31, 98–9, 145n2
biometrics
    border controls and 7, 73, 97, 109, 111
    concerns with 38, 125
    digital identities 108–11
    at eu-LISA Agency 23, 48–9
    IT systems for 26, 38, 132–4, 136–7
biopolitical turn 5, 8, 140n6
biopolitics 5, 8, 10, 140n7
Boltanski, Luc 3, 113–14, 116, 148n2
Border Management Today 37, 82–3, 90
borders
    about 4–5, 9, 140n5
    artificial intelligence (AI) 127–9
    biometric 7, 97, 109, 111
    dehumanization of 93, 101, 122–4
    digital infrastructures (*see* digital infrastructures)
    as experimentation sites 28–30, 38–9, *40*, 41
    networking European 82–3
    rethinking of 2–3
    security of (*see* security)
    smart (*see* smart borders)
    violent regimes 11, 19, 23–4, 27, 73, 89, 95, 101, 122–3, 124–5
border studies 4–5, 27, 140n2
Bowker, Geoffrey 141n11, 149n5
Broeders, Dennis 71
Busch, Lawrence 149n5
Bussolini, Jeffrey 141n11

C

Callon, Michel 29
Canada 134
capitalism 3, 35, 119, 147n18, 148n2

Castoriadis, Cornelius 11, 118, 119
Chiapello, Eve 3, 116, 148n2
CIR 99, 104–5, 109, 136–7, 147
civic epistemologies 72
Clarke, Adele E. 78, 79
Clarke, John 100
clubbability 72, 77–8
Cohn, Carol 24, 88, 95, 147n17
Cold War 3, 58
collective imagination
  and digital infrastructuring 27
  and future visions 10–13, 19, 29–30,
    120–1
  see also imaginaries; narratives
Commission see European Commission
Common Identity Repository (CIR) see CIR
Communication on Stronger and Smarter
  Information Systems for Borders and
  Security 102–3
Côté-Boucher, Karine 7
COVID-19 pandemic
  borders regimes during 3, 20, 85, 129–30
  virtual events during 17, 146n8
  visa applications during 132–3
Cowen, Deborah 91
crisis, narratives of 35–6, 102, 103, 111
Curtin, Deirdre 99

D

data
  migrants as 66, 93
  protection 39, 99, 102–3, 104, 108, 126
  quality 61–2, 90, 111, 127,
    144n10, 148n10
databases 1–2, 5–6, 8, 11
  see also digital infrastructures; EES;
    ETIAS; Eurodac; interoperability;
    SIS / SIS II; VIS
De Genova, Nicholas 99
dehumanization of borders 93, 101, 122–4
diffuse borders 7
digital borders see borders; digital
  infrastructures; interoperability;
  smart borders
digital identities 108–11
digital infrastructures
  about 7, 9, 52–3
  artificial intelligence (AI) 127–9
  as biological organisms 63–5, 64, 65–6
  for border security 6, 8–10, 83–5
  and collective imagination 27, 36–7
  COVID-19 and 129–30
  data quality 61–2, 90, 111, 127,
    144n10, 148n10
  "eventing" of 53–6, 58
  justifications for 113–17
  maintenance and repair of 9–10, 11, 59–60,
    141n14, 145n12
  for mobility governance 1–2, 26, 52

reaction formations 26, 99
standardization of 61–2, 65, 72, 76–7, 78, 83
Dijstelbloem, Huub 5, 71, 144n6

E

e-borders 7
EC
  border security, centralization of 14–15,
    31–2, 77, 82, 134, 135, 143n3
  interoperability 96, 102–3
  research, as focus of 17, 18
economy and smart borders 85–7, 145n2
ecosystem 89–90, 93, 147n20
ECRIS-TCN 6, 135–6
EDPS 18, 103, 104
EES 6, 26, 38, 73, 74–5, 86, 98, 134
Engels, Franziska 29
entextualization 53, 54
Entry/Exit System (EES) see EES
EPP 103, 104–5, 148n8
Ernst, Cornelia 148n6
ESP 136, 147n3
Estonia 44, 44, 45, 45–7, 51, 55–6
ethnography 2, 16, 17, 23, 53, 65, 75
ETIAS 6, 73–5, 86, 98, 134–5
eu-LISA Agency
  about 1–2, 13, 14–16, 26–7, 44,
    45, 143n20
  on artificial intelligence (AI) 127
  backup site (Pongau region) 15, 57–8,
    59–60
  Border Management Today 37, 82–3, 90
  concerns with 44, 125
  databases administered by 6, 14, 131–7
    (see also ECRIS-TCN; EES; ETIAS;
    Eurodac; SIS / SIS II; VIS)
  establishment of 31–2
  events 16–17, 24, 32–3, 36–7, 46–8, 51,
    53–6, 58, 68–70, 76–8, 146n7–10
  experimentation by 28–30, 38–9, 40, 41
  headquarters (Tallinn) 44, 44, 45, 45–7,
    51, 68, 69
  impact of 19
  interoperability (see interoperability)
  justification by 114–17
  maintenance (see maintenance; repair)
  narratives / shared imaginaries of 13, 32–3,
    35–7, 46–7, 57, 75, 115, 118, 120–1, 130
  operational centre (Strasbourg) 15, 17,
    47–50, 48, 49, 57–8, 58–61, 62, 64,
    143n3, 144n9
  pilot projects 38, 39, 41, 116, 143n5
  research on, experiences during 21–2
  security at 23, 45–6, 48–50
  smart borders (see smart borders)
  as a vanguard 15, 19, 27, 28, 30–2, 36
  on virtual world 2–3
  working groups 18, 92
Eurodac 6, 14, 26, 57, 98, 133

European Commission *see* EC
European Criminal Record Information System for Third-Country Nationals (ECRIS-TCN) *see* ECRIS-TCN
European Data Protection Supervisor (EDPS) *see* EDPS
European People's Party (EPP) *see* EPP
European Search Portal (ESP) *see* ESP
European Travel Information and Authorisation System (ETIAS) *see* ETIAS
European Union Agency for the Operational Management of Large-Scale IT Systems in the Area of Freedom, Security and Justice *see* eu-LISA Agency
events *see* backstaging; digital infrastructures; eu-LISA Agency; frontstaging
exclusion 4, 5, 10–11, 42, 126, 129
experimentation sites, borders as 28–30, 38–9, *40*, 41
Ezrahi, Yaron 11–12, 111

F

Feldman, Gregory 17, 36–7, 69–70, 78, 101, 146n10, 148n4 (chap 6)
field research *see* research
fingerprints
  of asylum seekers 26, 133
  at eu-LISA Agency 48–9
  at smart borders 73
  see also biometrics
Finholt, Thomas A. 141n14
Fleck, Ludwik 21
Foucault, Michel 5, 9, 140n7, 141n11, 141n13
France 15, 17, 48, 51, 57
  see also Strasbourg (France)
Fraser, Mariam 144n5
frontstaging 53, 54, 55, 56–8, 59, 65, 66
Fundamental Rights Agency (FRA) 18
future
  anticipation of 32, 36–7, 78–81, *81*, 89, 94, 114, 115, 141n13
  borders 17, 19, 120
  -making, digital borders 36–7
  (in)security, visions of 19, 26–7, 29–30, 120, 130
  technological visions 3, 10–13

G

Garkov, Krum 46, 47, *56*, 69, 82–3, 90, 116, 140n3, 146n9
geography of responsibility 125–6
Germany 48, 51, 89
global economy and smart borders 85–7, 145n2
Glouftsios, Georgios 31, 51, 59–60, 99
The Governance of Problems (Hoppe) 100
Griesemer, James R. 81
Guggenheim, Michael 29

H

Hacking, Ian 149n5
Halpern, Oliver Joel 76, 84
Hansen, Johannes Rübner 76, 84
Hausmann 64
headquarters (eu-LISA) *see* eu-LISA Agency; Tallinn (Estonia)
Heller, Charles 123
Hess, Sabine 4
High-Level Expert Group on Information Systems and Interoperability (HLEG) *see* HLEG
Hilgartner, Stephen 13, 27, 30, 53, 54
HLEG 103–4, 104–5, 136, 148n5
Hoppe, Robertus 100
Horst, Maja 54
Howarth, David 100
human factors 92–3

I

iBorders 7
"ID@Borders and the Future of Travel" (OSCE conference) 16, *34*, 77–8, 79, *81*, *87*, 89
identities 108–11
imaginaries
  about 12, 142n16–19
  of digital borders 36–7
  of smart borders 75–9, 120
  sociotechnical (*see* sociotechnical imaginaries)
  see also collective imagination; narratives
imagination *see* collective imagination
inclusion 4, 10–11, 124, 126, 129
inevitability, narratives of 32–3, 36, 41, 52, 118–19, 127
infrastructures *see* digital infrastructures
internal security *see* security
interoperability
  about 6, 14, 26, 39, 96, 105–6, 136–7
  biometric borders and 96–7, 133
  challenges with 98–9
  of databases, among eu-LISA 6, 14, 26
  data protection and 39, 99, 102–3, 104, 108, 126
  European Search Portal (ESP) 136, 147n3
  as experimentation 39, *40*, 41
  issue-experts 103–4
  justification of 114–17
  narratives 20, 102–3, 106
  policies 99–102
  as policy fiction 97, 99, 102, 108–9, 111–12, 119, 121–2
  simplification and 42–3, 97, 102, 105–8, 111, 121–2
iron curtain 4
Italy 23

J

Jasanoff, Sheila 12, 29–30, 72, 100
Jeandesboz, Julien 73, 88, 114, 145n2
Jensen, Ole B. 82
Johansson, Ylva 143n20

Jumbert, Maria Gabrielsen 100–1
Jünemann, Reinhardt 89
justification 113–17

K

Kalamaja (Estonia) 45–6
Kasparek, Bernd 4
Kim, Sang-Hyun 12, 29, 100
Knorr Cetina, Karin 29, 62–3
Kondo, Marie 107
Kuster, Brigitta 31, 145n2

L

laboratories 28–30, 41–2
  see also experimentation sites, borders as
Larkin, Brian 9, 10, 52–3
Lascoumes, Pierre 29
Latour, Bruno 11, 95, 149n5
Law, John 21, 53, 67, 101
Leese, Matthias 99, 109
Lemberg-Pederson, Martin 76, 84
Libya 23
Lincoln, Abraham 36
liquid borders 7
logistics 89–90
Longo, Matthew 5
Luxembourg 51

M

Maguire, Eileen Murphy 145n13
maintenance
  of digital border infrastructures 9–10, 11,
    59–60, 141n14
  eu-LISA and 15, 16, 31, 62, 65, 117
Marcus, George E. 142n17
market, border security 83–5
Martins, Bruno Oliveira 100–1
McCluskey, Emma 117
Mediterranean Sea 11, 142n15
method assemblages 21
Mezzadra, Sandro 2
Michael, Mike 54
MID 109–10, 115, 137, 147n3
migrants
  as data objects 66, 93
  digital identities of 109–10
  hyper-objectification of 42
  illegal 73, 145n4
  treatment of 11, 23, 125, 129–30, 132
migration
  autonomy of 25
  crisis 102–3
  management of 14, 26, 27, 74
Mitchell, Timothy 121
mobile borders 7, 84–5
mobility governance
  challenges with 42, 91–3, 125–6
  digital infrastructures for 1–2, 26, 52
Morozov, Evgeny 14, 100

Multiple Identity Detector (MID) see MID
Murphy, Michelle 78, 79

N

narratives
  of crisis 35–6, 102, 103, 111
  of experts / professionals 19–20, 24, 82,
    89, 97, 111–12, 120–4
  of inclusion / exclusion 129–30
  of inevitability 32–3, 36, 41, 52, 118–19, 127
  of interviewees 17–18
  of sociotechnical imaginary 11, 12–13,
    100, 127, 142n17–18
  standardizing of 13, 32–3, 35–6, 46–7, 57,
    75, 115
  of unidirectionality 33, 34, 35–6, 38, 41,
    119, 127
  see also collective imagination; imaginaries;
    sociotechnical imaginaries
Neilson, Brett 2
Netherlands 51
networking (of European borders) 82–3
Neuhof 47–8
  see also Strasbourg (France)
Niewöhner, Jörg 82
Nowotny, Helga 16

O

Ohmae, Kenichi 3–4
ontological singularity 101
operational centre (eu-LISA) see eu-LISA
  Agency; Strasbourg (France)
Organization for Security and Co-operation
  in Europe (OSCE) 16, 77
Oudshoorn, Nelly 125

P

pandemic see COVID-19 pandemic
Papadopoulos, Dimitris 6
Pelizza, Annalisa 66
Pezzani, Lorenzo 123
Pfotenhauer, Sebastian 29
Pickersgill, Martyn 30
Picum 129
pilot projects see eu-LISA Agency
platform 89–90, 93, 147n19
Poland 23
policies 99–100, 100–2
policy fiction 97, 99, 102, 108–9, 111–12,
  119, 121–2
politics of acceptability 117
Pongau region (Austria) 15, 57, 60, 143n21
Porter, Theodore 149n5
Pötzsch, Holger 7
PricewaterhouseCoopers 38

R

racism 23–4, 129–30
Rao, H. 55

reaction formations 26, 99
refugees 11, 102–3, 125, 129–30
repair 9–10, 59–60, 62, 65, 145n12
research
    acronyms, use of 24, 88–9, 121
    ethical implications of 22–3
    field (on eu-LISA) 21–2
    snowball sampling 18
responsibility, geography of 125–6
Ribes, David 141n14
Richardson, Tim 82
Riles, Annelise 17, 75
rituals 12, 36–7, 55, 72, 75–6, 77–8, 94–5
Rose, Nikolas 25
Ruhleder, Karen 52
Russia 23, 57
Rygiel, K. 7

S

Sabel, Charles F. 15
Sadowski, Jathan 75
sBMS 99, 136, 147
Schengen
    border security 6, 14, 73–4, 131
    digital infrastructures (see digital infrastructures)
    establishment of 51
    eu-LISA (see eu-LISA Agency)
    experimentation sites, borders as 28–30,
        38–9, 40, 41
    mobility governance 1, 52
    smart borders (see smart borders)
    visa policies 73
Schengen Information System (SIS) see
    SIS / SIS II
Schwertl, Maria 93
Scott, James 121
S&D (Alliance of Socialists and
    Democrats) 104–5, 148n8
Seaplane Harbour Museum (Tallin) 45, 45, 68
security
    apparatuses 9–10
    artificial intelligence (AI) 127–9
    biometrics and (see biometrics)
    border 3–4, 6, 52, 119
    economy and 85–7
    market, digital border 83–5
    (in)security, future visions of 19, 26–7,
        29–30, 120, 130
    state 2–3, 102–3
semantic coherence 55–6
Sennett, Richard 64–5
Shapin, Steven 75, 77
shared Biometric Matching System (sBMS)
    see sBMS
Sharon, Tamar 114
Sheller, Mimi 126
Simmel, Georg 4
simplification 42–3, 97, 102, 105–8, 111,
    121–2, 149n5

Singleton, Vicky 101
SIS / SIS II
    about 6, 14, 51–2, 131–2
    interoperability and 98
    management of 57–8
Slota, Stephen 141n11
smart borders
    about 7, 73, 80–1
    acronyms / terminology 88–90
    challenges with 42, 91–3
    databases for 73–5, 131–7
    experimentation 38–9, 40, 41, 82
    global economy and 85–7, 145n2
    interoperability (see interoperability)
    justification of 114–17
    literature on 71
    narratives and 19–20, 38–9, 75–9
    as a network 82–3
    opposition to 38
Smart Borders Package 38, 134
snowball sampling 18
social imagination see collective imagination;
        sociotechnical imaginaries
social scientific research see research
socio-digital borders 7
sociotechnical imaginaries
    about 10–13, 29–30, 100, 142n17–18
    of borders 2, 3, 18, 121
    of digital transformation 19, 27, 35–7,
        38–9, 41, 112, 119, 127
    see also collective imagination;
        imaginaries; narratives
solutionism 14, 26, 41, 95, 100–2, 114,
        119–20
Sontowski, Simon 38, 145n2
South Africa 129
standardization 61–2, 65, 72, 76–7, 78,
        83, 149n5
Star, Susan Leigh 9, 52, 81, 149n5
stateless people see third-country nationals
Stephenson, Niamh 6
Strasbourg (France) 15, 17, 47–50, 48, 49,
        57–8, 58–61, 62, 64, 143n3, 144n9
Strauss, Claudia 12
Süddeutsche Zeitung 44, 50
synthetic situations 62–3

T

Tallinn (Estonia) 15, 16–17, 44, 44–5, 45,
        47, 51, 56, 57, 68, 69, 143n3
Taylor, Charles 11, 142n16
Tazzioli, Martina 130
techno-determinism 117–20
technological borders see digital borders
technological infrastructures see
        digital infrastructures
technopolitics 10, 89, 119
techno-solutionism 88, 100–1
    see also solutionism

technostrategic effects 24, 72–3, 88, 95
terminology 89–90
Thévenot, Laurent 113–14
third-country nationals 38–9, 73, 85, 86,
    133, 134, 135, 136, 147n16
Torpey, John 74, 146n6, 147n15
traffic light system 109–11
transport companies 76, 86
Trump, Donald 149n7
Tsianos, Vassilis 6, 31, 145n2

U

Ukraine 23–4
unidirectionality, narratives of 33, *34*, 35–6,
    38, 41, 119, 127
United States (US) 74, 122, 129, 134, 149n7
urgency, narratives of *see* crisis, narratives
    of; narratives

V

Valuation Studies 114, 148n1–2
vanguard visions 13, 15, 27, 30, 32, 36, 142n18
violence (of border regimes) 11, 19, 23–4,
    27, 73, 89, 95, 101, 122–3, 124–5

virtual world
    borders and 7–8
    security in 2–3
    as solutionism 14, 26, 41, 95, 100–2, 114,
        119–20
VIS
    about 6, 14, 132–3
    biometrics 26
    visa overstayers 73, 134, 145n4
Visa Information System (VIS) *see* VIS
visas
    applicants, biometrics of 26, 132–3
    digitization of procedures 6
    and overstays 74, 86, 134, 145n4
Visvanathan, Shiv 42

W

Walters, William 52
Wentland, Alexander 29
world *see* virtual world

Z

Zeitlin, Jonathan 15
Zolberg, Aristide 86